A World Apart

A World Apart

Female Adolescence in the French Novel, 1870–1930

Beth W. Gale

Lewisburg
Bucknell University Press

Associated University Presses
2010 Eastpark Boulevard
Cranbury, NJ 08512

The paper used in this publication meets the requirements of the American National Standard for Permanence of Paper for Printed Library Materials Z39.48–1984.

Library of Congress Cataloging-in-Publication Data

Gale, Beth W., 1971-
    A world apart : female adolescence in the French novel, 1870–1930 / Beth W. Gale.
        p. cm.
    Includes bibliographical references and index.
    ISBN 978-0-8387-5730-7 (alk. paper)
1. French fiction—19th century—History and criticism. 2. French fiction—20th century—History and criticism. 3. Girls in literature. 4. Adolescence in literature. I. Title.

PQ663.G36 2010
843'.80935235—dc22
                                                            2009025566

Contents

Acknowledgments

DURING THE PROCESS OF CREATING THIS BOOK, I BENEFITED FROM THE support of various institutions and people, all of whom I cannot thank sufficiently. This project was born during a memorable conversation with Gerald Prince at the University of Pennsylvania. He, along with Lucienne Frappier-Mazur and Michèle Richman, deftly guided it through its infancy. I would like to thank colleagues from my year at Purdue University, especially Deborah Houk Schocket, Thomas Broden, and Marcia Stephenson, for guidance, sound advice, and all those great rides. Faculty at Hamilton College, especially Cheryl Morgan and Martine Guyot-Bender, provided me with significant dialogue and mentoring during my year with them.

The Higgins School of Humanities at Clark University generously provided funding for crucial summer research trips to Paris from 2002 to 2004. I thank the department of Foreign Languages and Literatures at Clark, especially Dorothy Kaufmann, Michael Spingler, Alice Valentine, Cathie Spingler, and Joanne Berg, for bolstering me professionally and personally since 2001. I am most grateful for the collegial support and encouragement of many other Clark colleagues.

Friends and family also helped immeasurably. As the book neared the end of its adolescence, Christine Wings Turkovich provided commentary and candy, and Stephen Levin offered critical insight and worthy suggestions for improvement. I thank the Gale family for unflagging affection and for understanding the need for all those trips to France. Since 1991, the Hamel-Lemée family has provided me with a welcoming home in France and a steady stream of generosity, slang, and galettes.

Romance Quarterly and Heldref Publications generously granted permission to use sections of my article, "Renée Mauperin as 'Vierge moderne': Documenting Adolescence." Passages from my article "Education, Literature and the Battle over Female Identity in Third Republic France" are published with the permission of Cambridge Scholars Publishing. I am grateful to Editions L'Harmattan for permission to use material from my article "Ni Rebelles ni soumises: les quasi-révoltées du roman d'adolescence en France."

This book is lovingly dedicated to the memory of Adeline Ellin, Mary Grace Connaughton Schwab, and Madeleine Wells Gale, each of whom was, in her own way, an important role model for the female adolescent I know best.

A World Apart

Introduction

In Rachilde's 1934 novel *La Femme-Dieu*, the narrator observes that
the adolescent heroine "semblait habiter un monde à part où elle demeurait seule maîtresse de ses actes ou de ses secrets" [seemed to live
in a world apart where she alone governed her acts or her secrets] (Rachilde 1934, 180). To the narrator, the adolescent inhabits a privileged
space, to which all others are denied access, where she reigns supreme.
At once positive because unique and negative because of its isolation,
the space of adolescence is a fascinatingly complex one, at least in the
eyes of Rachilde's narrator. The older observer may be prone to a view
of adolescence embellished by nostalgia, while the adolescent him- or
herself can be less enthusiastic. As the third millennium gets under
way, sufficient work has been done on adolescence for users of the word
to feel as though they understand its meaning. Adolescence, the period between childhood and adulthood, connotes bad skin and low
self-esteem, competition with peers, conflict with family, and constant
challenge of rules. At the same time, it is viewed as a period of unbounded idealism and of belief in open doors leading to an amorphous,
but certainly glorious, future. Adolescence marks the time when the
adult self is shaped.

Certain passages from the myriad books written on adolescence may
be helpful in defining the terms of this study. In one interdisciplinary
study, the authors observe that the Western concept of adolescence, a
stage of life distinct from childhood and adulthood, is a time for completing certain duties such as maturing physically, acquiring adult skills,
gaining autonomy, and establishing social connections. "In addition,
. . . society imposes specific expectations on the adolescent that shape
some of these tasks—for example, by encouraging extended education
in preference to early marriage and entry into the workplace" (Feldman
and Elliot 1990, 3). Hence adolescent experience in any given society
is shaped by that society's particular demands. The idea of conflict is
also intrinsic to understanding middle-class adolescence. In the intro-

duction to the third volume of his work on *The Bourgeois Experience*, Peter Gay writes of the conflicting impulses that find expression during adolescence: "Adolescence, certainly in modern middle-class culture, is a tempestuous time, exciting and excited. It is a time for testing and experimentation, a time that replays childhood dramas and revives childhood passions." Gay writes that desire for rebellion, coupled with fear of failure, create for the adolescent a mesh of "unsettling conflicts. Hence that extravagant oscillation of moods and the no less extravagant mixture of defiance and conformity that stamp so much behavior at this time" (Gay 1984, 31–32). Though Gay refers here to male adolescence, the themes he signals, as this study also suggests, are common to all Western adolescents, male and female. Gay's work places adolescence in a particular historical period, from Victoria to Freud, in an attempt to understand it in terms of its cultural context.

Indeed, contemporary studies on the subject have shown increasing interest in the historical evolution of the notion of adolescence, or what Catherine Driscoll refers to as "genealogy" of adolescence (Driscoll 2002, 3–4). As John Modell and Madeline Goodman note in their article about historical perspectives on adolescence:

> Changing social expectations for young people have been congruent with broad changes in the relationship of groups of people to one another, to production, and to the state. To understand adequately what adolescence is, we must also understand what adolescents are supposed to be and why. These questions can properly be answered only by placing them in a historical context. Our general argument is that the dominant political economy of an era helps define adolescence, both descriptively and prescriptively. (Modell and Goodman 1990, 93)

Thus any attempt to define or analyze adolescence benefits from historical and social contextualization. Modell and Goodman insist on the important role played by class in early understanding of adolescence:

> Adolescence, as it developed conceptually in the late nineteenth and twentieth centuries, was first and foremost a middle-class creation. It was a notion that initially made sense in those institutional contexts for young people that promoted their socialization as adults able to hold their own in the competitive middle class. Initially, young people not of the middle class were often perceived as having no adolescence. (102)

As Danièle Chauvin points out in the introduction to *L'Imaginaire des âges de la vie*, French adolescence can be linked not only to the rise of the bourgeoisie, but also to the changing shape of education for young people: "Adolescence is, essentially, a cultural determination, a creation of the liberal bourgeoisie that coincides with its rise to power, and in France, with the institution of the Napoleonian high school." Chauvin notes that adolescence creates a time of training or apprenticeship when scholarly pursuit takes precedence over more lucrative ones (Chauvin 1996, 11). Unfailingly, critics and social historians locate the birth of adolescence in the modern sense of the term somewhere between the mid-nineteenth and the beginning of the twentieth century.[1] This study will focus on the period between 1870 and 1930 as that encompassing the birth and explosion of French literary interest in female adolescence.[2]

In France, the creation of a social category called adolescence was dictated by various societal conditions. The word "adolescence" comes from the Latin *adolescere*, meaning to approach maturity, the past participle of which is *adultus*, meaning full-grown or mature (Kiell 1959, 260). Though the word appeared as early as the fourteenth century in French, it was not used as a feminine noun defining a person (adolescente) until later, around the fifteenth century. Despite the existence of these terms, words like "enfance" and "jeunesse" were more often used to indicate youth until the late nineteenth century, when adolescence became a separate age and social category with specific characteristics.[3] In French society, the word was first used to describe young men who were still living at home and subject to paternal authority, not yet participating in society as free and independent agents.[4] In the case of young women, the word "adolescente" appeared with increasing frequency toward the middle of the nineteenth century, as the shifting shape of French society created a new social group that demanded naming.[5] Literary portrayals of this new category followed in droves.[6]

The novel of adolescence can certainly be linked to the *Bildungsroman*, or novel of education, in its insistence on gaining knowledge about oneself and one's place in society. The novel of female adolescence, then, understandably appeared toward the end of the nineteenth century, when awakening concern about the instruction offered to young girls led to massive educational reform. Historian Michelle Perrot suggests that the distinction between various age-based female categories, including "petite fille, adolescente, jeune fille, jeune femme" [little girl, adolescent, young girl, young woman] was fueled by the late-nineteenth-century debate over female education and over the form of any such instruction for girls (Perrot 1991a, 122). This is not to say that adolescent girls seldom appeared in the novel before the end of the century. Balzac, for example, wrote several novels with adolescent heroines.[7] Yet George Sand was perhaps the most influential literary figure in drawing attention to a social group that she felt had been traditionally neglected in literature.

In 1854–55, Sand wrote: "Je trouve que les poètes et les romanciers n'ont pas assez connu ce sujet d'observation, cette source de poésie qu'offre ce moment rapide et unique dans la vie d'un homme. Il est vrai que, dans notre triste monde actuel, l'adolescent n'existe pas, ou c'est un être élevé d'une manière exceptionnelle" [I find that poets and novelists have not known enough about this subject of observation, this source of poetry offered by this rapid and unique moment in a man's life. It is true that in our sad world today, the adolescent either does not exist, or is a being raised in an exceptional way (Sand 1856, 119–20). Sand further suggests that educational practices destroy the "chasteté de l'imagination" [chastity of the imagination] and the "sainte ignorance" [holy ignorance] of adolescence. Though she here refers solely to male adolescents, it is not unlikely that Sand was also thinking of young women, given that she wrote several novels presenting adolescent heroines. In her article on George Sand, Marilyn Yalom writes, "When the history of female adolescence is written, it will be seen that the writing of George Sand offers a store of portraits and insights unparalleled in her time and place" (Yalom 1985, 204). Sand's contributions to novelistic understanding of female adolescence helped to break a path for later exploration.

George Sand's novels about young female characters include *La Confession d'une jeune fille* (1864), *La Mare au diable* (1846), and *La Petite Fadette* (1849).[8] Sand concerned herself particularly with the ways in which social class and education affected the behavior of young girls. Her precociously mature adolescent heroines use their intelligence, talent, and unique perceptiveness to analyze situations and to act appropriately in order to achieve their goal of finding good, honest, and wealthy husbands. In his article entitled "Growing Up Female: George Sand's View in *La Petite Fadette*," Michael Danahy suggests that the novel expresses "the plight that a young woman must endure in the absence of suitable consistent female role models and the important effects of a girl's mother on the full course of her humanization" (Danahy 1982, 49). To Danahy's comments, I would add that *La Petite Fadette* is, in the context of adolescence, an exploration of the relationship between appearance and social reality.[9] Fadette undergoes a physical transformation during adolescence that opens doors for her socially. Another adolescent character, Madelon, serves as a basis for comparison with Fadette. The former is more beautiful and enjoys a better position in the village, until Fadette's transformation reveals her intelligence and innate goodness, which contrasts sharply with Madelon's dishonesty and meanness. In the novel, Sand explores adolescent identity through tropes such as androgyny, paradox, and the contradiction between appearance and reality. Fadette learns to respond to society's demands, and her beauty, intelligence, and personal fortune allow her to marry the man she loves.

In *La Mare au diable*, Marie's level-headedness, intelligence, maternal instincts, and bravery seduce Germain during their two adventures near the haunted pool. Marie, like Fadette, presents an enchanting mixture of adult and childlike qualities. At once innocent and mature, naïve and capable, strong and vulnerable, Marie simply and deftly takes charge of difficult situations and gains access, through marriage to Germain, to higher social status. In *La Confession d'une jeune fille*, Lucienne, like Fadette and Marie, possesses an understated dignity, honesty, and intelligence that enable her to regain the fortune and social status that she loses during the course of the novel. Again, class differences play a major role: debate over Lucienne's family origins provides the central impetus for the plot. The novel suggests that proper education, including a loving household, and intelligence are more important than social class in determining a female adolescent's moral makeup and value to society. Sand's novels can be considered to be some of the earliest literary portrayals of female adolescence. Though Sand rarely veers from a traditional ending where the heroine succeeds in finding a husband, her novels present some elements of adolescence that had not been explored in such detail before, and that became key in later novels of female adolescence. In novels such as *La Petite Fadette*, *La Mare au diable*, and *La Confession d'une jeune fille*, Sand established new territory for later portrayals of female youth.

By the latter half of the nineteenth century, when French society began to consider and to debate the notion of providing a fuller education for France's young women, other writers were turning their attention to the increasingly important social group of adolescent females. Emile Zola wrote several newspaper articles regarding French society and its adolescent girls. In an 1868 article entitled "L'Education des filles" [girls' education], which was published in *La Tribune*, he attacked a pamphlet circulating in Paris that instructed adolescents on how to

find good husbands quickly. Zola wrote that such a method of instruction was inappropriate even for peasant girls, proposing that distribut-
ing pamphlets on hygiene would be "plus sain pour le corps et pour
l'esprit" [healthier for the body and the mind] (Zola 1969a, 126).[10] In
1880, he returned to the theme of female education in an article for *Le
Figaro* entitled "Types de femmes en France," in which he suggested
that education for girls was changing French society: "L'enseignement
s'infiltre partout, modifiant d'une manière décisive notre civilisation"
[Education has seeped in everywhere, definitively altering our civiliza-
tion] (357). For the middle class, Zola wrote:

> Toute l'éducation de la jeune Française peut se résumer ainsi: surveil-
> lance constante, et réclusion sévère qui ne se termine qu'avec le mar-
> iage. . . . On lui enseigne tous les jours l'hypocrisie de la jeune fille
> bien élevée. Celle-ci doit tout ignorer, doit être modeste, et elle simule
> la modestie et l'ignorance. Dès qu'elle atteindra dix-sept ans, toutes
> ses pensées se porteront vers le mariage, qu'elle désire et qui la rendra
> libre.

> [The entire education of the young Frenchwoman can be thus sum-
> marized: constant surveillance and severe reclusion that ends only with
> marriage. . . . She is taught daily the hypocrisy of the well-raised young
> woman, who must be ignorant of everything, must be modest and who
> simulates modesty and ignorance. When she is seventeen years old, all
> of her thoughts will lean toward marriage, which she desires and which
> will set her free.] (369)

Though Zola protests against the institutionalized hypocrisy of the
"well-raised young woman," he views marriage as the fortunate outcome of an unhappy period of reclusion and surveillance.

For Zola, women represent an impressive social force: "Elles sont
toutes influentes et toutes jouent le rôle de puissants agents sociaux,
lorsqu'un mouvement historique leur en fournit l'occasion" [They are
all influential and all play the role of powerful social agents, whenever
a historic movement provides them with an occasion] (Zola 1969a, 377),
yet the novelist clearly values above all their social roles of wife and
mother. Zola criticizes social codes when he attacks the generalized
"ignorance" demanded of young girls, but he returns to tradition in his
view of marriage as the necessary and positive end result of their period
of feigned innocence. The ideas Zola expresses on education, social
class, family influence, hygiene and the body, marriage, and forms of
liberty can be found in his and other period novels of female adoles-

cence. I include Zola's journalistic commentary on young women in order to expose the intimate relationship between literary and social reality for girls at the end of the nineteenth century. It is essential to understand the social context of literary portraiture of girls, particularly, as I argue in my study, at the time when female adolescence was just emerging as a social and literary category.

Another important element of literary discussion of youth is its inherent political commentary. Rosemary Lloyd writes in her book *The Land of Lost Content: Children and Childhood in Nineteenth-Century French Literature* that the last decade of the nineteenth century signaled "an alteration in attitudes towards the theme of childhood and adolescence in French literature" (Lloyd 1992, 3–4).[11] Literary interest in childhood proved to have a certain degree of political power: Lloyd writes that C. S. Parker's 1925 *The Defense of the Child by French Novelists* "postulates a direct relationship between literature and political change when he argues . . . that the changes that were instituted by the Third Republic were largely a response to the depictions of childhood in the literature of the time" (4). The idea that literature may hold some political clout is not new; its use in the context of childhood and adolescence is. Lloyd also signals a shift in portrayals of childhood toward the end of the nineteenth century:

> There is . . . a significant change of tone as the gushing and patronizing view of children is gradually replaced by an increasing awareness of the role of childhood traumas in forming the adult personality. And finally, the century is marked by a growing interest in adolescence as a state separate both from childhood and from adulthood. Although I have deliberately excluded from this book any study of adolescence as such, it is abundantly clear that both thematically and narratologically it would provide the basis for further explorations. (244)

Though Lloyd does not refer to Justin O'Brien's 1937 study of the novel of adolescence in France, it should be signaled as the first book-length work on the subject. In his study, O'Brien explains his decision to ignore female adolescence by claiming that puberty affects girls far less, spiritually and intellectually, than it does boys.

My study fills the void indicated by Lloyd and left by O'Brien by demonstrating that French novels that sought to portray the separate world of female adolescence became, at the end of the nineteenth century and the beginning of the twentieth, a key vehicle for the documentation and promotion of changes in social reality. My study is the only one, as far as I know, to examine female adolescence of the time through a variety of lenses: historical, political, sociological, but above all, literary. To deepen my analysis and to contextualize it in terms of broad cultural trends, I include critical voices from the past, such as prolific and opinionated social critic Octave Uzanne and literary analyst Jules Bertaut, and present, such as feminist historian Christine Bard and literary scholar Diana Holmes. These voices offer differing, and even contradicting, views, because they represent different fields, time periods, and agendas; I incorporate them in order to create a multilayered tableau of the conventional wisdom surrounding literary adolescence both then and now. During the sixty-year period covered by this study, the adolescent character became a site for conflicting portraits of what young women were, could, and should be, as novelists competed to create the definitive literary example of the young woman of their time, even as the category of female adolescence itself was just being defined and therefore shifting constantly. In France, as this study shows, adolescent heroines provide a medium for the expression of fears and of enthusiasm about various aspects of social change, particularly with regard to gender roles. In other words, they represent France and its future.[12]

Each chapter of this study begins with an introduction to the two decades that it covers and a first subsection covering an important theme of that time, followed by discussion of themes common to all periods but differently interpreted in each: the body, the mind, education, and love/sexuality. Chapter 1 surveys some of the earliest novels of female adolescence, written by the Goncourt brothers, Emile Zola, and Rachilde. The novels reveal the influence of stringent moral authority in representations of young women. In them, the adolescent character is a stagnant, objectified embodiment of ideology that undergoes little development. The decadent movement in vogue at the time also colored portrayals of female adolescence; girls in these novels are doomed to illness and death. In Chapter 2, I consider the new spaces of female adolescence as revealed in the novels of the Belle Epoque, as well as the reasons behind increasing distinctions between portrayals of young heroines by men and by women. The novels here show increasing valorization of the young woman as progressing subject, not merely as static object, and mirror the improving position of female adolescence in France. Chapter 3 documents the effects of thinking about the unconscious mind on novelistic representations of adolescence. It also corresponds to a time at which female adolescence is more firmly established in French society. These novels come the closest to portraying social reality through literary representation. They focus on the personal experience and perspective of individual characters, thereby illuminating adolescent subjectivity to a greater extent than before and completing the movement from stasis to progress across the three chapters. Perhaps because of this increased focus on female subjectivity, this final chapter covers a period of time during which women novelists began to dominate the field of female adolescence. In the Conclusion, I suggest that the initial wave of interest in the female adolescent, which lasted about sixty years, merely paved the way for increasing exploration of adolescence in life and in literature, both in France and elsewhere.

1
The Decadent Vision
(1870–1890)

THE DECADENT AESTHETIC, OPERATING IN FRANCE AS THE NINETEENTH century nears its end, influenced the portrait of the adolescent heroine in the novel of the period. Though the dates of the decadent movement prove difficult to specify with any precision, critics tend to agree that the period from 1870 to 1889 witnessed the height of the decadent reign.[1] I propose to trace the formation of the notion of adolescence during this period, and to explore the ways in which decadent aesthetics and stringent moral ideologies helped shape the portrayal of female adolescence in the novel. An outline of the understanding of youth and its societal role in France just before the period in question, especially in terms of girls, will facilitate my analysis of the phenomenon of female adolescence and its novelistic representation during the period just before the fin-de-siècle.

The position of youth in French society changed rapidly during the nineteenth century. The debate on the ideal age for marriage and the ensuing delay of nuptials led to a prolonged period of economic dependence on the parents well after biological maturity.[2] Before the marriage controversy, girls were married as early as sixteen years of age. Afterward, they enjoyed at least four additional years of youth unhampered by concerns for husband and children. This freshly created category of young people, physically and often mentally ready to participate in society, but prevented by medical concerns from entering into the inevitable social roles of spouses and parents, helped shape the new understanding of adolescence.[3]

"Adolescents" and their experience during this prolonged time of life preceding adulthood differed dramatically according to sex and gender roles. For boys, adolescence was a time of learning, both official, in the various educational institutions offered to young men, and unofficial, in terms of social and sexual exploration. For male adolescents, questioning and experimentation were considered natural character traits. For young girls, however, the traditional lack of education kept them within strict boundaries. Gabrielle Houbre observes two boundaries of "youth" for girls, which "begins with the dark red of the first menstrual period and ends with that of nuptial deflowering" (Houbre 1997, 25).[4] In other words, a girl's youth is hemmed in on both sides by bloody and potentially traumatic experiences. In between these rites of passage, Houbre notes, female existence all but disappears: "Adolescence thus strongly resembles a parenthesis in the progress of feminine existence" (26). Especially in the middle and upper classes, this time offers little in the way of stimulation to the girl, nor is she considered an important part of society until her official presentation as a potential wife. Indeed, attracting an appropriate husband was a momentous challenge for young women, one that will be discussed in greater detail later in this chapter. Michaela de Giorgio has observed that "a nineteenth-century adolescent girl's duty was to aspire to a pleasant appearance, a beautiful voice, and a happy marriage" (Giorgio 1991, 187). Before the time when they became available to men seeking wives, adolescent girls fell into a void, escaping the interest of the outside world for several years.

During this period of several years, girls were granted limited intellectual and social options. The public and private spaces allowed to girls, the leisure activities they could indulge in, and access to knowledge were all controlled by a strict team representing moral authority, led by religious figures and parents, the mother in particular. "Education" of young girls was handled by religious institutions and/or by the women of the family. Fearing the corruptive influence of knowledge, particularly of the reproductive process, educators and parents kept girls ignorant of even the most basic physiological processes.[5] The cult of the celestial and nurturing mother figure, embodied by the Virgin Mary, was evoked as an eternal feminine ideal of innocence and selflessness. Girls were raised to be submissive, blissfully ignorant, and above all, chaste. Destined to be faithful and loving wives and mothers, girls were scrupulously watched and steered away from any possible sources of information deemed potentially pernicious. As Jean-Claude Caron remarks, the instruction of girls was delayed because the church "remained attached to the idea of woman as privileged messenger of Christianity to coming generations, specifically during a century when dechristianization was all the rage." Woman, in the eyes of the church, is "the redemptress, the intermediary between God and men, she who maintains social cohesion" (Caron 1996, 193). Transformation of the female role through *enseignement* thus posed a serious threat to the social order.

Though the educational situation of young women in France began to change in the latter half of the nineteenth century, progress came slowly and was not always motivated by feminist concerns. As Caron points out, the church represented the main obstacle to female instruction:

> The ferocious opposition of the Church, which considered that education of young women was exclusively part of its domain, explains in large part the slow progress in this arena; added to this reason is the weight of mentalities which both on the right and left of the political spectrum and in society as a whole, stalls the development of a movement whose benefits are not clear. (Caron 1996, 194)

Those who felt strongly about the benefits of educating girls were thus struggling both against a willful and powerful religious institution and against the general mentality of the French public, who failed to see the usefulness of the proposal. Yet progress came, albeit slowly. The development of new educational options for girls was marked in particular by a speech in 1867 by Jules Simon in which he criticized the insufficient and inappropriate schooling of girls, saying it turned them into dressed-up idols rather than inspiring study companions (Mayeur 1977, 114). Soon thereafter, Victor Duruy, the Ministre de l'Education publique under Napoleon III, attempted to create classes for girls, but such classes suffered from poor attendance and led to strong protests by the Catholic Church (114). The law Camille Sée of 1880, which established female *lycées* in France, appears to be a positive step toward emancipation, which of course it became. Initially, however, educators of young women did not aim to open their eyes to new possibilities and changing social roles. Rather, the political interest in young women was partially motivated by a desire to wrest them from the grasp of the church. As Jules Ferry said in an 1870 speech, "Il faut que la femme appartienne à la science ou qu'elle appartienne à l'Eglise" [Woman must belong to science or to the Church] (Caron 1996, 196). Debates over educational possibilities for girls thus revealed an inherent possessiveness: women were territory to be claimed by one institution or another.

The possibility of claiming and possessing women through education appealed to religious and political leaders, but also to husbands. Ferry's speech, along with others of the same period, reveals that the plan for female education was partially inspired by a desire to provide more interesting and stimulating wives for Frenchmen. This idea could be viewed positively, as Antoine Prost reveals in his comments on the history of education in France: "D'une part, en effet, on veut pour [les jeunes filles] un enseignement différent de celui des garçons, car on tient à respecter leur 'féminité.' Mais de l'autre on veut combler en partie le fossé qui sépare intellectuellement les deux sexes" [On one hand, in fact, girls' teaching ought to be different than that of boys, so as to respect their "femininity." But on the other hand, it was important to fill in the gaps that separated the sexes intellectually]. It was difficult to conceive of a form of instruction that would bring women closer to men intellectually while respecting the basic differences between them. Prost goes on to describe the outcome of this quandary: "On concevra donc un enseignement ouvertement culturel—au sens de désintéressé—car il ne s'agit nullement de préparer les jeunes filles à excercer une profession; mais en même temps on voudra développer l'habitude de raisonner positivement, pour qu'hommes et femmes parlent un langage commun." [Thus an openly cultural—meaning objective—teaching was conceived, for there was no question of preparing girls for a profession; but at the same time girls should develop the habit of reasoning positively, so that men and women speak a common language.] Reason was long considered to be a strictly masculine domain, as opposed to feminine emotion. It was considered most logical therefore to teach women some reason, so that they might better communicate with their husbands. Yet Prost confirms that instruction for young women can be seen as an offensive against the church: "Par là l'enseignement féminin apparaît comme un moyen de lutter contre la superstition, le mysticisme et l'influence cléricale" [In that way, teaching girls appears as a way of fighting superstition, mysticism and clerical influence] (Prost 1968, 262). The idealistic goal of a shared language for men and their wives merely veiled the objective of escape from the clutches of the church. It was nonetheless a powerful argument for education, once it became clear to concerned conservatives that traditional roles would not be threatened. Camille Sée, the author of the 1880 law that created high schools for girls, insisted that educational reform was not meant to lead women away from their true vocation as homemakers and mothers (Caron 1996, 197). For these reasons, the schools differed greatly from boys' schools, and subjects were chosen to reflect a traditional feminine role in society; there were no courses in science, math, Latin, or Greek, and no physical education. Pupils came from all social classes, and attendance was erratic and sparse: many families chose to keep their daughters at home or send them to religious schools rather than to the newly created high schools. Nonetheless, the new wave of interest in female education, albeit powered by often dubious male agendas, marks a clear change in the position of the young woman in France at the end of the nineteenth century.

Literary portrayals of female adolescents from 1870 to 1890 do not necessarily document the educational options opening up for women, but they do reflect an intent gaze directed at the social phenomenon represented by this newly created group of young women. Novelistic portrayals before 1870 tend to paint adolescent girls from a perspective specific to the author. For example, Gabrielle Houbre suggests that Balzac "projette . . . ses propres obsessions en lieu et place de l'imaginaire des jeunes filles"[projects his own obsessions in the place of the young girls' imaginary], a practice far from unusual during his time:

> In this he merely adopts a male strategy characteristic of the early 19th century, for men are caught in a trap that they themselves helped put into place. They asked insistently that young girls stifle or model their personality so as to better bend to the normative demands attached to their condition. (Houbre 1997, 175)

Balzac and others of his period thus portray a certain kind of adolescent girl, one who silently and obediently conforms to the dictates of her social role. After the Commune, however, portraits of female adolescents show a clear attempt to document a new social phenomenon and to explore the experience of young women more fully. This important change coincides with the development of a decadent literary vision.

Though it is difficult to arrive at a simple and clear definition of the decadent aesthetic, some explanation of the phenomenon will clarify my use of terms and provide a backdrop for my discussion. In his article "Définir la décadence," Michel Décaudin suggests that the concept springs from the "observation that one is arriving too late into an aged world, that one carries mortal fatigue of life in the flesh and spirit" (Décaudin 1980, 6).[6] Decadence entails fatigue, yet this weariness affects not just the individual, but the entire *milieu* he or she inhabits: "The physical and moral exhaustion of the society in which they live is in fact an idea shared by all those who call themselves 'decadents'"(7). Décaudin traces some of the results of this decadent torpor, including the "temptation of the artificial because nature has already given everything, recourse to all the refinements and all the excesses, giving in to neurosis, sexual transgression"(7). In art, decadence manifests itself through artifice, neurosis, and transgression of all sorts.[7]

The adolescent character lends itself perfectly to this decadent art form, for at the end of the century, female adolescence, as a concept, remains inchoate. Writers who undertake a portrayal of female adolescence at the end of the nineteenth century are necessarily exploring this new category by examining it in terms of the society that has produced it. According to Pierre Citti, the goal of the novel around 1870 is a "'social inquiry' that aims to reveal to the public something that it didn't know" (Citti 1980, 46).[8] Furthermore, Citti adds, "The novel isolates a character structurally from its milieu, even if the author wishes not to separate the two. . . . Paul Bourget explains decadence by the predominance of the individual over the collective and the victory of the organ over the organism" (51). For many reasons, the study of the adolescent girl incorporated all of these themes: her specificity as an element of society made her stand out against her milieu, and the very definition of adolescence depended on a privileging of the female sex organs over the entire body.[9] The female adolescent character thus became a central focus of certain writers associated with the decadent movement, and perfectly embodied decadent torpor and overwhelming fatigue.

The Archetype of the "Modern Virgin"

Renée Mauperin, by Edmond and Jules de Goncourt (1864), is an excellent source for describing and understanding the new social phenomenon of adolescence, though it predates the period analyzed by several years. Fresh and shockingly modern, both in the eyes of the reading public and in those of the authors, Renée Mauperin was hailed in 1910 by Jules Bertaut, writer of the earliest and most comprehensive studies of the girl in French literature, as the quintessential "vierge moderne," or modern virgin (Bertaut 1909, 144).[10] Thus even in the early twentieth century, when portraits of adolescent girls had become more common and more developed, this novel was still considered by at least one critic to represent an archetype. In a new preface to the novel, written in 1875, Edmond de Goncourt writes the following: "Les auteurs, en effet, ont, préférablement à tout, cherché à peindre, avec le moins d'imagination possible, la jeune fille moderne telle que l'éducation artistique et garçonnière des trente dernières années l'ont faite" [The authors have in fact tried above all else to paint, with as little imagination as possible, the modern young girl as the artistic and boyish education of the last thirty years has made her] (Goncourt 1923, 1–2). The themes of decadence play a key role, not only in this novel, but also in much of the Goncourt brothers' writings. In an 1870 letter to Zola, one of the brothers wrote: "Songez que notre œuvre, et c'est peut être son originalité, originalité durement payée, repose sur la maladie nerveuse" [Think that our work, and this is perhaps its hard-fought originality, rests on nervous illness] (Bourget 1993, 328). Therefore, the model literary adolescent girl springs from the pen of authors who were deeply influenced by the decadent aesthetic.

What is it that makes Renée Mauperin so modern? To begin with, this is a young woman (twenty years old) who has clearly decided to avoid marriage. Though affectionate with her family, especially with her father and brother, and with her female friends, Renée rejects every potential mate brought home by her parents in hopes of sparking her interest. Complaining about Renée's refusal of all suitors, her mother explains the source of her daughter's stubbornness: "J'aimerais bien mieux qu'elle fût un peu moins intelligente"[I would far prefer that she be a bit less intelligent] (Goncourt 1923, 74). Here, then, intelligence is clearly linked to suspicion of traditional social roles, a notion that echoes the themes of the debate over educating young women. Though she possesses many of the necessary attributes to make her an appealing mate in the eyes of the bourgeois society she inhabits, Renée decides to create an existence on her own, without linking herself to a man. Such a subversive decision in a character from the mid-century wins her Bertaut's approval as the model or icon that successive portrayals of young female characters can only seek to emulate.

Renée's "modernity" lies not only in her rejection of marriage (in the course of the novel, she turns down no less than fourteen suitors), but also in her general freedom of speech and behavior, which violates social mores regulating female behavior in the mid-1800s. Gabrielle Houbre notes the price of such linguistic liberty for the adolescent girl: "When a girl decides to converse a bit freely, she is immediately discredited in society's eyes" (Houbre 1997, 167). Girls were expected, as was suggested earlier, to keep their opinions to themselves, and to speak softly and only when necessary. Renée not only speaks when she wishes to, but also says exactly what occurs to her, without filters. Concerning language, Robert Ricatte, author of a book on the Goncourt brothers, observes that it is Renée who consciously manipulates her vocabulary in the novel. Far from being a generalized phenomenon, her shocking and innovative language is a device used in particular situations to express her boredom, or her disapproval of a proposed spouse. In fact, she is quite consciously playing the role of the modern young woman: "One must therefore often look for the real Renée underneath this cunning or modest disguise of language" (Ricatte 1953, 232–33). Ricatte's suggestion that a "real" Renée exists behind all the linguistic screens is interesting. Whereas in Balzac's time a girl's personality was hidden behind a mask of ceremony, here the personality itself is almost a mask. Renée's loud, boisterous behavior may be a calculated façade designed to hide her true feelings. In any case, it signals a marked shift in portrayals of young women during the late nineteenth century.

In the novel, and as seen in criticism thereof, Renée's behavior clearly trangresses gender role boundaries. Jules Bertaut points out Renée's "virility," encouraged only by her father (Bertaut 1910, 149). In the first scene, Renée discusses with a would-be fiancé her passions, such as horseback riding with her father, and her frustrations, such as being forbidden to seek out male company when bored at dances (Goncourt 1923, 7–9). These expressed likes and dislikes belong to a code of behavior radically diverging from that which she is expected to follow. She thus calculatingly pushes her male interlocutor into reacting negatively to her and breaking off his plans for engagement. Both the content and the form of her conversation are clearly coded as masculine. From the beginning of the novel, Renée's tomboy tendencies are accented by her brother's calm, prudent, near-effeminate nature and her sister's traditionally feminine role of wife and woman of the world, preoccupied with social visits, dresses, and balls. Renée's sabotage of her parents' desire to find an appropriate husband for their daughter is both humorous and revealing: she dances freely at the dinner table, runs to play a boisterous polka (that she has written), gives an impromptu haircut to one of the dinner guests, and snatches her father's cigarette for a scandalous puff (40–45). This scene indicates Renée's conflictual relationship with her mother, who represents conventional codes of female conduct, and her complicity with her father, who merely laughs at her rebellious behavior.

The Goncourt brothers use a discussion between Renée's brother and the "adopted son" of the family, Denoisel, to express the dramatic changes in the role of the girl in society. Denoisel, who applauds what he views as a positive transformation, represents the more progressive camp, while Henri represents conservative society and more traditional views of gender roles. In a long monologue, Denoisel announces the end of the age of "pretty little misses" that speak like "wind-up dolls":

> Aujourd'hui, ce n'est plus ça. Le procédé de culture est changé. . . . On demande à une jeune fille des impressions, des expressions personnnelles et naturelles. Elle peut parler, et elle doit parler de tout. C'est passé dans les mœurs. Elle n'est plus tenue de jouer l'ingénuité, mais l'intelligence originale. Pourvu qu'elle brille en société, les parents sont enchantés.

> [Things are not like that anymore today. Cultural processes have changed . . . Young girls are asked for impressions, for personal and natural expressions. She can and must speak of everything. This is now acceptable. She is no longer obligated to act ingenuous, but rather originally intelligent. As long as she shines in society, her parents are delighted.] (Goncourt 1923, 47)

According to Denoisel, then, young women can and should speak up about their impressions and opinions. Unlike many of his contemporaries, Denoisel values outspoken intelligence in a young woman. One important element of this new conception of the young girl, as voiced by Denoisel, is the education accorded to her, which includes the development of her particular talents, and courses with true artists as teachers (47). Denoisel sticks to traditional territory in discussing possible areas of study for these modern young women: music and art. Yet he does suggest that they ought to have lessons with real professionals, so as to better develop their natural talents. Denoisel goes on to underline the role of even the best, kindest father in the development of this new social phenomenon: "Suppose que ce père ait souri à toutes les audaces, à toutes les jolies gamineries d'un garçon dans une femme; qu'il ait laissé sa fille prendre peu à peu ces qualités d'homme dans lesquelles il retrouve avec orgueil la tournure de son cœur . . . " [Suppose that this father had smiled at all boldness, at all the pretty childish behaviors of a boy in a woman; that he had let his daughter slowly take on these male qualities in which he recognizes with pride the shape of his own heart . . .] (47). Unfortunately, Denoisel cannot finish his thought, for Henri scolds him for his indulgence with Renée, saying that her boyish pranks are getting tiresome. This interruption can be read as a prudent decision on the part of the authors to cut off a speech that some readers might view as excessively subversive. Still, Denoisel manages to underline some of the key elements of a nascent conception of female adolescence: new freedom of demeanor, quality instruction, and a privileged relationship with the father. Henri, who significantly truncates Denoisel's speech, represents (along with his mother) traditional society, one that fails to understand and appreciate Renée. She spurns societal demands that she behave in ways that she views as dishonest, boring, and pointless. Yet Denoisel voices a change in French attitudes, predicting an easier future for the female adolescent.

Renée's modern vision of love distances her from the romantic heroines preceding her and announces a new attitude toward romantic attachment. She is well aware of the existence of love, but spends her time analyzing it rather than experiencing it. Ricatte considers this "absence of love in Renée" to be "a gap filled with richness. An entire section of the novel is comprised of dialogues where Renée wonders about tenderness and love, and it is a fertile new thing to have replaced, in this portrait of a girl, all love scenes with as many scenes where she fascinatedly considers love" (Ricatte 1953, 236). Intellectual inquiry replaces direct experience, and allows for a more detailed and intricate portrait of the adolescent psyche. Renée asks Denoisel if he thinks girls her age don't read novels and sing love songs. She then expresses her frustration with novels, which are all "remplis d'amour, il n'y a que ça! Et puis, dans la vie, on n'en voit pas" [filled with love, that's all there is! And then in life, none can be seen]. This revelatory metatextual moment merits further commentary: Renée bewails the inconsistency between portraits of life and the real thing, or more particularly, portraits of youth and the experience thereof. She fails to see the interest of love as portrayed in literature: "Moi, du moins, je n'en vois pas; je vois, au contraire, tout le monde qui s'en passe, et très bien. Il y a des jours où je me demande si ce n'est pas fait seulement pour les livres, si ce n'est pas une imagination d'auteur, vraiment" [I, at least, don't see any; I see, on the contrary, everyone doing very well without it. There are days where I wonder whether it isn't just made for books, if it isn't really an author's imagining] (Goncourt 1923, 105).[11] Renée has a critical distance missing in the romantic young heroine, who takes novelistic portrayals of life for reality.[12] When asked if she has ever been in love, Renée confesses that she began to feel love for Denoisel, but turned it into a superior feeling of friendship and respect for his moral and intellectual lessons. Romantic love seems to Renée to be an unnecessary and unrealistic part of life, which she replaces with solid friendship and filial attachment. She is aware of the novelty of her ideas, considering them to be "romanesque," which she defines as follows to Denoisel:

C'est d'avoir des idées . . . pas comme tout le monde . . . c'est penser un
tas de choses qui ne peuvent pas arriver. Tenez! une jeune personne est
romanesque quand ça lui coûte de se marier comme on se marie, avec
un monsieur comme les autres, un homme qui n'a rien d'extraordi-
naire. . . . Vous ne me croyez pas de cette pâte-là, j'espère?

[It's having ideas . . . not like everyone else . . . it's thinking a bunch of
things that can't happen. Listen! A young person is romantic when it
costs her something to get married like most do, with a gentleman like
all the others, a man who is nothing extraordinary. . . . I hope you don't
think I'm like that?] (207–8)

Renée has great respect for Denoisel, and values their intellectual complicity more than a romantic relationship. Her resistance to a traditional marriage is clear, and her horror of being seen as a typical young
woman who follows convention speaks volumes. By acknowledging the
"cost" of marriage to an unimpressive husband, Renée rejects the role
attributed to her by her bourgeois society. Interestingly, she seems well
aware of the novelty of such a radical position. She criticizes her society
and its expectations with a surprisingly lucid perspective.

Like most of the other decadent heroines, Renée's life ends in the
space of the novel. That a decadent character should die is hardly surprising, though the death of an adolescent, a being on the brink of
adulthood, necessarily strikes the reader. It is interesting to note that,
in his article on the Goncourt brothers, Jean-Pierre Richard should
choose to evoke adolescence when discussing decadence:

The Goncourts don't live in a climate of adolescence. Sick, precociously worn out, they bear deeply inscribed in themselves the signs of
that fin-de-siècle spirit that is concurrently wreaking havoc in most of
their literary contemporaries. Nervousness, refinement, delicacy, all is
translated in their work in terms of decadence. (Richard 1954, 278)

The contrast is interesting: the portrayal of youth at a time of generalized fatigue, an end fascinated by a beginning. Richard adds that youth
and old age are "the only two moments in life where the internal action
of life lets itself be seen" (279). His observation may help explain why
the fin-de-siècle writer would be inspired by adolescence, for in it can
be seen the inner workings of life. The decadent world view is one of
pessimism, of exaggerated suffering, of the inevitability of death, so it
seems appropriate that the heroine should perish within the boundaries
of the narrative. Richard observes that the Goncourt brothers "present

characters coming apart and whose essence is affirmed through that destruction. . . . [A]ll of their great novels concern the same subject, the painting of a case of degeneration: as if their heros could only exist under the threat of illness" (280). The Goncourt novel would then seem to depend on, or at least to revolve around, physical or mental degeneration.

Renée dies from general weakness and heart trouble. Ricatte suggests that the Goncourt brothers had a particular ailment in mind, documented by several texts on heart disease published earlier in the century: "Renée's unusual death reproduces exactly the phenomena that had been called to their attention in a young cardiac patient, and that happen . . . in enlargement of the heart" (Ricatte 1953, 241). This medical research confirms the decadent obsession with physical decline. Richard writes of "a completely exterior and therefore perfectly inhuman fate that gets the better of the Goncourt characters; and it is no coincidence that this fate most often wears a medical appearance that exacerbates its progression" (Richard 1954, 281). Renée's terminal illness fits the notion of generalized degeneration, a key element of the decadent world view.

Such an illness of the heart has symbolic significance as well. Renée, a character who has refused traditional forms of love, seems to suffer from her increasing love for Denoisel, a love that remains unstated, and that appears indirectly to contribute to her demise. Moreover, her discussion with her brother Henri, in which she realizes that he is willing to change the family name for an important marriage (with the daughter of his mistress), provokes her illness, which drags on in the form of sadness after being cured: "Elle demeurait triste d'une tristesse que le temps ne guérissait pas" [She remained sad, a sadness that time didn't heal] (Goncourt 1923, 194). Renée encourages, even welcomes, her own sadness. As she says to Denoisel:

> Il y a des jours où il fait du soleil, on ne souffre de rien, on n'a aucun ennui, pas de chagrin devant soi. Eh! bien, on a envie d'être triste, on se cherche des idées noires. Il faut qu'on pleure. Je me suis vue des fois dire que j'avais la migraine et aller me coucher, tout bonnement pour pleurer en enfonçant la tête dans mon oreiller: ça me faisait un bien! . . . Et on a dans ces moments-là une lâcheté à se secouer, à se sortir de là; c'est comme quand on commence à s'évanouir: il y a une douceur à se sentir le cœur s'en aller.

> [There are days where the sun shines, there is no suffering, no problem, no grief in sight. Well, you want to be sad, you think of dark things.

You have to cry. I have heard myself say that I had a migraine and go
to bed, just to cry with my head in my pillow: it did me so much good!
. . . And at those times you feel lazy about getting a hold of yourself,
of getting out of that place; it's like when you start to faint: there's a
sweetness to feeling one's strength leaving.] (200)

Renée's joy in her simulated illness and search for "idées noires" reveal
the decadent influence. As we will see later in this study, adolescence is
already construed of as a time of mental and physical languor, therefore
the adolescent heroine perfectly suits the decadent aesthetic, which
portrays such degeneration as the symptom of a moment in sociocul-
tural time.

The decadent heroine, the earliest form of the "new woman," a social
phenomenon to be traced later in this study, exists under the sign of
illness and death. Despite her apparent autonomy, liberty of word and
deed, and heretofore unheard-of lack of constraints from social institutions, the adolescent suffers from an apparent incapability to love, or
at least to "love" in a traditional, socially acceptable manner. Despite
her refusal of certain social tenets, she has a strong moral code, which
Ricatte calls a sense of "virile honor," and which forgives no transgression, even from a beloved family member.[13] Horrified at her brother's purchase of a name, Renée sets in motion a chain of events that
ends with his death in a duel. Therefore, feelings of guilt (vis-à-vis her
brother, whom she has betrayed, and Denoisel, whose opinion of her
matters more than even she realizes) contribute to the depression and
despair that weaken Renée's health. Her illness, a "sickness of the heart"
confirmed by the doctor, represents at once her refusal of her feelings
for Denoisel and of her brother's act, both of which violate her moral
code. Renée dies, leaving her parents in a state of profound grief.

The death of the heroine can be read in several ways. First, it can
signal the dangers of the new opportunities offered to young girls, of
the liberal and indulgent education Renée receives from her adoring
father. One can also see in her death an insistence on the purity of the
adolescent: death of the innocent as a symbolic reference to the traditional view of the female adolescent as virginal and naïve. I read Renée's
end as a message about the temporary incompatibility of the new young
woman and the rapidly changing society she inhabits. Ricatte observes
that, in literature of the mid-nineteenth century, "Young women who
have already begun to think or to act for themselves put excessive tension into it. Renée escapes effortlessly from her milieu, usually laughing." He goes on to point out that this "fresh and joyous creation"

nonetheless scandalized the literary public (Ricatte 1953, 230). This paradoxical figure, full of health and happiness, who so rapidly succumbs to physical and spiritual decline after the shock of her brother's affair and his death in a duel soon thereafter, cannot thrive in a society that expects her behavior to fit a neat, long-standing pattern of feminine submission and devotion, and that permits and even encourages dishonesty in the name of social ascension. The decadent adolescent, as represented by Renée Mauperin, has a difficult time finding a niche in the society she inhabits. Her rebellion against existing societal patterns comes too soon, and the world is not yet prepared to rethink its habits. She dies in frustration, unable to accept the world as it is or to effect a positive change.[14]

If the presence of death in the novel clearly indicates the decadent frame of mind that colors the novels to be discussed, the very nature of the new young woman Renée represents fits the decadent model. The intellectual atmosphere in late nineteenth-century France reveals a sense of decline, loss of control, impotence, physiological weariness, and genetic breakdown at the time that manifests itself in literature as inversion, androgyny, and sterility.[15] Yet the preponderance of literary production at this time reveals the potential "productivity" of such generalized decline. In fact, the decadent movement rests on paradox. Behind the pessimism and despair lies an inevitable hope for some kind of reconciliation: intrinsic to the death of God signaled by Nietzsche is the potential for a rethinking of spiritual values; in the deconstruction of humanity to its most basic processes is the hope for reproduction. The adolescent female, still in nascent form at the end of the nineteenth century and herself inevitably marked by conflict, paradox, and general uncertainty, effectively symbolizes the concerns of the decadents and their hope against hope for the future.

In the novels I have chosen to represent this decadent image of adolescence (as already glimpsed in *Renée Mauperin*), *Chérie* by Edmond de Goncourt, *La Joie de vivre* and *Le Rêve* by Emile Zola, and *La Marquise de Sade* and *Minette* by Rachilde, the patterns established above repeat themselves with fascinating variations.[16] Though the heroines vary greatly in personality, milieu, and experience, together they give a clear picture of the decadent, morally constrained, stagnant vision of the female adolescent at the end of the nineteenth century. Themes such as sexual maturation, changing forms of religion, the escape from reality via the mind, forms of sterility, and the influence of illness and death reveal this vision.

THE AWAKENING OF THE BODY

In the middle of the nineteenth century, the female body became a
principal focus of scientific/medical inquiry. As a result, new information about female puberty appeared. Christine Planté points to the
discovery of the functioning of the female sex organs and the menstrual cycle in the 1840s.[17] This is the era of physical education for
girls, where they were permitted to exercise without corsets and many
of them discovered the natural movement of their bodies for the first
time.[18] The maturing female body disturbed nineteenth-century parents, educators, and religious figures; all of these saw in it a potential
for sexual temptation and corruption. Therefore, girls were kept in the
dark about their bodies' sexual functions, and toiletries were often per-
formed clothed (Knibiehler 1991, 361). Marie-Françoise Lévy points
out that the religious festivities during the month of May had a very
concrete purpose: to channel the sexual energy of adolescent girls into
religious practices. Lévy writes that the goal was to "intervene as a prevention of sensual disorder brought about by this natural effervescence.
Spring, earth and nature are associated with a blossoming sexuality
that might jeopardize the young woman's virginity. This is a religious
discourse of prevention" (Lévy 1984, 61). Religious ecstasy was a safe
outlet for the emotional and physical turbulence of puberty.

As has already been suggested, medical research on the female body
and its functions, such as studies about the age of the onset of menstruation, encouraged doctors to urge parents to delay marriage, thereby
creating a new social class.[19] In her study of the history of girlhood,
Joan Jacobs Brumberg notes that nineteenth-century doctors thought
early marriage to be a mistake because a girl's pelvic development was
considered incomplete until the age of twenty. A largely Christian society would struggle to provide a safe time between menarche and marriage for teenage girls (Brumberg 1997, 11). Brumberg traces the crisis
of the 1870s and 1880s about what to do with the huge group of sexually
mature but unmarried girls created by the delay of marriage.[20]

Clearly, menstruation marks an important change in biological and
social status: "Menstruation makes a sexual being of a little girl and
plays a large part in an implicit rite of passage from one age to another"
(Houbre 1997, 156). Yet for most girls, this passage was not accompanied by preparatory conversations or instruction, and it often came as
quite a shock. Brumberg notes that, when girls entered high schools
and colleges in the latter decades of the century, their lack of knowl-

edge about their bodies became blatantly obvious (Brumberg 1997, 12–13). Many attributed girls' ignorance to their mothers' decorum-induced silence.[21] Mothers believed that, by saying nothing, they were protecting their daughters' virtue from the increasing sexual danger linked to later marriage. They also tried in various ways to retard the onset of menstruation, believing that early menstruation was a sign of a libidinous or sexually licentious society (16). Sexuality was repressed in various ways: reading material linked to love and the developing body was taboo, and social groups for young girls developed in the 1880s to provide girls with a "safe" place to interact without sexual temptation (17). Fear that teaching about menstruation would lead to discussion of intercourse kept girls ignorant of their developing bodies (35). It was believed that sexuality could be repressed through external controls; therefore, a girl's doctor enlisted her mother's help in monitoring certain dangerous behaviors such as excessive exercise, and hot or cold baths (36). Also during the 1880s, the rise of the germ theory led to increased interest in cleanliness of house and person (38). For Victorian mothers and grandmothers, Brumberg observes, menstruation was merely a question of hygiene.

In France, similar attention was paid to cleanliness after the mid-nineteenth century, when Pasteur alerted the French to the existence of the bacterial world (Vigarello 1983, 202). Alain Corbin notes that the young girl's bedroom was surveyed with particular care, as she was considered to be fragile and vulnerable to illness (Corbin 1982, 195). Though toilets appeared in schools during this time, girls were encouraged to avoid indulging their bodies: "Female educators firmly recommend that their students restrain themselves; a respectable woman must prove that she can resist her bodily impulses by mastering her physiological needs" (203). Educators hoped that, by training girls not to listen to their physical impulses, they could control the development and expression of sexual desire. Baths were frowned upon, as they could provide the girl with dangerous stimulation were she to observe her body too closely: "By bathing too often, the young woman even risked debility" (209–10). George Vigarello agrees that bathing, especially in hot water, was considered to lead to immoral or prurient behavior. Indeed, cleanliness began to be considered a part of a girl's moral education (Vigarello 1983, 174). At puberty, the girl was taught proper hygiene, linked less to physical cleanliness and more to the use of clean and good-smelling linen (211). However, the girl was forbidden to use flowers and perfumes on or near her body, as they were linked to seduction and considered to cause mental illness (214–16). The natural, untainted smell of the virgin was in any case the most highly prized fragrance (207, 214). This is fortunate, for given the many and varied restraints regarding hygiene, actual cleanliness was kept to a minimum.

In the quest to preserve the innocence of the adolescent girl, at least until her marriage, her body was clothed in ways that reinforced its purity. Yvonne Knibiehler has commented on the nineteenth-century garment, which underlined the innocence of the young girl. She writes of the heavy significance of the color white, " . . . the transparent muslin of the first ball gown that veils intact modesty. The young lady is a lily, a dove. Her candid freshness evokes the spring of the world" (Knibiehler 1991, 355). Moreover, the female garment traces the girl's progress toward adulthood:

> Dress underlines the various stages of growth, the formation of personality. The young woman's skirt touches the ground, and her hairstyle is elaborate. The "big girl," who is going through the crisis of puberty, braids her hair or puts it in a net, her skirt comes to her ankle. The "little girl" before the age of reason wears her hair loose; her dress shows her boots and even her pantaloons. (355)

These cultural dress codes marked a girl with clear signs of her age, of her progress toward marital eligibility.

Medical advances that established the specificity of the female reproductive system also facilitated the development of new theories about female behavior, and the notion of hysteria, the "maladie du sexe faible," was born.[22] During puberty, according to the doctors of the late nineteenth century, "The nervous system . . . proved to be the most fragile and most exposed to attacks of epilepsy, hysteria, . . . idiocy and other ills that afflict women" (Houbre 1997, 157). Hysteria can be linked to the idea of a weakened will, another *leitmotif* of decadence. Though later than the period discussed here, Havelock Ellis's studies on sexual inversion of the 1890s showed the appeal of knowledge about the human body's form and function and the ensuing influence on behavior.[23]

Such scientific study of links between bodily functions and behavior interested novelists such as the Goncourt brothers, who wished their portrayals to be as close to the truth as possible. In the preface to his novel *Chérie*, Edmond de Goncourt writes that he hopes to give a realistic portrayal of the girl, unlike the majority of contemporary writers:

Je crois pouvoir avancer qu'il est peu de livres sur la femme, sur l'intime féminilité[24] de son être depuis l'enfance jusqu'à ses vingt ans, peu de livres fabriqués avec autant de causeries, de confidences, de confessions féminines . . . Je n'ai pu me résoudre à faire de ma jeune fille l'individu non humain, la créature insexuelle, abstraite, mensongèrement idéale des romans chic d'hier et d'aujourd'hui.

[I believe that I can state that there are few books about woman, about the intimate femininity of her being from childhood to twenty years of age, few books created with so many chat sessions, confidences, feminine confessions. . . . I could not resolve to make my young woman the inhuman individual, the asexual, abstract, dishonestly ideal creature of the chic novels of yesterday and of today.] (Goncourt 1926, ii)

Goncourt dismisses earlier novelistic portrayals of girls in favor of a more realistic version that takes into account the actual characteristics and behavior of late nineteenth-century adolescents. In the postface, J. H. Rosny Aîné of the Académie Goncourt writes of Goncourt's sources of information on female coming-of-age: mothers and daughters who wrote him anonymous letters explaining their experiences. The novel is a serious attempt to document social fact, not a mere invention of the imagination. The novel gives surprisingly detailed descriptions of the physical changes Chérie experiences during puberty, and of her mental reactions to them. Her early puberty is marked by a loss of grace, of femininity: "Une métamorphose étrange: en ce corps de Chérie qui était . . . la grâce même, depuis des mois se glissait quelque chose de laidement garçonnier." [A strange metamorphosis: in Chérie's body which was . . . grace itself, for several months something had started to slip in that was ugly and boyish]. Her gestures are "maladroits, gauches, presque comiques" [maladroit, awkward, almost comic] (101). She becomes "un être qui n'était plus une petite fille et pas encore une femme, un être au sexe comme indécis et non définitivement arrêté et en train de se chercher, un être mystérieux mû par des impulsions d'une spontanéité irréfléchie et contradictoire, jaillissant au dehors avec une rudesse parfois sauvage" [a being who was no longer a little girl and not yet a woman, a being of seemingly undecided sex, not definitively stopped and searching for itself, a mysterious being moved by the impulses of ill-considered and contradictory spontaneity, gushing out with a sometimes savage harshness] (102). This description of adolescence as intrinsically androgynous, hybrid, and unpredictable reveals a strong influence from decadent aesthetics, which embraced hybridity and excessive or problematic sexuality.

At the same time, Goncourt's novel occasionally yields passages of detailed and accurate descriptions that seem far removed from the decadent imagination. The description of the onset of menstruation in the novel is perhaps one of the most explicit and certainly one of the earliest of its kind: "Sous le désarroi momentané des manifestations extérieures avait lieu, dans le corps de Chérie, l'occulte transformation de la fillette en une créature d'amour, en une femme réglée" [Under the momentary disarray of exterior manifestations in Chérie's body, the secret transformation of the girl into a creature of love, into a menstruating woman, was taking place]. In a passage motivated by concern for scientific accuracy, Goncourt mentions the difference in age at the time of the first menstrual period among various populations: Parisians menstruate earliest (Goncourt 1926, 102). Goncourt goes on to document his statement in a strange, hardly novelistic passage, which gives the "fait constaté par la médecine" [fact noted by medicine] that Parisian puberty occurs at thirteen to fourteen years of age, outlines letters received from mothers about earlier occurrences, and suggests that the exciting atmosphere of salons might lead to early puberty (102–3). Goncourt thus explains the passages on Chérie's "jouissances" artistiques.

There follows a passage in which Goncourt analyzes the arrival of the first menstrual period and the girl's perception thereof.[25] He evokes:

> un sommeil trouble ou, parmi les cauchemars, ont lieu la sourde et tourmentante élaboration de la femme dans la jeune fille, le détournement du plus pur de ses veines pour les fonctions de la maternité, le chaud éveil d'un organisme encore végétant; c'est le sommeil, pendant plusieurs mois, des vierges impubères, jusqu'à la nuit de fièvre où elles se réveillent dans la terreur de ce sang inattendu.

> [a troubled sleep where, among nightmares, the deaf and tormenting elaboration of the woman in the girl, the detour of her purest veins for the maternal functions, the warm awakening of a still vegetating organism take place; it is the sleep, for several months, of the immature virgins, until the night of fever where they wake up in the terror of unexpected blood.] (Goncourt 1926, 103)

Unprepared girls felt "terror" at seeing the "unexpected" blood, because none of the older women in their lives prepared them for the shock in any way. Goncourt awakens readers to the basic injustice of the traditional system by insisting on this unpleasant experience, both in general and in particular. After the narrator's commentary, there follows what is made to look like a censored passage, then a return to Chérie and her consternation at seeing the blood (104). In this way, Goncourt convincingly documents the ineffectiveness of female education, for Chérie "resta cependant assez longtemps un peu honteuse de cette perte de sang comme d'une infirmité, comme d'une souillure apportée à sa nette et propre humanité, comme d'une indignité" [remained for a long time slightly ashamed of this loss of blood like an infirmity, like a soiling of her clean and neat humanity, like a disgrace] (104). Because of the lack of instruction given to girls about their bodies, the onset of menstruation provoked fear, guilt, and embarrassment. Menstruating girls felt as though they were ill or unclean, rather than accepting their experience as a normal part of life. In referring to this state of mental and emotional upset, Goncourt indirectly argues for increased education, a topic dealt with in greater detail later in this study.

Throughout the ensuing discussion about the after-effects of menstruation, it is often difficult to tell which passages refer to Chérie in particular and which are simply statements gathered from Goncourt's research. In any case, he is one of the first novelists to acknowledge in such detail the subtleties of female existence and the emotional burden of changing physicality (Goncourt 1926, 104).[26] The interior changes in the adolescent girl were mirrored by exterior changes, most frequently the lengthening of skirts and the putting up of the hair.[27] Goncourt explores the unstable position of the girl in relation to the event: she feels disgust, then pride, followed by a feeling of solidarity with the mother in sharing a secret that one hides from one's friends, and finally a new interest in womanly occupations (105–6). Physical maturity brings with it a new timidity, especially around men (106). This passage exposes the very male perspective of Goncourt's narrator, despite his seemingly progressive interest in documenting the reality of young females. He finds "charming" the embarrassment, torment, and fear of man that he observes in young women during puberty. Other results of the first menstrual period, according to the narrator, include sensitivity and a preference for being alone in her room, dreaming of love (108). Just as in the other novels, physical awakening and flights of the imagination seem to coexist. Another side effect is passionate attachments to female friends (108).[28] Goncourt adds one last bit of information about the maturation process: different populations mature at different speeds;

Chérie's early development is explained by her mother's Spanish blood (132). This whole episode is notable not only for its physiological and psychological detail but also for its double focus on the character and on the population she represents.

As Goncourt's character continues to mature, she reveals an increasing awareness of her physicality. She fears unpleasant breath and bewails the darkening of her hair (Goncourt 1926, 154–56), yet remains ignorant of physical love. As the narrator comments, "Ce qu'on ne croirait guère, c'est que cette jeune fille, femme depuis des années, et dont l'imagination était uniquement occupée d'amour, ne savait encore rien de l'union des sexes et du mode de procréation des enfants" ["What one could hardly believe, was that this young girl, a woman for years now, and whose imagination was uniquely occupied with love, still knew nothing of the sexual union and of the method of procreation"] (189). Chérie believes babies come from natural springs, and passes up all opportunities to discover the truth through observation of statues or animals, discussion with friends, or the reading of "bad books" (190–91). Her education comes with the unintentional discovery of a book on the Amazons (193). Soon thereafter, her nights are troubled by erotic visions (221). She surrounds herself with perfume and sleeps in perfumed sheets, still entertaining illusions about physical love until a letter from a newly married friend destroys all of her fantasies about married life (236–39).[29] After this definitive loss of innocence, Chérie's physical and mental degeneration begins. Of the period novels considered, *Chérie* gives the most detailed account of the physical awakening of the adolescent, and of her discovery of her body and its functions.

For Zola's female characters, the physical transformation is suggested, rather than stated outright. Angélique has increasingly sensual "religious" daydreams. Pauline observes new smells and other changes in her body, and the transformations bother her:[30]

> C'étaient en elle des changements qui la troublaient, un lent développement de tout son corps, des rondeurs naissantes, comme engorgées et douleureuses, des ombres noires, d'une légèreté de duvet, au plus caché et au plus délicat de sa peau. Quand elle s'étudiait d'un regard furtif, le soir, à son coucher, elle éprouvait un malaise, une confusion, qui lui faisait vite souffler la bougie. Sa voix prenait une sonorité qu'elle trouvait laide, elle se déplaisait ainsi, elle passait les jours dans une sorte d'attente nerveuse, espérant elle ne savait quoi, n'osant parler de ces choses à personne.

[There were changes in her that worried her, a slow developing of her entire body, nascent curves, swollen and painful, black shadows, light as down, on her most hidden and most delicate skin. When she studied herself with a furtive glance at night, while going to bed, she felt a faintness and confusion that made her blow out the candle quickly. Her voice took on a tone that she found ugly; she didn't like herself this way; she spent her days in a kind of nervous waiting, hoping for something, she wasn't sure what, not daring to speak of these things to anyone.] (Zola 1964, 852)

Though the family doctor actually cautions Pauline's aunt about the danger of panic and horror if young women are not prepared for the onset of menstruation, the aunt fails to heed his warning: "Elle avait pour système d'éducation l'ignorance complète, les faits gênants évités, tant qu'ils ne s'imposaient pas d'eux-mêmes" [Her education system was based on total ignorance, bothersome facts avoided, as long as they didn't present themselves] (853). When Pauline has her first period, she panics and assumes the worst: "'Tout est fini, je vais mourir'" [It's all over; I'm going to die] (853). Afterward, Pauline feels anger at having been kept ignorant: "Elle gardait une surprise et une rancune du silence de sa tante, de l'ignorance complète où celle-ci la maintenait. Pourquoi donc la laisser ainsi s'épouvanter? ce n'était pas juste, il n'y avait aucun mal à savoir" [She remained surprised and bitter at her aunt's silence, at the total ignorance that her aunt had kept her in. Why let her be so horrified? It wasn't fair; there was nothing wrong with knowing] (855). Here, Zola clearly criticizes the senseless practice of allowing girls to approach puberty completely ignorant of the workings of their bodies. Even long after her first period, Pauline still thinks of her physical transformation as potential illness: "Plusieurs fois, elle se crut souffrante, sur le point de faire une maladie grave, car elle se couchait fiévreuse, brûlée d'insomnie, emportée tout entière dans le tumulte sourd de l'inconnu qui l'envahissait" [Several times, she thought that she was ill, about to become seriously ill, for she went to bed feverish, burning with insomnia, swept away entirely in the muffled tumult of the unknown that overran her] (868). Despite her conviction that something is wrong with her, Pauline displays robust sensuality, particularly with regard to her cousin Lazare. In the scene of near rape between Pauline and her cousin Lazare, Pauline's desire is clear: "Elle s'abandonnait . . . , la face rouge et gonflée, les yeux fermés, comme pour ne plus voir. . . . Il lui donna un baiser, qu'elle lui rendit furieusement, en le serrant au cou de toute la force de ses deux bras." [She gave in . . . , her face red and swollen, her eyes closed, as if not to see . . . He gave her a kiss, that she returned furiously, squeezing his neck with all the force of her two arms.] Her movement is described as a "secousse de son corps vierge" [tremor of her virgin body] (1071). Despite the supposed frailty of Pauline's body, at which the author hints repeatedly, its sexual response is quite normal. Given these two seemingly contradictory extremes, physical weakness and robust sexuality, Pauline can be seen as a typically hybrid decadent character.

In Rachilde's novels, new knowledge of the female body is always viewed through the lens of decadence. In *La Marquise de Sade*, Mary Barbe is marked from her early youth by the sight of blood, and it colors her dealings with those around her. Mary matures precociously: at ten years of age she has "cheveux de femme," "coquetterie de femme," and "désespoirs de femme" [womanly hair, vanity and despair] (Rachilde 1981, 78, 104, 115). When Mary is fifteen, her transformation from child to adult woman is most prominent. In keeping with the decadent aesthetic, maturation manifests itself in the novel as illness: as fever, smallpox, insomnia (178, 188, 189). "Mary prit des maladies de langueur, elle passa par toutes les fièvres de croissance, et, un matin, elle se réveilla nubile, ayant quinze ans révolus, bonne à marier, revêtue de la pourpre mystérieuse de la femme" [Mary had langorous illnesses, she went through all of the growing fevers, and one morning, she woke up nubile, fifteen years old, ready to be married, wearing the mysterious crimson of woman]" (178). This image of menstrual blood, though metaphorical, resembles the more explicit expression of coming-of-age found in *Chérie*. In *Minette*, the main character's physical maturation is also figured as illness, suffering, and fever, after which "elle n'avait plus l'air d'un enfant, elle tenait de la femme" [she no longer looked like a child; she took after woman] (Rachilde 1889, 46–47). Later descriptions of her insist on the woman slowly appearing in the child (110, 127), as evidenced by a womanly smell and a sexual response to a kiss (232–33). The final scene, just before her decision to end her life, shows the influence of strong physical desire that nearly conquers the warnings of her conscience.

All of these novels explore either directly or indirectly the adolescent girl's physical transformation, often decadently represented through illness, and the heroine's reaction to it. Goncourt and Zola reveal the conspiracy of silence surrounding menstruation and the developing body, resulting in shock and shame for unprepared girls, while Rachilde addresses the changes in her characters in a more veiled way.

The female adolescent character provided an ideal canvas on which novelists could project their ideas about the developing female body as the century neared its end. When viewed with decadent aesthetic principles, the adolescent girl's body is at once both sexualized and suffering, and the character experiences physical changes as illness without understanding what is happening to her. As the next section shows, some of the young girl's ignorance can be explained by the powerful role of religion in her life.

Religion Re-imagined

In all of these texts, religion is a dominant theme. Understandably so: until the various laws changing the way girls were educated in France, notably the Camille Sée law of 1880, a girl's education came from priests, confessors, her mother, and various religious manuals written for the purpose. "The girl is almost always perceived with a spiritual halo," Houbre observes, possibly because "her education is under the total authority of the Church which directs her, along with her mother" (Houbre 1997, 167). The central goal of these various sources of education was to prepare the girl for a life of marriage and domesticity.[31] As Houbre observes, "Marriage is . . . an almost irresistible culmination in Catholic families where the most important thing is to preserve the girls' chastity" (165). Preserving their chastity required, in the eyes of the church, a strong insistence on motherhood as the feminine ideal. The Virgin Mary, being the image *par excellence* of innocence, purity, devotion, and motherhood, became the inspiration of an entire religious/educational phenomenon for young girls, "le culte de Marie" [the cult of Mary]. While Protestants moved away from a valorization of virginity, "Catholicism, on the contrary, deliberately made it sacred, particularly through the celebration of the cult of Mary" (166). The Catholic Church's dominance of female education allowed for only one model of female behavior, that of the virginal wife and mother.

In her book on *L'Education des petites filles chez la Comtesse de Ségur*, Marie-Christine Vinson observes the constrictive nature of female spaces and ideals of feminity: "The young girl is a prisoner: of very defined, authorized, luminous but closed spaces . . . ; also prisoner of more or less drawn models: the virgin (the cult of the virgin was proclaimed by the Vatican in the 50s), or the spouse, high destiny" (Vinson 1987, 6). Whether girls were being taught at home or in a

number of religious institutions, they spent their time memorizing
prayers to the Virgin and learning how to be more like her (Lévy 1984,
95). Ignorance of all female bodily functions was an essential element
of this powerful inspirational tool, an ignorance that female family
members did little to combat: "Mothers and older sisters used silence
or the artifice of language to maintain the opacity of privacy regarding the female body" (Houbre 1997, 156). Houbre also points out that,
once married, girls were expected to keep quiet about the secrets of
conjugal life when talking to unmarried friends (172). The young girl
found herself surrounded by a conspiracy of silence where those who
could easily enlighten her about certain facts of life were those least
inclined to do so. This organized hypocritical ignorance frustrated
certain writers. In her dissertation on the question of female emancipation in three naturalist writers, L. Chantal Jennings acknowledges
Emile Zola's irritation with Catholic methods of educating girls. Zola
felt that traditional education led to trouble and was unhealthy because
it kept the girl ignorant of the realities of life (Jennings 1969, 150–51).
It is important to note that, for Zola, such realities were the inevitable
roles of wife and mother.[32]

Girls were taught to elevate the spirit and keep thoughts of the body
to a strict hygienic minimum. Giorgio observes the link between the
cult of Mary and the adolescent body:

> In the 19th century, it was discovered that female adolescence hid a
> dream reserve that was hard to control, which worried Catholics (as
> well as seculars). In the eyes of the Church, it was no coincidence that
> the month of May was consecrated to Mary—the Madonna's protection
> to preserve female innocence must act in the middle of the many temp-
> tations that come during the beautiful season. (Giorgio 1991, 188)

In order to keep the time in which girls could dream and think about
taboo topics to a minimum, convent schools kept pupils to extremely
stringent schedules, where every moment of the day was devoted to
some closely watched activity (Houbre 1997, 190). Moments of prayer
to the Virgin were the only moments where the imagination of the
girl could take flight: hence her enthusiasm for the cult of Mary. Girls
lived and breathed adoration for the Virgin, erecting tiny chapels in
their rooms and placing statues and other likenesses around their beds.
Even Renée Mauperin, whose behavior consistently violates common
codes of conduct for adolescent girls, prays to the Virgin twice in the
novel, once when asking that her death precede her father's, and once

after her brother's death and soon before her own (Goncourt 1923, 100, 303).

It is no wonder then that religion should influence the lives of young female characters. Yet when seen through the filter of decadence, the religious fervor expected of female adolescents is distorted, either called into question or transformed into something else entirely. In Rachilde's *La Marquise de Sade*, Mary Barbe's "religion" is seeking violent revenge on the men she sees as merciless destroyers of innocence, including her own. For many adolescent girls, the desire to be loved, which leads them to choose various love objects as childhood becomes adolescence, is closely linked to their affinity for the boundless love and acceptance promised by religion. As the pull toward romantic love becomes stronger, aided by the romantic adolescent imagination, the conflict created facilitates a slippage, or even merging, of the mental spaces devoted to romance and to religion. For Minette, in the novel of the same name, her growing love for a married farm worker can only be a punishment from God for her purportedly scandalous familial origins. Minette associates her passion with her religious fervor (Rachilde 1889, 216). In *Le Rêve*, the role religion plays in Angélique's romantic dream signals this facet of the adolescent imagination. Longing for a very real, physical experience fixes itself on a wholly acceptable, symbolic object of desire. Due in part to her readings of the lives of the saints, where her active imagination brought them to life, Angélique comes to believe that the prince who haunts her dreams is none other than the Saviour himself. Romantic vision and religious dogma mingle in the adolescent mind.

Strong religious faith, coupled with a physical awakening, is often figured as a spiritual marriage. Lévy points out that the first communion, an important event in the girl's spiritual life that took place around twelve years of age, was described as an "angelic wedding party," as a physical penetration of the body by that of Christ, which provoked a feeling of ecstasy (Lévy 1984, 110). *Chérie* describes the heroine's preparation for her first communion as an act of love: "La première communion est le premier amour de la femme, amour qui s'éveille au milieu de la prise de son imagination par des idées d'adoration ... , c'est le don du premier sentiment d'amour humain éclos en la petite fille sous ... la dévotion, et qu'elle offre inconsciemment à un amant céleste" [The first communion is the woman's first love, love that awakes in the midst of the capturing of her imagination by ideas of adoration ... , it is the gift of the first feeling of human love blooming in the young girl beneath . . . her devotion, that she offers unconsciously to a celestial lover] (Goncourt 1926, 85). Philippe Mendousse observes this precise phenomenon of conflating the spiritual and the sensual in his book on the female adolescent soul:

> And if in young imaginations nascent sensuality transposes itself, as we have seen, into ideal loves, it can only give to devotion a sentimental form where the almost erotic language of the most ardent passion will dominate: words like fiancée, spouse, ineffable union, ravishing . . . return continually in the mystical effusions imitated in books of piety. (Mendousse 1963, 122)

For many adolescents, religious rites are described in passionate, sensual terms. Angélique takes this figurative marriage one step further, and dreams of a marriage to a physical embodiment of Christ: "Mais c'est Jésus que je veux!" [But it's Jesus that I want!] (Zola 1928, 54). She hopes to meet a spiritual prince, an incarnation of her religious fervor. Chérie's white dress makes her think of weddings, and leads to thoughts far removed from the solemnity of the religious rite of passage. This appropriation of mysticism for one's own pleasure is one of the common subversive qualities of female adolescent reverie, as revealed in the novels analyzed here—subversive because it transposes the teachings of the church to a much more material realm.

Sensual interpretation of the scriptures was hardly the intention of those charged with the education of young girls, yet it was a way for adolescents to reconcile dogma and desire. Ironically, the force intended to keep young girls out of reach of sexual awakening became the very instrument of sensual epiphany. Whether or not the decadent aesthetic influenced this portrayal of eroticized religious fervor is debatable, but such a subversive vision of devotion does signal a decline in the power of the church, once thought to be omnipotent.

EDUCATING THE MIND AND SENSES

Despite the presence of religion and its strong pedagogical aims in several of these novels, the heroines educate themselves in other ways. The institution destined to replace the church in controlling girls was the school. But from 1870 to 1890, girls had limited access to official instruction, and the novels reflect this. L. Chantal Jennings writes that Emile Zola wished to depict young female characters free of religion, ignorance, and stupidity, whose balanced instruction imbues them with moral qualities and sufficient occupations to keep them from the dangers of idleness (Jennings 1969, 227). Female adolescence in this time period is marked by an overpowering need to escape from the realities of the quotidian in dream and in creative activity. All of the adolescent girls in these novels, without structured education to occupy their minds, invent stories, read whatever they can find, and imagine. Yet their escape from reality into imagined worlds borders on unhealthy and neurotic, and reveals the decadent attachment to the notion of hysteria.

Female adolescent characters tend to gravitate toward spaces that offer simultaneous entertainment and education.[33] Such spaces reflect the adolescent and reveal information about her most intimate self.[34] John Neubauer notes several "adolescent spaces," including the garden, the room, the school, and the street (Neubauer 1986, 64–74). My reading suggests that, during the period in question, particularly *female* adolescent spaces were more limited, including neither street nor school. Natural realms and the bedroom are the most important spaces in the life of the female adolescent, with the possible addition of the church. One of the most personal spaces for the young girl is her bedroom, where she can lose herself in daydream.[35] Minette wanders outside, visits her friend the *curé*, or remains shut in contemplation in her room. Mary Barbe explores nearby rose gardens, or sits dreaming in her room. Chérie has a favorite part of the park behind her grandfather's house (Goncourt 1926, 42).[36]

In such intimate spaces, reading tends to be a favorite pastime. As Christine Planté observes, reading is often the only "individual experience" for young women, "because their life has been organized since childhood in a tightly controlled schedule that gives each of their minutes and each of their acts a familial, social, and religious finality." Planté argues that the necessarily religious education given girls emphasized "moral development and collective life" rather than autonomy. Therefore, the reading of novels became a rare solitary experience for young women, "and these stories that, speaking to them of themselves, made them dream of other things, became the occasions, even distorted and illusory, to establish a rapport with the self that perhaps only religious practice allowed them in other forms" (Planté 1989, 76). Reading allowed the woman to experience her mind and her emotions alone, without concern for the good of a collective entity, giving her a new freedom.

Yet reading indicates curiosity, which was viewed by the educators of young girls to be a source of corruption.[37] "Reading is dreaming, therefore getting away, therefore escaping from contingencies, norms and conventions, it is doing exactly the opposite of what was allowed women in (good) 19th-century society" (Hoock-Demarle 1991, 156). Educators make every attempt to keep a watchful eye on the reading material made accessible to girls. "During the entire 19th century and the beginning of the 20th . . . women's reading was attentively policed. The novel represented the highest degree of danger . . . A respectable girl did not read books about love" (Giorgio 1991, 180). The novel is viewed as particularly dangerous for its effect on the body and on the mind: "It is the pretext for longing daydreams or equally inopportune feverish exaltations" (Houbre 1997, 183). Such frivolous imaginings could lead to the construction of illusory and pernicious utopias. Hoock-Demarle comments: "The adolescent girl who devotes her time to reading novels . . . denies her initial innocence and creates for herself an artificial paradise" (153). Ironically, in the courses created for girls during the nineteenth century, literature was one of the only subjects deemed acceptable for their impressionable minds, but the texts selected for study were of course chosen carefully by educators concerned mainly with sheltering the readers (Houbre 1997, 189). Girls had to struggle to gain access to the only allowed source of knowledge, but the obstacles merely enhanced the pleasure of eventual success.

For Edmond de Goncourt's character Chérie, reading provides a sensual release. When she catches scarlet fever, reading becomes "une prise de possession absolue de la lectrice, et Chérie . . . disait que chacune de ses maladies de ce temps se représentait à sa mémoire par le souvenir d'un délicieux enfoncement dans un livre" [an absolute possession of the reader and Chérie . . . said that each of her illnesses at the time was represented in her mind by a memory of a delicious slide into a book] (Goncourt 1926, 75). Listening to music also gives her mysterious sensual pleasure (78–79). Chérie sneaks into her grandfather's study at night to read a forbidden "roman-feuilleton," her pleasure heightened by her racing heart and trembling hands (110–12). She also reads *Paul et Virginie*, finding it to be the ideal love story, but embellishes the reading experience by dipping her books in perfumes (113). Several scenes of reading become very sensualized, for example when "indolemment somnolente, les yeux demi-clos" [indolently drowsy, her eyes half-shut], she hears two servant girls outside talking of love (118). The scent of orange flowers, the heat of the afternoon, and the sound of her native patois make this a powerful scene of sensual awakening linked with the deliciously dangerous act of reading.

For Rachilde's Mary Barbe, reading is a way of gaining power. If, as Houbre suggests, the justification for keeping girls ignorant of their physical functions was to keep control of them, Mary Barbe proves such a theory to be at least partially founded.[38] Mary convinces her uncle to allow her to read a book on the body and its functions, knowledge that serves her later to dominate her husband and the other men in her life, including her uncle. Escape through reading inspires in Mary Barbe a desire for more concrete movement toward the outside world. She finds her uncle's home prisonlike in its monotony and in her inability to leave. As she says to her uncle, "J'ai quinze ans . . . , je m'applique à vous obéir en tout et vous me traitez comme une prisonnière qui serait coupable. . . .Quand je veux sortir, [on] me dit que vous le défendez . . . Ici, je ne trouve pas le soleil, j'irai le chercher ailleurs" [I'm fifteen years old . . . , I try to obey you completely and you treat me like a guilty prisoner. . . . When I want to go out, I'm told that you won't allow it. . . . Here, I find no sun, I'll go seek it elsewhere] (Rachilde 1981, 182–83). Books allow her to imagine a more exciting life and empower her to seek it.

For the heroine in Zola's *Le Rêve*, Angélique, reading provides similar escape and release. She builds a dream world around the religious statues and characters that people her physical and mental landscape, and around the idealized male figure that appears to her in a dream. Twelve-year-old Angélique discovers an engraved book on the saints that inculcates her religious passion and encourages her tendency to dream, so much so that she forgets daily life and the passing of time (Zola 1928, 25). Her enthusiasm for these stories springs from their dramatic nature, which plunges her into an elevated, marvelous other world (30). Her imagination embellishes her reading, bringing the characters to life. In particular, she is attracted to the saintly virgins, for whom she feels a "tendresse fraternelle" [fraternal tenderness] (32). The adolescent need for company, normally fulfilled by flesh-and-blood friends, causes Angélique to fill her solitude by animating the characters that people her books. She finds another creative release in embroidery, which employs her passion for the saints and her creative impulses (42). Angélique incorporates elements from her environment into her mental landscape and the material representations she creates thereof.

The spaces surrounding Angélique also provide fodder for her fantasies. Like many female adolescent characters, Angélique finds a soothing shelter in her room: "C'était avec la joie d'une véritable récréation qu'elle se retrouvait seule dans sa chambre, le matin et le soir: elle s'y abandonnait, elle y goûtait l'escapade de ses songeries" [It was with the joy of a real break that she found herself alone in her room, morning and evening: she gave herself up to it, tasting there the escapade of her thoughts] (Zola 1928, 54). There she can peacefully indulge in her spiritual reverie, which, the narrator points out, has given her new force to meet the battles of existence. Her new home, nestled against a church, has provided a nurturing milieu that has saved her from an otherwise dubious fate. Yet the embellishment of faith comes from Angélique herself. Out of various external and internal elements, she imagines a dream "milieu" that she controls and that she then uses to help her confront the battles of life (65). Angélique creates her own religion, which then becomes a source of comfort for her. Her fervor grows slowly as she reaches maturity, and in the tumult of physical change surrounding puberty her state of mental excitation reaches its height (66). The space inhabited by Angélique fosters her imaginative flights, and facilitates the development of her creative mind.

Angélique's sensual nature and love of the spiritual, combined with her slow sexual awakening, produce the dream of the title: that one day she will marry a prince and revel in his wealth, goodness, and beauty (Zola 1928, 50). Her vision evokes physical pleasure: "Elle continuait tout bas, elle montait plus haut, plus haut encore, dans l'au delà du désir; et tout le disait en elle, sa bouche que l'extase entr'ouvrait, ses yeux où se reflétait l'infini bleu de sa vision" [It continued softly, grew louder, louder still, beyond desire; and everything in her said it, her mouth opened by ecstasy, her eyes where the infinite blue of her vision was reflected] (53). The dream even becomes a part of her work (53). Angélique blends faith, creativity, and awakening sensuality, creating with these elements a romantic vision. Anthony Greaves has observed that the tendency to idealize love is a key decadent element in Zola's novels, leading to the downfall of the character:

> Even if he escapes the dubious intentions of a third party, the individual is completely capable of destroying himself. This tendency manifests itself especially in amorous relationships. Rather than being content with earthly love, perhaps limited, but solid and safe, one seeks love touching the limits of perfection, well beyond the real world. (Greaves 1980, 94)

Moreover, he adds, "The forces of illusion find the most appropriate field in religion" (95). Angélique fits this analysis perfectly: her religious fervor, combined with her desire for a perfect love, renders her incapable of inhabiting reality, as the end of the novel makes clear. Her illusion has become her world, and she can conceive of no other.

The collision of reverie and reality comes soon enough. When Félicien, who belongs to a higher social class, proposes that they run away together, Angélique imagines herself the heroine of a fairy tale: "Des musiques l'enivraient; elle voyait leur royal départ, ce fils de princes l'enlevant, la faisant reine d'un royaume lointain" [Music intoxicated her; she saw their royal departure, this son of princes taking her away, making her queen of a faraway kingdom] (Zola 1928, 175). Yet when she tries to leave, she is retained by holy visions warning her against a rash and potentially catastrophic departure. Her new dream is to die pure and chaste, like the saints who people her dreams. The hard truths of reality drive her eternally back to a dream world bolstered by faith.

Reading, imagining, and artistic creation provide outlets for the female adolescent mind, constricted by the religious instruction that often governed adolescent existence. These heroines find ways of incorporating religious themes into their fantasy worlds, thereby satisfying their need for sensual and emotional release while respecting the education they have received. They reveal the complexity of the adolescent mind, capable of rationalizing flights of fancy. The meanderings described here as natural to the adolescent mind fit the decadent fondness for neurosis and transgression. Fantasy and mental escape to dream worlds reinforce the image of the hysterical girl out of touch with reality. Conjuring up the danger of unsupervised reading and the specter of hysteria in the novel proved to be a powerful argument against allowing girls to cultivate their mental space, and therefore slowed the process of educational reform.

Fin de siècle/Fin de race

Given the enthusiasm for scientific exploration of heredity (Zola's determinism) and for the theory of the inevitable degeneration of the human organism toward the end of the nineteenth century, the decadent passion for social and genetic decline is easily explained. The novel of adolescence of the period questions reproduction by creating female characters with absent or problematic parents. Though Renée's parents are both alive, it is clear that her relationship with her mother is conflictual, and her relationship with her father based on camaraderie rather than paternal authority. The orphans among the heroines of the other novels include Zola's Angélique and Pauline, and Rachilde's Minette (though the potential paternity of the Abbé is hinted at). Mary Barbe loses both of her parents during the course of the novel; Chérie's father is dead, and her mother, plagued by insanity and shut up in a guesthouse on the family property, dies during the narrative, leaving Chérie to be raised by her grandfather. The absence or demise of all of the parents in the novels from 1870 to 1890 raises some interesting issues, principally that of the decadent fascination with genetic break-down. These novels call into question the family tree, not only by de-picting the precarious health of the offspring, but also by eliminating and/or undermining the progenitors.

In addition to her problematic ancestry, each novel's heroine is her-self marked by sterility in one of several ways. In some cases, by her own choice: Mary Barbe of *La Marquise de Sade* announces to her hus-band that she has no intention of giving him children: "Louis, je suis décidée à ne pas vous donner d'héritier, et comme il faut être deux pour ces sortes de décisions . . ." [Louis, I have decided not to give you an heir, and as two people must make this kind of decision . . .]. When her husband protests, Mary explains: "*Je suis assez*, EN ETANT, et si je pouvais finir le monde avec moi, je le finirais" [*I am enough*, JUST BEING, and if I could finish the world with myself, I would finish it] (Rachilde 1981, 214, emphasis Rachilde's).[39] This speech shows sev-eral interesting marks of the fin-de-siècle subversiveness of Mary's discourse. First, the fact that she has been granted access to medi-cal texts explaining the functioning of the sexual organs is enough to shock period readers. Second, that she dare approach her husband to discuss such a topic as contraception—having already made a decision, no less—transgresses all the social codes governing communication between spouses, particularly in the mouth of an eighteen-year-old virgin. Finally, Mary states very clearly her sense that she represents the end of the line, the end of an age.[40]

For Rachilde's Minette, the chances for a traditional marriage are al-ready slim, given her marginalized social position. The last descendant of a noble family, she represents a class to which none of those who live nearby can aspire. To complicate matters even further, the suspicious origins of her birth give rise to malicious gossip about werewolves. She is in fact the daughter of her beloved confessor, a fact that has its own scandalous connotations. Were none of these reasons enough to ruin Minette's chances for marriage, such a possibility disappears entirely when she falls in love with one of her farm workers, a married man.

Rachilde eliminates one by one all chances for her heroine's future happiness.

In Zola's *La Joie de vivre*, the end of the family line is figured less physiologically and more financially.[41] Madame Chanteau slowly pilfers Pauline's personal fortune until nothing remains. At the end of the nineteenth century, a plentiful dowry had everything to do with a young girl's success in finding a husband and starting a family, especially if she were an orphan. Apart from her total devotion to her cousin, which provides another obstacle to a healthy marriage elsewhere, Pauline's lack of fortune and family connections suggests that she is doomed to a life as an old maid. Yet this becomes her choice. When her cousin Lazare asks why she doesn't marry, toward the end of the novel, she answers, "Me marier! jamais de la vie, par exemple!" [Marry! Never ever, honestly!] (Zola 1964, 1129). She explains that "qu'elle voulait rester fille afin de travailler à la délivrance universelle" [she wanted to remain a girl in order to work for universal deliverance] (1129). Though such a humanist aim corresponds poorly to decadent thematics, the end result, voluntary failure to reproduce, resembles that found in the other novels. For Zola's other heroine, Angélique, her name already announces the absence of sexuality and of fertility. There are other signs, however, such as her identification with the saints from her religious readings, her "creation" of various embroidered religious characters, and the innocence of her imagined marriage with an asexual, divine prince. Neither of Zola's characters are overtly sexual beings; for both, marriage and reproduction seem unlikely options.

Like the others, Goncourt's Chérie is not a candidate for marriage and motherhood. Chérie enjoys being admired so much that she develops a passion for group seduction at each ball yet avoids marriage, considering that she has plenty of time and need not rush into binding social contracts. There are several obstacles to her nuptials, however: her grandfather's lack of fortune, her mother's madness, and her spoiled childhood. These obstacles prove sufficient to convince Chérie to stop trying to find a husband. In her case, it is not lack of will to marry, as she wants to do so more than anything else toward the end of her life. Chérie's precarious social and biological conditions simply make her an undesirable spouse.

For all of these characters, marriage and reproduction are excluded for a variety of reasons. Each heroine lives in a sterile world, either by choice or for reasons beyond her control. The theme of androgynous behavior in many of the texts also corresponds to the pessimistic view of the biological future held by the decadents. In these decadent literary works, female adolescence is a tight, impenetrable space that closes in on itself, destroying the possibility of realizing the nineteenth-century feminine maternal ideal.

In addition to the theme of sterility, the decadent school of thought relies heavily on the metaphor of illness. For the decadents, the entire civilization is ailing, and each individual becomes infected by the general malady. As Anthony Greaves writes in his article on "Zola et l'esprit décadent":

> An exacerbated feeling of weakness and defeat is the most striking feature of the decadent hero. The generosity and enthusiastic zeal of the first romantics dissipates too quickly, giving way to a mix of despair, cynicism and bitterness. Convinced of the uselessness of any reaction, the decadent allows himself to be carried away by events, waiting for death to deliver him from the tortures of a poorly made existence. (Greaves 1980, 90)

Though these female adolescent heroines cannot truly be described as "waiting for death," their physical fragility participates both in the contemporary discourse surrounding the female sexual organs and their often pernicious control of the body and mind, and in the decadent obsession with degeneration/decline. Yet according to the decadent template, illness is often a combination of the physical and the mental, a nervous state of excitation that may seem to conflict with the notion of fatigue, of disenchantedness with the experience of living. These heroines are both prematurely tired and overexcited, a paradox that perfectly fits the decadent model, as well as the topos of hysteria. They are both pessimistic and desperate.

Zola's Pauline has clear physical problems and weaknesses that are established early in the novel. Her physical awakening brings on attacks of fever, which are mirrored toward the end of the novel when her beloved cousin's relationship with another woman provokes a more serious struggle with illness that leaves her weak. Yet Pauline is constantly surrounded by illness. She is the voluntary nurse of her dying uncle, whose slow agony she has witnessed firsthand during her years as part of his household. Pauline refuses any opportunities to escape caring for him, and his hopeless agony mirrors her own, both in terms of illness and in her powerlessness to transform her life through marriage and motherhood. Pauline's illness is a natural extension of the larger theme of illness and doom that dominates both the household and the novel.

In Zola's *Le Rêve*, Angélique yearns for a new life—in particular, access to a new social rank through marriage to the noble Félicien—yet fears taking the necessary steps to realize her dream. The day after her refusal to run away with Félicien, Angélique's health begins to fail. Moved by her innocent struggle and her devotion to his son and to God, Félicien's father gives them his permission to marry. Angélique interprets this as a sign of the inevitability of her dream (Zola 1928, 198). During the wedding, she has similar thoughts of triumph: "C'était enfin la réalisation de son rêve, elle épousait la fortune, la beauté, la puissance, au delà de tout espoir" [The dream was finally coming true; she was marrying fortune, beauty, power, beyond all hope] (204). After the ceremony, as she prepares to leave the church, Angélique realizes that marrying and entering the world signals the end of the part of her life dominated by her dream, and the beginning of a period dominated by reality (207). On the threshold between her familiar dream world and the frightening unknown of actual marriage, Angélique dies suddenly.

One may be tempted to dismiss Angélique's death as the end of an excessively romantic and/or neurotic character that is poorly prepared to face the complexities of life. Her dreams have accustomed her to an artificial, embellished, and asexual reality, and the shock of leaving the maternal space of the cloister proves to be too much for her delicate and sensitive nature. The end can also suggest a veritable, albeit precocious, completion of a life, an ideal ascension based on goodness and purity of thought and deed, a kind of spiritual marriage that rapidly replaces her more terrestrial one. This reading is problematic, though, in the sense that Angélique has longed not only for spiritual union, but also for wealth and power and luxury, which may undermine the purity of her love for Félicien.[42] Yet another interesting nuance is that the narrator reminds the reader that "tout n'est que rêve" [all is but a dream] (Zola 1928, 208), suggesting the illusory nature of much of reality, or the realism of dream. Angélique has given herself to the imaginary, to the point that her own existence can no longer be distinguished from it. The mind of the isolated adolescent clings to the dream world she has constructed from various elements of her environment, and can no longer rejoin reality, nor terminate the transition to adulthood in any sense of the term. She dies, still pure and ephemeral, like the fictional virgins she so wished to resemble. Adolescence (and life) ends with the realization of the dream.

Like the others, Goncourt's Chérie dies in the space of the novel. She is already of a "délicatesse nerveuse toute particulière" [quite particular nervous fragility] until her bout of scarlet fever around the age of twelve, at which point she develops a more intense sensitivity (Goncourt 1926, 75) that increases again when she is around seventeen years of age and her friends begin to marry (32). When Chérie realizes that she has no suitors, she makes a conscious decision to stop seeking a husband, ceases to dress and go out, and falls into a torpor, an almost painful mix of worry, sadness, and fatigue that develops into serious illness (242). Interestingly, giving up on marriage seems to deal the protagonist a fatal blow. She begins to sleep longer and more deeply, "d'un sommeil d'anéantissement, d'un sommeil où il y avait de la mort" [a sleep of exhaustion, a sleep where there was something of death] (246). The doctor, "spécialiste des maladies nerveuses" [specialist of nervous illnesses], diagnoses her problem as lack of reproduction: "L'ovulation appelle la fécondation" [Ovulation calls for fertilization], he says, and confirms that such depression can be fatal in young girls (249). In the last scene of the novel, Chérie goes out one last time (to the theater with a friend) and faints constantly. The last chapter gives her death announcement; she dies at nineteen years of age.

The implications of Chérie's death are clear: girls must express their sexuality, even passively, through fantasy or daydream. The presence of the doctor as a representative of the moral majority assuages the fears of readers and critics who conceive of female sexuality only in the context of marriage. When hope for socially approved expression of sexuality in the form of marriage dies, the result can be fatal, Goncourt's novel seems to suggest. The heroine's depression leads rapidly to physical decline; this aspect of the novel reinforces the link drawn by the decadents between mental and physical well-being.[43]

For Rachilde's Minette, sexual repression also proves fatal, though as is often the case with Rachilde's heroines, Minette chooses death. For her, suicide is the only remaining option when, totally isolated in her room, the need for love coupled with sexual temptation prove stronger than her desire to remain pure and close to God. Her trajectory from her room to that of her potential lover is interrupted by a sudden, impulsive detour that leads her outside into the drifted snow, where she freezes to death. Again, sexual repression leads to death.[44]

The adolescent heroine navigates a complicated social space, negotiating between a yearning for independence and the need for affection and guidance, between the expanding demands of the mind and the changing construction of the body, between the constrictive forces of socialization and the unbounded flights of the youthful imagination. Marie-Françoise Lévy notes that, for nineteenth-century girls, the conflict between various societal messages and roles often proves too much, and she turns, first to God, then to death, as the only solution to the inescapable tension:

> The young woman in this crisis where identity and vocation, adolescence and distress are in question, lives the forbidden when she must go from the closed world of her family or her boarding school to the gaze of others, judged, weighed as a prospect, as a dowry. Tossed between the real and the imaginary, absorbed by her obsessive worry about purification, sacrifice and saintliness, she turns to God. She even comes to evoking—invoking—death. (Lévy 1984, 149)

The pressure and tension of leaving the safety and acceptance of home for a world where she becomes merchandise prove traumatic for the young woman. Death resolves the clash between religious and daily life, particularly in the case of an "exemplary death," which was considered ideal in the eyes of many girls (149). These heroines do not or cannot embrace the social structure within which sexuality is sanctioned, and the tension arising from their attempts to seek happiness (including sexual fulfillment) outside of marriage often leads them to a moral impasse from which the only available escape is death.

One possible reading of these novels is that the authors are intentionally critiquing moral and social constraints by painting portraits of heroines who cannot find happiness, or even continue to live, within them. Both Zola and the Goncourt brothers were displeased with the state of education for young women and wished for a changed social role for adolescents. Their novels may suggest, albeit indirectly, that better and more honest education, particularly about sexual matters, might prevent some misunderstanding, terror, suffering, and even death for the female adolescent. It was not until several decades later, though, that novelists began to argue explicitly for sexual education.

In these late nineteenth-century novels, female adolescence is simultaneously progressing, carving out a literary space, and regressing, as that space proves to have no exit due to the influence of moral authority and decadent aesthetics. The literary vision of the adolescent girl is taking shape, and though she may be physically weak and socially doomed, she is attracting plentiful attention, enough to ensure a future in novels to come. The fact that the decadent novels discussed here end with an adolescent death can be read as a warning of the girl's precarious societal and literary position at the end of the nineteenth century. The writers may in fact be arguing that the female adolescent in literature and in life should gain access to a larger space, for her own good and for that of society in general.

Many critics writing about adolescence locate the explosion of literary interest therein just after the period discussed here.[45] Indeed, this first wave of interest in the adolescent barely preceded what became an international concern in various fields soon thereafter. As novels after 1891 will show, themes of illness and the specter of death continue to haunt such literary portrayals of adolescent girls. Yet the novelists of the Belle Epoque will create a new social and literary space for female adolescence, despite such recurrent and inevitable growing pains.

2
Shifting Spaces
(1890–1910)

THE EARLIEST TRUE EXAMPLES OF THE FRENCH NOVEL OF FEMALE ADO-
lescence tended to support the aesthetic notions and ideologies dominant at the time rather than to portray social reality. Though some of
the novels discussed in the previous chapter present nearly believable
adolescent characters, the writers all succumb at some point to the
decadent mindset in vogue at the end of the nineteenth century, imbuing their characters with physical and mental fragilities and/or idiosyn-
crasies that entertained period readers. Already an amorphous being,
the adolescent girl becomes, when seen through the decadent literary
optic, a pallid, emotionally unstable character. She is at odds with her
peers, family members, and the world around her. Indeed, she has occasional moments of willful extroversion, phenomena that parallel the
beginnings of educational reform in France, which sent a clear message to the general public that women had brains and could use them
to consider things beyond needlepoint and the latest recipes. Yet these
moments are few, and often tinged with irony. The reader understands
that the character will have to defer to the moral conventions of her
society or remain forever at its margins, an exile often figured in these
novels as premature death. The decadent world had no use for adolescent characters, except perhaps as screens onto which were projected
self-conscious displays of contemporary scientific theories about the
female body and mind.

The novels of female adolescence written at the turn of the century
reflect the improving position of the young woman in French society,
and, indeed, in the world, and therefore conceive of their protagonists
more as complex subjects than as objects, as in the decadent novels
from the previous chapter. In fact, many of these novels show marked
progress in adolescent girls' lives. In 1904, G. Stanley Hall published

his imposing work called *Adolescence: Its Psychology and Its Relations to Physiology, Anthropology, Sociology, Sex, Crime, Religion, and Education*, in which he also pondered related subjects such as morality and literature. According to Patricia Meyer Spacks, by reaching an international audience, Hall's study "inaugurated a period, still continuing, in which the adolescent assumed a place of pivotal importance in sociological, psychological and literary thought and in the popular imagination as well" (Spacks 1981, 228). Spacks notes that Hall's work served to "create a large space for a group that previously had no 'official' space at all. . . . After the turn of the twentieth century, adolescent protagonists in fiction assume a new aspect, more aggressive, more complicated in feeling, more *significant*" (235–36). In France, the educational reforms of the 1880s ensured that girls from most social classes were attending private *cours* or public schools, and learning about an increasing number of subjects, including those formerly reserved for boys, such as mathematics and the sciences. New spheres were opening to them, and thus one might expect portrayals of this transformation to be jubilant and unsullied by the kind of pandering to aesthetic or moral ideals revealed in earlier works. As reform progressed, representations of adolescence accordingly became less ideological and closer to portraying social reality. The period considered here (1890–1910), which we will refer to as the fin-de-siècle and the Belle Epoque,[1] did witness the publication of several landmark novels of female adolescence embellished by the kind of unforgettable character that becomes part of literary memory for decades to come, the best example of which is probably Colette's Claudine. Yet many writers chose to present stereotyped female characters representing some general principle, political position, or social status.

Though I have tried to avoid classifying writers according to gender, Belle Epoque novels of female adolescence tend to fall into two groups, and these two groups most often fall on either side of the gender line. There are exceptions, of course, but to simplify matters, I will briefly describe the broad characteristics of each category before moving on to a more detailed discussion of the novels that represent it.

Male writers and critics of this time period had varying reactions to the rush of female writers and female characters onto the French literary stage. Some of them praised novels supposed to be written by men, only to revise their commentary when the author was revealed to be a woman.[2] Others avoided discussing woman writers, opting instead, when prompted, for a commentary on the influence of women as *read-*

ers.[3] Most criticism of female novelists and their work at this time is undeniably negative,[4] and the rare appreciative word, due to tone or to the use of disclaimers, sounds much like an attack.[5] Yet male novelists themselves were beginning to pay attention to the increasingly important slice of society represented by female adolescents, or at least to the rapidly growing number of female readers, and to write novels based on a young female protagonist. As Jules Bertaut writes in *La Jeune fille dans la littérature française*, the young female character has become an "official being" by this time: "Literature was becoming enriched with a new species to study, not one of the least curious, and each tried to paint one of its truths" (Bertaut 1910, 175). Inspired by the novelty of this new "species," writers vied to write the truest, most accurate description thereof. Bertaut goes on to describe the powerful fascination of the young female character:

> The young girl, having conquered her rank in the world, endowed to literature a new type, extremely interesting because it is extremely complex, that seduced observers immediately. By her flexibility, the indecision of her too new feelings, by this unknown sense of something unfinished that always subsists even among the most decided girls whose personality seems most certain, she allows oscillating feelings about her, she appears subtle, mysterious, elusive.[6] She irritates and amuses, arouses curiosity and rejects it, makes advances and pulls back, has all whims, graces and mischief. (176)

Bertaut's commentary suggests that the appeal of the female adolescent lies in her unpredictable nature, her mystery tinged with "devilish" whim and grace. This very quality fascinated the authors who then tried to reproduce it in their works, and the critics who studied and classified the works, such as Bertaut: "She has been much studied for about twenty years, many of her good qualities and flaws have been recognized, she has been classed into genres, sub-genres, and species, and we have not yet, thank God, exhausted all of what she brings to literature" (177). This new and exceedingly rich matter from which to mold a novel led to dramatically varying portraits, and Bertaut acknowledges that there is plenty more to write. He attributes this wide range of portrayals to the rapidly changing female adolescent:

> The young girl, like all living beings, is in a state of perpetual evolution . . . She who by her style, her customs, her language and her gestures was the most "current" yesterday, is today, at this moment, already outdated by the appearance of a slightly younger friend who brings to

us the image of tastes, passions and hates of a different generation. And often this image is so opposed to the first that all must be redone. No social type will change more rapidly than this one, now that it has its naturalization papers, and is recognized and studied by all. (177–78)

For Bertaut, then, the nature of adolescence makes it particularly subject to change; it naturally transforms itself to reflect a given historical moment. Certainly the differences between adolescent heroines can be partially explained by such "generational" changes, or shifts in fashionable behavior for girls, but the undeniable rifts between male and female portrayals of adolescents lead to the natural assumption that the two sexes had very distinct perspectives with regard to the adolescent character.

   The novels of female adolescence written by men differ from those of the same period written by women in several significant ways. First, they are nearly always written in the third person, from the perspective of a supposedly omniscient but clearly male narrator or from that of a male character. Second, the male novelist is far more apt to preface his text with a consideration of the social phenomenon, the principle, or even the geographic location that the heroine is intended to represent.[7] The mere titles reveal the presumption that the heroine represents some larger principle (*Les Vierges fortes* by Prévost and *Almaïde d'Etremont ou l'histoire d'une jeune fille passionnée* by Jammes, for example). These novels of female adolescence written from a male point of view are far from uninteresting, as they suggest some key aspects of the societal attitude toward female adolescents during the fin-de-siècle and the Belle Epoque, both in content and in narrative technique.

   Female novelists of the time (Tinayre, Colette, Noailles, d'Houville) portray adolescent heroines in an entirely different manner. It should be noted, however, that despite the differences between the sexes in terms of how they construct their female characters, the characters remain just that: constructions, based on a novelist's idea of what a young girl is or could be. In this comparison of male and female constructions, it is possible to think of the young girl as territory that novelists competing for literary accuracy attempted to claim. In his study of *La Littérature feminine d'aujourd'hui*, Bertaut lauds these female novelists, not for blazing a literary trail, as the Goncourt brothers and Emile Zola had already dealt with the young female character, but rather for providing a depth of analysis previously unattained by male novelists: "In the analysis that they have made of this young heart, this young sensitivity, they naturally found accents, provided details, gave precisions that we have not yet seen under the pen of writers of the other sex" (Bertaut 1909, 33). Bertaut interestingly fuels the competitive fire between novelists by suggesting that, although men did stake the first claim to the character, women created richer and more detailed portrayals of adolescent girls. First, the novels of female adolescence written by women tend to be first-person narratives. The "I" may allow for freer exploration of the psychology of the female adolescent, and for greater detail in characterization.[8] As Bertaut observes, "States of being usually so vague when they are evoked by writers who can only speak of them by hearsay have never been expressed in such a precise way. This is, if you will, documentary literature" (33–34).[9] Unlike the works of male novelists, in which the adolescent heroine is understood to stand for some societal phenomenon, and indeed the narrator often tells the reader as much, female novelists rarely profess their characters to have some representative value besides that of a young girl of the time. However, it may be suggested that, by "faithfully" representing the "real" experiences of an adolescent, without imbuing her acts with some greater meaning, the female novelist succeeds in creating a more accurate representation of Belle Epoque adolescent reality.[10] This reality consists of school, friends, and family, much the same elements as those of novels of male adolescence of the period, but the female novelist adds a new element by showing the struggles of the girl to advance in a society that doesn't necessarily recognize her as a cognizant being.

Yet these portraits are not extreme feminist manifestos, making use of adolescence as a moment of nascent adult identity to argue for female emancipation. The subtle yet ubiquitous feminism of the Belle Epoque endorses transformation and progress from within existing social structures.[11] Female novelists do not suggest that adolescent heroines refuse traditional roles such as those of wife and mother, but rather that they seek more autonomy and happiness within those roles. As stated much earlier by Jules Ferry and Camille Sée during the debate over what would become the 1880 Camille Sée law, reform of education for girls was intended not to encourage the avoidance of marriage in young girls, but to provide French men with more interesting spouses (Caron 1996, 196–97). In a certain sense, female novelists complete this notion: rather than struggling against traditional structures, they suggest that educated and autonomous young women find greater happiness in marriage by making more appropriate and discerning choices of husbands, and by working to establish a more equal balance of power within the relationship.

While the primary thematic concerns in the period from 1870 to 1890 are the adolescent's physical changes and their effect on her thoughts and behavior, the novelists of the Belle Epoque tend to focus more closely on wider concerns such as the spaces of female adolescence, both literal and figurative. In the decadent novels considered in the first chapter, the domestic space dominated the narrative; here, domesticity and the family are often abandoned entirely, and new structures replace the traditional familial one. In these novels, the adolescent girl, bereft of parents or endowed with problematic role models, finds replacement parental figures in friends, teachers, and romantic interests. These sources of the love, comfort, and support traditionally associated with the family lead the adolescent into hitherto relatively unknown spaces: school, café, restaurant, and even workplace. When presented with a different reality than that of the parlor, garden, or dining room, she is able to discover aspects of herself and the world that might never have surfaced in the sheltered interior of the family domicile. In the following, I will trace the various spaces opened up to the female adolescent in these turn-of-the-century novels and their effect on her blossoming identity.

The novels of female adolescence written by men during this period—Marcel Prévost's *Les Vierges fortes: Léa* (1900), Francis Jammes' *Clara d'Ellébeuse* (1899), *Pomme d'Anis* (1904), and *Almaïde d'Etremont* (1901), and Romain Rolland's *Antoinette* (1908)[12]—tend to show the adolescent most at home in natural and domestic spaces, while novels such as Marcelle Tinayre's *Avant l'amour* (1897) and *Hellé* (1899), Colette's *Claudine à l'école* (1900) and *Claudine à Paris* (1901), and Anna de Noaille's *Le Visage émerveillé* (1904) show the adolescent learning to navigate in various other geographic, social, and mental spaces. These generalizations are in some cases erroneous, yet on the whole, the female novelists clearly promote a more mobile conception of the female adolescent. At this point in literary history, the female adolescent character is on the move.

Spaces Natural and Unnatural

The spaces of adolescence in these novels tend to break down into two groups: domestic and nondomestic, indoor or outdoor, country or city. The outdoors is often presented as one of the spaces in which the child or adolescent is most at home, in contrast to the domestic indoor space.[13] Indeed, representations of the actual homes of female adolescents reveal domestic spaces to be sources of trauma and unhappiness. One of the *leitmotifs* of the novel of female adolescence since the mid-nineteenth century has been an untraditional family structure. In nearly all of these novels, at least one of the heroine's biological parents is missing, and in many of them, the heroine is orphaned within the span of the narrative. Moreover, relationships with remaining parent figures are often conflictual and even abusive. The adolescent can flee from a space (the structure of the family) where she feels misunderstood or even threatened to a soothing natural space, such as a garden. But is a "garden" always a garden? As John Neubauer writes:

> The garden is the mythic habitat of the child. What are the spaces of the adolescent who has outgrown the paradise of childhood? Literary adolescence is full of nostalgic references to mythical gardens, but the "real" gardens of adolescence are in the city, and urban spaces represent its changing scenery. Unspoilt nature is an object of yearning; the often abhorred but irresistibly fascinating cityscape is where events take place. (Neubauer 1986, 64)

When compared to the reality of the novels of female adolescence studied here, Neubauer's quote seems ironic: while the female novelists' work tends to corroborate his claims, the works by male authors reveal a different conception of female adolescence, closer perhaps to what Neubauer would call childhood.[14] As Neubauer notes, the exciting city is "often abhorred," and the protagonist may find herself overwhelmed by the mastery of new social codes and longing for the simplicity of the provincial setting of her youth. In any case, in the novels space itself is problematized, as is the movement between them. There is nearly always tension in each space that causes the adolescent to seek solace elsewhere.

   Though the characters of Francis Jammes live near villages, their experiences take place in spaces dominated by the presence of nature. They are also all part of a family unit that is untraditional or destabilized in some way. Clara d'Ellébeuse has both parents, neither of whom understands her very well. Her father harbors secret fears about her sanity. Clara spends her time riding near her parents' estate, or wandering in the park behind the house. Pomme d'Anis was born the day her father died, and is being raised by her mother and an uncle named Tom. Pomme plays with her friends in the natural settings necessary for her uncle's botanical studies. Almaïde d'Etremont is an orphan. Her mother died when she was thirteen, and her father was institutionalized soon after. Almaïde lives with an uncle who keeps her prisoner: "un oncle infirme et taciturne qui trouva son avantage à gérer les biens de sa nièce et à l'éloigner le plus possible du monde" [an infirm and taciturn uncle who found it advantageous to manage his niece's assets and to keep her as far as possible from the world] (Jammes 1899, 158). She flees the domestic space: "Elle éprouve une joie à se sentir loin du château qu'elle déteste, loin de ce parc dont chaque fleur lui paraît triste" [She feels joy at being far from the château that she hates, far from the park whose every flower seems sad to her] (158). Almaïde escapes from the confines of her uncle's château to the mountains and riverside where she finds solace in the soothing balm of nature. For all of these characters, which Bertaut refers to as "jeunes filles de province," nature is an important part of their environment. It enables them to wander, to think, to feel peace. Their lives are built around simple encounters with natural settings.

The other male novelists follow this pattern of representing untraditional family structures. Antoinette of Romain Rolland's novel of the same title loses her father to suicide at sixteen years of age, soon after which her mother dies. Alone with her brother Olivier, Antoinette reveals her strength and capacity for self-sacrifice, but dies without knowing love or success. Antoinette symbolizes devotion to family and home.[15] Marcel Prévost's characters Léa and Frédérique are orphans. They have lost their mother and have two different fathers. Frédérique is the daughter of a rich gentleman who refused to acknowledge her at the time of her birth, while Léa's father is an alcoholic who dies early in the first novel. Both girls are adopted by a community of women, who give them help in finding jobs and support them emotionally. For Léa and Frédérique, whose various homes are located in urban centers, contact with nature is limited to occasional visits to parks and gardens. Yet Léa's epiphanic moments nearly always take place in a glorious natural setting. For these characters by male novelists, nature becomes a site of leisure, nostalgia, and protection, Neubauer's "mythic habitat" of childhood.

In the works by female novelists, the family and natural spaces function somewhat differently. The family still tends to be incomplete, yet it may be noted that it is most often the mother who has disappeared from the family circle. In Chapters 4 and 5 of her book on *Feminist Novelists of the Belle-Epoque*, Jennifer Waelti-Walters notes that the mother/daughter combination is indeed rare in the works by female novelists, and proposes several possible explanations: either it was difficult for female novelists or for their narrators to face the possibility that their daughters might repeat their own struggles, or portraying independent women educating their daughters to be similarly autonomous would have been too threatening for the contingent of the reading public who wanted gender roles to remain comfortably stable (Waelti-Walters 1990, 82).[16] In any case, Waelti-Walters observes, these novels present girls with fathers as role models and protectors; the father held the power to see to the education of his daughter while warning her about the dangers of love and sex. Jean Larnac draws a parallel between lack of appropriate family structures and the young girl's escape to nature in the "countless portraits of little girls and young girls offered by contemporary feminine literature":

> One would say that all of our women writers were raised deplorably, since they paint with such complacency savages liking to prowl through gardens, woods and shores, without a care for anyone but their senses always greedy for pure air and natural beauty. Claudine likes to get lost in the woods of Montigny. The heroines of Mme de Noailles, those of Mme Marcelle Tinayre . . . , even those of Mme Gérard d'Houville have this appearance of young, free animals. (Larnac 1929, 227–28)

Larnac claims that such wild behaviors in adolescent heroines stem from the author's lack of education. In these novels, the theme of weak family bonds returns repeatedly, and helps to explain the characters' need to seek emotional fulfillment outside the home. Larnac observes that nature becomes a panacea for all of the heroine's emotional aches and pains, including those inflicted by the family, a lover, or disappointment in the educational system (229–36).

In Marcelle Tinayre's book *Avant l'amour*, orphaned Marianne, adopted by the Gannerault family, strives to find happiness despite her illegitimacy and lack of dowry. Like Colette's Claudine, Marianne repeatedly refers to her lack of friends or role models. In several passages, she clearly expresses her sense of being misunderstood and isolated: "A qui parler, à qui confier mon intime misère, le mal d'ennui et de désir qui me tourmentait? Je me sentais étrangère à tout et à tous" [Who could I talk to, to confide my private misery, the pain of boredom and desire that tormented me? I felt like a stranger to everything and everyone] (Tinayre 1897, 41). She insists on the need for a mentor, a moral guide sadly lacking during the crucial period of her adolescence: "A ce moment critique et décisif de la puberté morale, je me sentais sans guide et sans soutien" [At this critical and decisive moment of

moral puberty, I felt like I was without a guide and without support]
(42). As a result of this lack, Marianne spends much of her time alone
in the garden of her adoptive home, suffering from loneliness and
marginality.

Tinayre's other character, Hellé, is also an orphan, raised by her
aunt and uncle. Her aunt dies when she is sixteen years old (20), and her
beloved uncle's death three years later serves to complete the bucolic
and nostalgic aura surrounding Hellé's childhood home. In the novel,
an opposition is established between the natural setting where Hellé
spends her early life and receives her initial education, and the city,
where she learns the subtleties of social behavior. When she returns
to the country, she experiences a blissful state of freedom and sensual
pleasure, far from the books, lessons, and curious gazes of the city (117).
The inevitable conflict between Hellé's education and the demands of
her adopted "monde" causes a retreat from the city to the natural setting of her youth. After the sudden end of her engagement, she flees to
her childhood home for solace (325). In Hellé, the province, an open,
nurturing and domestic space, provides a contrast to the city, one of
strict and stifling social codes.

In Colette's *Claudine à l'école*, Claudine's father, a scientist who spends
his time engaged in experiments and pays little attention to his daughter, represents her only family. Claudine spends much of her free time
alone in the countryside surrounding her home in Montigny. At the
beginning of the novel, she describes with great emotion the scenery of
her village and of its region. The trees are her friends, and the natural
woodsy setting is for her filled with emotional memories of wandering
and of discoveries (10). Yet leave them she must, for her father realizes
that in the city she will enjoy new experiences and enhanced educational opportunities. Claudine leaves reluctantly, but after a period
of transition during which she feels lonely and miserable, even falling
ill for a time, she soon takes a liking to the adventures to be had in
Paris, to the chance encounters waiting at every street corner. Claudine's Paris is a space of social visits, of outings, concerts, and meals
in restaurants. Colette, like Tinayre, establishes the contrast between
the soothing "familial" experiences to be had in the provinces and the
more exciting social scene in Paris. Claudine's movement from one to
the other naturally echoes her progression toward adulthood.

The nun in Anna de Noailles' novel has left the domestic life behind for a quieter life in the convent. In *Le Visage émerveillé* (1904), the
presence of nature coupled with the young nun's creativity and active

imagination allow her to appreciate to the fullest the austere life of the convent. Each moment of her existence, with the help of her poetic sensibility, becomes one of priceless beauty. The smallest elements of nature take on new meaning due to the creative power of her young mind. Nature holds her captivated: the other sisters laugh at her way of standing near a rosebush, transfixed (28). The simple force of her description comes often from a mixing of various senses to create a powerful image. She describes extreme heat visually, as "flocons bleus" [blue flakes] (15). Her description of the sound of a passing train also rests on synesthesia: "Ce bruit du train est beau comme un parfum traîné vite sur beaucoup d'espace, le parfum de la tubéreuse et de la jacinthe rouge" [The sound of the train is beautiful like a perfume carried quickly through a lot of space, the perfume of tuberose and red hyacinth] (5). The train comes to symbolize access to an exotic world (7). Yet when given the choice, the nun chooses the natural setting she knows best over faraway lands. The convent and its garden are for her a comforting, safe, familial space that she has no intention of leaving for exotic but unknown, and therefore threatening, vistas.

These heroines use natural spaces to compensate for the things lacking in their domestic lives. Yet as John Neubauer points out, the urban spaces experienced by some characters provide more stimuli and aid the adolescent in developing her intellectual and social faculties. Nature soothes and nurtures, but it can also serve as a crutch, keeping the adolescent from advancing in life. The characters that embrace a natural idyll may find happiness, but in doing so they reject society and the opportunity to take on new and more active social roles thanks to educational reform. Indeed, both Hellé's uncle and Claudine's father decide to relocate to the city in order to provide their *protégées* with more challenging social and intellectual experiences. Though the heroines of novels by women find solace, companionship, and emotional fulfillment in nature, they succeed in navigating through urban spaces as well, learning how to use each sort of space for personal development.

CHANGING BODILY DIMENSIONS

We have seen the ways in which the decadent aesthetic and increasing knowledge of the female anatomy affected the novelist's portrayal of the adolescent girl's corporeal experience. During the period from 1890 to 1910, the decadent fascination with physiological functions has all but disappeared, and is replaced by a more subtle awareness of the adolescent's physicality, often filtered through her own gaze.

At the end of the nineteenth century, social transformation led to a change in the adornment of the female body of any age. In his book on fin-de-siècle France, Eugen Weber writes of the links between social progress and changes in female dress. He notes that practical considerations became the most important factor in determining dress; for example, the rejection of corsets came both from the recent biking craze and new medical theories about the detrimental effect of corsets on breathing, digestion, and fertility (103).[17] At this time, female bodies were becoming less bound and more subtly dressed. Weber refers to the Nouvelle Mode of 1900, which first valorized the slender aesthetic: "Women were trying to lose weight, eating less, crying less, and fainting less" (104). Weber wonders whether these changes were caused by looser garb, looser social restrictions, or both, suggesting that women saw a changing image of themselves reflected in fashion (104). With an entire society paying closer attention to the female body and its representation, it not surprising that contemporary portrayals of the female adolescent should reflect this trend.

In Chapter 3 of her book *The Body Project*, Joan Jacobs Brumberg notes that around 1900 the American girl of ages twelve to thirteen wore a one-piece "waist" or camisole with no cups or darts in front.[18] When she developed breasts, she wore different styles of the same garment with more construction, stitching, tucks, and bones, which slimmed her waist and shaped her bosom without cups. The bosom was worn low, revealing society's lack of interest in uplift and cleavage. According to Brumberg, the French word "brassiere," meaning infant's undergarment or harness, was first used in *Vogue* in 1907 (70). She also signals new thought about skin: G. Stanley Hall, whom many consider to be the father of modern adolescence, claimed that all adolescents have a "dermal consciousness," albeit more intense in girls than boys, and that they read blemishes as signs of moral failure (60, 64). Brumberg points to the new presence of mirrors in bathrooms, a turn-of-the-century creation: city girls used department store mirrors and shiny windows to look at their faces (67). Adolescent girls of the Belle Epoque began to confront their image constantly, which led to a new focus on physical appearance.

The male novelists of the time often describe the female adolescent body from the perspective of an outside observer, rather than from the adolescent's point of view. Francis Jammes' adolescents have a repressed physicality, discouraged by those around them and the circumstances in which they live. The narrator's observations contribute to this image, to the extent that it becomes unclear whether the characters are distorted or embellished by the narrator's gaze. At the beginning of *Pomme d'Anis*, the narrator comments enthusiastically on adolescent "fraîcheur" [freshness]: "Fleurs qui n'avez pas été touchées! Venez . . . Que votre innocence m'enchante" [Flowers as yet untouched! Come . . . let your innocence enchant me] (29). In a scene where two female friends dance together, the narrator emphasizes the sensual movement of the virgin girls' dancing knees (34). Clearly, these passages reflect a point of view exterior to the adolescents themselves, and the narrator's enthusiasm for their fresh and innocent young bodies reveals marked subjectivity. In these novels, on the rare occasions when the narrator reveals the adolescent's perception of her own body, self-awareness is often clouded by doubt and fear.

For example, body awareness in Jammes' *Pomme d'Anis* operates under the sign of imperfection: a limp. Pomme suffers from her infirmity, unrelieved by a visit to Lourdes as a child. When an attractive young man shows interest in her, Pomme d'Anis assumes that he cannot possibly love her (87). She refuses to believe his declaration of love during a return trip to Lourdes, dismissing it as an expression of pity (94). Despite repeated manifestations of affection, followed ultimately by a marriage proposal, Pomme refuses to consider herself desirable. When her admirer accepts her refusal and marries her best friend, Pomme comes to regret her decision, deciding to cut off her hair and to become a nun. Her conviction of being unfeminine and undesirable drives her to refuse sensual pleasure and to choose a life of religion. In this book, Pomme's physical awakening is never discussed. Because of her infirmity, she refuses to accept her own desirability and therefore never embraces her maturing body. For her, a less-than-perfect body condemns one to a life of chastity. This is an extreme example of the adolescent body-image concerns appearing around the turn of the century.[19]

Another Jammes character, Clara d'Ellébeuse, resembles the decadent adolescent character in her ignorance of her body, caused by insufficient education. The narrator observes her childish "grâce charmante et maladroite" [charming and awkward grace] (Jammes 1899, 75), yet Clara has no experience of her body apart from the daily moments spent on personal hygiene (84). "Elle se déshabille lentement, mais avec une pudeur excessive, la crainte de fixer trop longtemps ce que cache la robe . . . Elle se dit qu'il est permis de regarder ses bras exposés à l'air tout le jour, mais qu'il ne faut pas toucher ou regarder à son corps inutilement, en dehors de sa toilette" [She undresses slowly, but with excessive modesty, fearing to look too long at what the dress hides. . . . She tells herself that it is allowed to look at one's arms that are exposed to the air all day long, but that one must not touch or look at one's body unnecessarily, outside of bathing] (85).[20] Clara's ignorance of the body and its functions allows her to believe she is pregnant after hugging a male friend. Her ensuing, probably psychosomatic, illness provokes the decision to commit suicide. Ironically, it is just before her suicide that Clara seems to achieve a new awareness of her body. She first cleans herself carefully, then takes the bottle of laudanum from the medicine cabinet and hides it between her breasts. Just before taking the poison, she experiences a moment of unexpected sensuality from the cold flask between her breasts (119), yet her perception of her body is still sadly inaccurate; she thinks that her stomach has grown from her supposed pregnancy (147). Clara's ignorance of her body is affected by her mental instability, whether genetic or otherwise, yet it is clear that her death is in part caused by her lack of knowledge about her body. The rudiments of sexual education, Jammes seems to propose, would probably have prevented her tragic death, or at least would have reassured her as to the impossibility of pregnancy.

Almaïde d'Etremont, another Jammes heroine, resembles Clara in that she is completely uneducated about her body. Almaïde has a natural propensity for sensuality that has been curbed by her strict and cold uncle, who confines her both physically and mentally. Her lack of social contact has preserved her naïveté for an unusual period of time; she is twenty-five years old. Almaïde regularly escapes her uncle's prisonlike chateau and flees to a nearby, secluded spot where she savors nude dips in a river, noting "le tremblement de ses jambes charmantes" [the trembling of her charming legs]. "Elle frissonne à peu à peu entrer tout entière dans la fraîcheur verte et liquide . . . Elle suffoque et ses épaules frémissent quand elle y est baignée tout à fait" [She shivers while entering gradually but completely into the green, liquid coolness. . . . She suffocates and her shoulders quiver when she is completely in the water] (Jammes 1901, 158). Her swim becomes for her a sort of therapy, an opportunity to relax and forget about her daily life. But her bath is also a sensual experience, where the young woman rejoices in her body: "Souvent elle vient ainsi, à la tombée du jour, étreindre sur sa gorge polie et ronde la douceur des eaux. Elle sait que nul ne passe en ces retraites. Et d'ailleurs, jamais d'extrêmes pudeurs ne l'effrayèrent. On la grondait, au couvent, de courir riante et peu vêtue au milieu du dortoir" [She often comes here like this at the day's end, to clasp the softness of the water to her polished and rounded bosom. She knows that no one passes by this hiding place. In any case, she has never been alarmed out of extreme modesty. She was often scolded at the convent for running through the dormitory, laughing and scantily clad] (158).[21] Her body responds to the caresses of the water, and it is in this state of heightened sensuality that she sees an adolescent goat-herd pass by. This unexpected sighting troubles Almaïde sexually; she blushes and cannot sleep that evening due to "tristesse fièvreuse" [fe-verish sadness] (159). Almaïde is well aware of her physical attributes. At one point she contemplates "avec un sentiment d'amer orgueil la rondeur parfaite de ses bras" [the perfect roundness of her arms with a feeling of bitter pride] (32). She is the most sensual of the heroines discussed here, though she is also the oldest and the one with the least social contact.

The *Vierges fortes* books by Marcel Prévost give the greatest range of body types and attitudes toward them of the novels discussed here, yet the tendency to conceive of female characters as representative types is omnipresent. The leader of the feminist movement, Romaine Pir-nitz, has a shriveled body that no longer possesses any feminine allure. Her powerful influence upon the two main adolescent characters and her angular, unsightly form operate as a warning about the dangerous pursuit of feminist ideals to the exclusion of the traditional roles of wife and mother. Pirnitz is a living suggestion that one's convictions imprint themselves on the body. The scientific concern with the case of the virile woman, who denied or refused her femininity, was expressed at this period by Havelock Ellis in his book on *Sexual Inversion* (1897) and by other sexologists of the time.[22] Judith Walkowitz refers to the influence of Ellis's work in her article on the dangerous sexualities of the late nineteenth century. "The congenital invert was the aggressive and masculine woman represented by the popular transvestite," she writes (Walkowitz 1991, 416). Prévost may have based his portrait of Pirnitz on these theories.

Though Pirnitz wears traditional female clothing, the stigma of the unfeminine woman is upon her, inciting suspicion among those who wish to denigrate the cause of educational reform. The danger of feminism, as certain of Prévost's characters (and probably many of his readers) seem to think, is that it provokes a loss of feminity in women. Untraditional ideas manifest themselves in an unfeminine, unsightly body. The power of these arguments on the reading audience of scientific texts such as that of Ellis and of literary texts such as Prévost's can be predicted. At a time when a girl's ability to please men helped ensure her financial future, hearing that subversive thought would deform the body probably kept most girls comfortably safe from answering the call to independence trumpeted by feminists. Despite the appeal of Pirnitz's wisdom, the descriptions of her androgynous body, combined with her school's failure at the end of the novels, were more likely dissuasive than persuasive factors. The two main characters, sisters Frédérique and Léa, represent intelligent, hard-working girls, as yet untouched by the destructive effect of feminist thought, whose beauty reaches its height when they reject the feminist principles and pursue more traditional roles. In these books, the rejection of marriage and motherhood leads to the atrophy of the feminine qualities so coveted at the end of the century.

Worse still, the books illustrate, celibacy can lead to symptoms of hysteria. In the second *Vierges fortes* book, *Léa*, the developing madness of one of the young characters is attributed to her repressed sexuality. When the doctor examines Geneviève after her first attacks, his diagnosis is that she must marry: "Il faut que cette petite se marie. . . . [L]a patiente a besoin d'une vie conjugale régulière" [This little one must marry. . . . (T)he patient needs regular married life] (Prévost 1900, 225). Her best friend and roommate, Daisy, reacts violently and expresses her scorn immediately: "Mariez-vous! c'est la panacée. . . . Une jeune fille est mal en point: vite, un homme dans son lit, et tout s'arrangera. Ah! les farceurs . . . c'est encore un des moyens par lesquels ils nous tiennent, en se prétendant indispensables à notre santé . . . " '[Get married! Men never have anything but that remedy to offer you. Get married! That's the panacea. A young girl feels bad: quick, a man in her bed, and everything will be fine. Ah! The jokers . . . this is yet another way that they keep a hold on us, by claiming that they are indispensable to our health . . .] (226). In this scene, Prévost allows for two opinions to be expressed on the causes of madness in a young and otherwise healthy girl. The traditional view is that of the doctor, for whom hysteria and madness result from sexual repression.[23] Daisy calls into question the reasons behind this perspective, yet interestingly provides no other explanation for Geneviève's behavior. Regardless of Prévost's intentions, this episode probably served to reinforce the opinions of those readers inclined to believe the doctor, as well as to incite doubt in feminist sympathizers.

The *Vierges fortes* books do give at least one positive example of a woman who escapes from the ideological clutches of Pirnitz and the other feminists and, in doing so, salvages her beauty and femininity. In opposition to Geneviève, who has chosen to live without marriage, Léa chooses, albeit belatedly, the love of a man over a lifetime of advancing the feminist cause. Her coquetterie and sensuality, qualities considered both natural and feminine, which she repressed during her years of work with the feminists, return when she leaves them in Paris and begins preparations for a reunion with her fiancé (Prévost 1900, 405–6). For most readers of the *Vierges fortes* books, Léa has probably made the right choice: she has abandoned the floundering school and come to search for her fiancé, choosing marriage over a life of celibacy. Her beauty flourishes after this decision, but she has waited too long to make up her mind, and her growing awareness of physical desire causes her to fall ill (406). Léa dies without having blessed her marriage with a child, and leaving the reader wishing she had made her decision much earlier. The book suggests that a woman must choose love and tradition over the temptation of a short-lived intellectual principle that threatens one's health and very femininity.

Though Marcel Prévost was lauded as one of the rare male novelists of the Belle Epoque to interest himself principally in the woman and in her changing role in society,[24] his *Vierges fortes* books leave the modern reader unsatisfied; the ideal they propose proves itself in the span of the narrative to be an unpracticable one. Despite the many pages spent listing the virtues of the feminists and their goals, at the end of the novel both heroines have recognized the importance of traditional female roles, not for society's sake, but for the health and happiness of the individual woman. Sensuality can be positive, the novels suggest, as long as it guides the young woman toward a man and toward marriage. In some respects, Marcel Prévost resembles Emile Zola in his thinking about women and gender roles. Though both believe in educating girls better and differently, they believe that marriage and motherhood are ultimately the most satisfying and appropriate roles for women, for their own good and for that of their society.

In Romain Rolland's *Antoinette*, the title character plays a role of self-sacrifice and self-denial that prevents her from pursuing this female ideal. Her choices carry her away from love and marriage, not in support of feminist causes, but in order to help support her brother. Yet when she is young, Antoinette's beauty allows her to entertain romantic notions about her future (Rolland 1908, 10). She is curious about her

maturing body, a source of endless delight, as revealed in one scene
where she hides a stolen rose between her growing breasts (13). She
finds other sources of sensual pleasure: "Une volupté aussi, exquise
et défendue, était d'enlever ses chaussures et ses bas, et de s'en aller,
pieds nus . . . Couchée à l'ombre des sapins, elle regardait ses mains
transparentes au soleil, et elle promenait machinalement ses lèvres sur
le tissu satiné de ses bras fins et dodus" [Another exquisite and forbidden pleasure was to take off her shoes and stockings and to walk away
barefoot . . . Lying in the shadow of the pine trees, she looked at her
hands, transparent in the sun, and she moved her lips mechanically
on the satiny material of her fine, plump arms] (13). These sensual
descriptions of self-appreciation differ enormously from the scenes of
suffering and fever that one finds in the decadent novels. Antoinette's
self-esteem is encouraged and bolstered by her father's admiration. At
sixteen years of age, Antoinette "jouissait de savoir son corps et son
âme fleurissants, de se savoir jolie et de se l'entendre dire. Les éloges
de son père, ses paroles imprudentes eussent suffi à lui tourner la tête.
Il était en extase devant elle; il s'amusait de sa coquetterie, de ses œil-
lades langoureuses à son miroir" [enjoyed knowing that her body and
her soul were in bloom, knowing that she was pretty and being told so.
Her father's praise, his imprudent words would have sufficed to turn
her head. He was in ecstasy before her; he was amused by her vanity,
by her langorous glances at the mirror] (23). Her father's appreciative
gaze assures Antoinette of her seductive power and seems to promise
her future success in attracting worthy admirers from whom to pick a
husband.

   Antoinette's life changes dramatically after her parents' financial
ruin and ensuing death. She begins a life devoid of sensuality, working
herself to the point of illness in order to finance her brother's studies.
Her sexual awakening comes largely from her discoveries regarding his
private life (68). Yet despite her purity and moral refusal of any sexual
thoughts, she is still aware of her "grand charme" [great charm] and
her effect on men (70). Yet until her death, Antoinette denies her own
sexuality. This novel, like the *Vierges fortes* books, states the dangers
of refusing the call of one's body, of avoiding marriage, though in this
case the heroine places a fraternal relationship above all others. Antoinette's selflessness can be admired to some extent, but she pushes
it to an uncomfortable extreme where her self-denial becomes almost
masochistic. Her martyrdom frustrates the reader, who watches her
miss one opportunity after another to realize her potential as a sensual

woman, and to let her brother realize his on his own. The reader is left wishing that she had acted on her feelings of love in order to heal her overworked body and to express repressed desires.

All of the works by male novelists surveyed here depict the adolescent's relationship to her own body as one of repression, doubt, and denial. The women novelists portray a different attitude toward the body, perhaps in part because they had firsthand experience with the social taboos concerning the young girl's body and its apparel. However, they make no more references to the changing body of the female adolescent than do the male novelists. Illness is rampant, as it is in the novels by male authors, though it is often difficult to distinguish between physical and mental malady. In her article entitled "Corps et coeurs" [Bodies and Hearts], Yvonne Knibiehler writes of the attempts on the part of educators and parents to keep the body and its functions secret from adolescent girls. Given the conviction that washing the body, particularly its more intimate parts, too frequently (more often than once weekly) or too readily revealed inherent libertinage, girls were encouraged to change linens instead (Knibiehler, 362).[25] Possibly because of this intentional societal repression of encounters with the body, references to it in these novels are reduced to fleeting glances on the part of the adolescent herself, or brief allusions to her body in comparison with those of the girls around her.

Colette's Claudine has a straightforward and seemingly healthy attitude toward her body. She is well aware of her physical appearance and of its impact on others, as revealed in a passage where she frankly appraises her physical charms, including her nails, hair, eyes, and figure (21). When preparing for the visit of the Minister of Agriculture, Claudine again judges her own physical appearance: "Mes cheveux font bien 'le nuage'. Petite figure toujours un peu pâlotte et pointue, mais je vous assure, mes yeux et ma bouche ne sont pas mal" [My hair is doing "the cloud" well. Little face always a little pale and pointed, but I assure you, my eyes and my mouth are not bad] (152). These self-appreciations are always refreshingly honest; in these descriptions the reader is treated to both a visual image of Claudine and an awareness of her personality.

Claudine manipulates dress to assert herself or to elicit a response in others. In *Claudine à l'école* she describes rites of passage associated with clothing: "Quand j'ai eu quinze ans sonnés, j'ai allongé mes jupes jusqu'aux chevilles . . . Les jupes longues, mes mollets les exigeaient, qui tiraient l'œil, et me donnaient déjà trop l'air d'une jeune fille" [When

I turned fifteen, I lengthened my skirts to my ankles . . . My calves, which were attracting attention and making me look too much like a young woman already, made long skirts necessary] (Colette 1989, 11). The interesting juxtaposition of elements here suggests that, just as the school is being renovated and improved, so is she physically changing and progressing. For her lessons with a recently arrived young male teacher, she intentionally dresses to please, while attempting to hide her efforts from her friends (37). Claudine's practical yet sensational way of dressing makes her a role model and source of distraction and entertainment for the other students. Yet she is careful to feign nonchalance, as in the matter of the gowns worn for the distribution of the year's awards: "Parmi les élèves, c'est très bien porté de ne point paraître s'occuper de sa toilette de distribution. Toutes y réfléchissent un mois à l'avance, tourmentent les mamans . . . —mais il est de bon goût de n'en rien dire" [Among the students, it's good not to seem like you worry about your outfit for prize day. Everyone thinks about it a month in advance, torments the moms . . . —but it is in good taste not to talk about it] (137). She is always aware of the reactions of others, both negative and positive, yet seeks her own approval above all: "On ne peut pas contenter tout le monde et soi-même. J'aime mieux me contenter d'abord" [You can't please everyone and yourself. I prefer to please myself first] (152). Still, Claudine appreciates the approval of others, which confirms her seductive powers: "Je pensais bien, je voyais bien que ma toilette me seyait, . . . mais les regards sournois, les physionomies soudainement figées des jeunes filles qui se reposent et s'éventent m'en rendent certaine et je me sens mieux à mon aise" [I thought so, I saw that my outfit was flattering, . . . but the sly glances, the suddenly frozen physiognomies of the girls resting and fanning themselves convince me of it and I feel better, more at ease] (165). Though she claims to worry first about her own opinion, Claudine feels best when she sees approval of her appearance reflected in the eyes of others.

Claudine's descriptions of her body and its dress occasionally reveal her sensuality. Even the most simple descriptions of her outfits can be sensually charged, as when she describes the movement and sound of her dress and the way it caresses her slippers (152). In another scene, she describes the liberties she takes with dress during hot weather by replacing her stockings with socks, and the shocked reaction of her classmates (97). Here, her violation of the dress code serves multiple purposes: it provides some relief from the oppressive heat, and it earns her the attention and admiration of her classmates. During the exams, Claudine makes unexpected and precocious mental connections between her present physical experience and later conjugal life: "Les examinateurs reparaissent enfin, ils s'épongent, ils sont laids et luisants. Dieu! Je n'aimerais pas être mariée par ce temps-là! Rien que l'idée de coucher avec un monsieur qui aurait chaud comme eux . . . (D'ailleurs, l'été, j'aurai deux lits). [The examiners reappear at last, sponging themselves; they are ugly and shiny. God! I wouldn't like to be married in this weather! Just the idea of sleeping with a man as hot as they are . . . (Anyway, in the summer, I'll have two beds)] (123). She goes on to describe the awful smell in the room and wishes that she could leave. Her commentary is both innocent and incisive: she harbors few illusions about the joys of conjugal life or about her classmates' personal hygiene. She proposes practical solutions to each quandary (two beds for couples in hot weather; leaving a hot, stuffy, and malodorous room). Claudine's descriptions of her own body and garments and those of her comrades reveal a far more developed physical and sensual awareness than that of the heroines discussed above.

In *Claudine à Paris*, Claudine announces that she has begun keeping her journal again after an illness that has deprived her of her hair. Her awareness of her physical appearance seems heightened: "Si j'allais paraître trop maigre? Assise dans mon cuveau, toute nue, je constate que je me remplume un peu; mais il y a encore à faire" [What if I were to seem too thin? Sitting in my basin, completely naked, I notice that I am putting some weight back on; but there is still a ways to go] (197). Later in the novel, another bath scene provides more information: "Je m'étudie et m'attarde minutieusement. Ce duvet-là, ça ne compte pas comme poil sur les jambes, au moins? Dame, les bouts de mes nichettes ne sont pas si roses que ceux de Luce, mais j'ai les jambes plus longues et plus belles, et les reins à fossettes" [I study myself in great detail, taking my time. This down doesn't count as leg hair, I guess? Hey, the ends of my boobs are not as pink as Luce's, but I have longer and more beautiful legs, and dimples behind my waist] (289). This close observation of her body distinguishes Claudine from most adolescent heroines preceding her, who have been taught to avoid looking at their bodies, even while bathing. Claudine widens the gap even further by describing the breast size contests she and her girlfriends would hold at school: "L'exhibition terminée, nous refermions nos corsages, avec l'intime conviction, chacune d'en avoir beaucoup plus que les trois autres" [At the end of the exhibition, we would close our blouses, each one of us privately convinced of having much more than the three others] (198). Claudine reveals an unabashed interest in her own body and its development, but also in the way her body compares to those of her friends.

However, what interests Claudine most of all is the effect she produces on her primary suitor, Renaud. When her "uncle" pays her a compliment, Claudine reveals her natural vanity, saying that she knows that her short hairdo flatters her and that she can tell by her reflection in mirrors (264). Renaud inspires unfamiliar physical desire in Claudine, experienced as "une mollesse inconnue" [an unfamiliar weakness] (269). When he asks her to observe the color of his hair, Claudine feels a similar physical response (276). These passages show Claudine's observation of her body and its sensations, a facet of adolescent life hitherto represented in the novel as languor or even illness.

Claudine differs from the heroines of the male-penned novels in that her physical awareness, unabashed sensuality, and subversive behavior remain largely uncriticized by other characters.[26] The reader cannot help identifying with and admiring Claudine, a reaction far removed from the pity, frustration, and sadness engendered by the male novelists' heroines. Claudine gets the best of her adversaries in nearly every situation, and though the reader observes her self-doubt and worry about her appearance or about her future, Claudine adjusts well to any obstacles and twists in the road. She takes advantage of her sensual nature, and enjoys herself to the fullest, as opposed to Frédérique, Léa, and Antoinette, who deny themselves pleasure in allegiance to some greater principle.

One cannot rationally expect a young nun to be as liberated a heroine as is Claudine, and Anna de Noaille's character confirms these expectations. In *Le Visage émerveillé*, the adolescent nun makes few references to her physical appearance, apart from simple comments based on dress or health, or comparisons between her body and other familiar objects (Noailles 1904, 4, 9). Either because youth is a source of optimism or because it distinguishes her from the other sisters, she revels in it (13). Jubilation over her youthful difference is for the nun a subtle form of physical awareness.

The young nun's first meetings with Julien, the young man who awakens her to the charms of nonreligious love, turn her appreciation of youth into a more sensual savoring of its trappings: "Je sais que je suis jolie, que je suis jeune, je le sens. Je sens ma vie et ma jeunesse à chaque minute; je sais que j'ai, sous ma robe droite, mon corps qui est doux, mes jambes qui ont des mouvements" [I know that I am pretty, that I am young, I feel it. I feel my life and my youth at each minute; I know that under my straight dress I have my soft body, my legs that move]. She begins to recognize her new physical sensations as the manifestation of desire: "Je ne veux pas être pure, Seigneur; je ne suis pas pure, je sens tout le temps l'âme de mon corps et toutes les parois brûlantes de mon âme. C'est cela le désir" [I don't want to be pure, Lord; I am not pure, I feel the soul in my body and all the burning surfaces of my soul all the time. That is what desire is] (44).

Due to her ignorance of her body and its functions, the adolescent nun often misinterprets new sensations as signs of illness (Noailles 1904, 47–48). This attempt to rationalize her own physical responses carries over into Julien's acts of affection, which she tries to justify to herself (59). Because the nun finds her sensations agreeable, she decides not to worry about the possible immorality of her conduct with Julien. She recognizes the strength of her sensations, and secretly believes that they have the power to awaken long-denied life forces in other nuns. This unstated wish is yet another attempt at rationalization of her desire: the need to view sexuality as a healing force.

The nun gradually loses all self-control and realizes that she desires her friend as much as he desires her (87). Her enthusiasm causes her to forget temporarily the teachings of the church, choosing sensual pleasures over the fear of sin: "Qu'importe tout l'univers, tout le péché! Il y a cette flamme, cette ivresse, cet enivrement! . . . La volupté! tout est volupté. . . . Il veut, je ne veux pas, je veux" [Who cares about the whole universe, all the sin! There is this flame, this exhilaration, this intoxication! . . . Sensuality! Everything is sensuality . . . He wants to, I don't want to, I want to] (92). These passages powerfully evoke the physical awakening of the least likely of female adolescents, a nun. They suggest the sensual capacities of even the most innocent and sheltered young girls.

Though the nun seems thoroughly overcome by her physical awakening and addicted to the new sensations she experiences, when Julien proposes that she leave the convent to travel with him, she hesitates and finally refuses. The outside world has never satisfied her needs, nor made her want to learn its rules. When her mother and sister come to visit her, rather than appreciating their fancy clothes, she sees them as disguising the soul, concluding that each is proud of her own costume (144). Despite the nun's obvious sensuality, she cannot conceive of life outside her nun's habit. With Julien, she finds a way of temporarily exploring her body's sensations without, in the long run, permanently jeopardizing her commitment to God. In a certain sense, the nun manages to have the best of both worlds.

Like Claudine, Marcelle Tinayre's heroines express the emotions they experience as they observe their changing bodies. Marianne of *Avant l'amour* is the only character who notes that the mind and the body do not mature at the same speed. She feels that her fifteen-year-old body holds back her twenty-year-old soul (Tinayre 1897, 39). Her self-appreciation, provoked by a glimpse of her reflection in a mirror, resembles that of Claudine in its honesty. Marianne wishes that her face could be slightly longer and her mouth more delicate. In general, though, her appearance satisfies her (36). Her main consideration, like that of many girls raised at the turn of the century, is whether her beauty will attract love: "Suis-je assez belle pour être aimée? . . . Serai-je aimée, un jour?" [Am I beautiful enough to be loved? . . . Will I be loved one day?] (36). Interestingly, her wording reveals an interest in love, not in marriage. While Antoinette, for instance, thinks of her beauty as a way of attracting a successful husband, Tinayre's character thinks in terms of love.

She is not totally naïve, however. Her reflection in the mirror reminds her of her development during adolescence (Tinayre 1897, 40). In keeping with her education, Marianne senses quite early that beauty will serve a concrete purpose: "De la chrysalide de l'adolescente s'évada une femme que je ne soupçonnais pas. . . . Elle devinait la puissance de son sexe; elle se révélait sa propre beauté. . . ." [From the adolescent chrysalis a woman escaped that I didn't suspect. . . . She guessed at the power of her sex; she discovered her own beauty . . .] (43–44). Marianne is not unaware of her sexual power over men and of what she represents as a potential wife. Yet she decides not to use her charms for superficial flirtation, waiting instead for a true, pure love (263).[27] Marianne expresses the economic value of beauty and rejects such material values for more spiritual ones. In *Hellé*, the title character expresses a similar dismissal of the material value of beauty: "J'étais belle, je le savais, et je considérais ma beauté non comme un trésor qu'on peut exploiter pour de bas intérêts, mais comme un don précieux qui porte avec soi une joie sereine" [I was beautiful, I knew it, and I considered my beauty not as a treasure that can be exploited by base interests, but as a precious gift that carries with it serene joy] (77). In these two novels, Marcelle Tinayre explores the societal importance placed on beauty, and offers her heroines ways of escaping from this trap.

Though well aware of their charms, these adolescents do not exploit their beauty, preferring to be appreciated for other less material qualities. There is also in their words the suggestion of agency in matters of love. They can select their object of affection, rather than waiting passively for a marriage proposal. Of the four novels discussed here, Tinayre's grant the young female the greatest power in terms of recognizing and controlling their own desire. Yet all four show movement away from the decadent portraits and from those by contemporary male novelists in the sense that the adolescents are much more accepting and appreciative of their physical form, albeit as a means of attracting men.

THE ADOLESCENT MIND/MOOD

Though the understanding of the social category of female adolescence has developed somewhat since the decadent portrayals, the male novelists' Belle Epoque characters tend in certain ways to repeat patterns of mental behavior associated with decadence. The decadent adolescent spends much time in a state of mental torpor, triggered by romantic reverie or by the adolescent's changing body. The inner life becomes dramatically important, and the adolescent often escapes to a dream world for solace and protection. Moodiness here is not counterbalanced with a validation of the adolescent's mental agility and capacity for reason.

The mental space of the Jammes character Clara d'Ellébeuse is a complex one, marked by rapid mood change. In the very first scene, the reader observes the transition from pride about her family name and situation to sudden anguish (Jammes 1899, 62). Her obsession with her great-uncle's physical relationship with his fiancée, as revealed in their correspondence, is for her a source of great guilt (63). Clara's sensitive mind and nature allow her to be heavily influenced by the letters, to the extent that she spends more time lost in her attempt to recreate the mysterious events than living in the present. She loses the capacity to distinguish between reality and the content of the letters, and slowly identifies with the female character in the drama she has created, with the help of details found in the correspondence. When Clara's health fails, she assumes that, like the Laure of the letters, she must be pregnant—an unfortunate condition caused, in her opinion, by an embrace with a young male friend. Her worried father, who knows that madness runs in the family, believes that her illness is a sign of "maladie nerveuse" [nervous illness] (140). When her health declines even further, Clara decides suddenly to commit suicide with laudanum, seemingly unaware of what she is doing: "Elle ne s'étonna pas elle-même de son acte. Elle ne le ressentait plus qu'avec difficulté, comme son corps. Elle éprouvait la paralysie presque totale de ce qu'elle accomplissait" [She herself wasn't astonished at her act. She felt it only with difficulty, like her body. She felt the almost total paralysis of what she was doing] (118). The spontaneous decision to put an end to her life is the ultimate expression of the randomness of Clara's thoughts and impulses. How much of her decision can be attributed to the rashness of adolescence and how much to the family history of madness is unclear. Yet Jammes expresses in this short novel the disorder of the adolescent female's mental space, which often resembles that of Zola's character Angélique.

For the female novelists, atypical thought patterns and rapid mood shifts are valorized rather than criticized as signs of psychological disorder. Claudine's mental space, albeit surprisingly lucid, resembles in some ways that of Clara. Yet Claudine typically manages to use her agile mind to her advantage, as demonstrated during her history oral exam, where her quirky, insolent comments take the examiner aback but convince him of what he views as an unusual mental competence in a young girl (120). The following passage suggests the complexity of Claudine's mental space, her ability to glide from one thought to another, observation, analysis, apprehension, confession:

> Je ne me sens pas trois idées nettes, la chaleur, la fatigue. . . . Ma robe est prête, elle va bien. . . . Je serai jolie demain, plus que la grande Anaïs, plus que Marie: ce n'est pas difficile, ça fait plaisir tout de meme. . . . Je vais quitter l'école, papa m'enverra à Paris chez une tante riche et sans enfants, je ferai mon entrée dans le monde, et mille gaffes en même temps. . . . Comment me passer de la campagne, avec cette faim de verdure qui ne me quitte guère? Ça me paraît insensé de songer que je ne viendrai plus ici. . . . [J]'aurai du chagrin de ne plus vivre ici. . . . Et puis, pendant que j'ai le temps, je peux bien me dire quelque chose: c'est que Luce me plaît, au fond, plus que je ne veux me l'avouer.

> [I don't feel three clear ideas, the heat, fatigue. . . . My dress is ready; it is great. . . . I will be pretty tomorrow, prettier than big Anaïs, prettier than Marie: it's not hard, but it makes me happy all the same. . . . I will leave school, Papa will send me to Paris to stay with a rich aunt without children, I will come out into society, making a thousand blunders at

the same time. . . . How will I live without the countryside, with this
hunger for greenery that barely leaves me? It seems crazy to think that
I won't come here anymore. . . . I will grieve not to live here anymore.
. . . And yet, while I have time, I can tell myself something: it's that I
find Luce attractive, more than I care to admit to myself.] (150)

In this passage, Claudine drifts from thoughts about the present (heat),
the near future (her dress for the next day), and the future (the end of
her education). She predicts her own discomfort in a place lacking the
landmarks she has come to know and count on, and then slides into a
confession that may surprise the reader. Claudine reveals the capri-
ciousness of her young mind, but also her capacity for analysis of her
own thoughts, even those buried far beneath the surface.

In *Claudine à Paris*, Claudine displays her uncanny ability to analyze
her thoughts with perception and humor:

> Claudine, ma vieille, tu ne te corrigeras jamais de ce besoin de fouiner
> dans ce qui ne te regarde pas, de ce petit désir un peu méprisable de
> montrer que, finaude et renseignée, tu comprends un tas de choses au-
> dessus de ton âge! Le besoin d'étonner, la soif de troubler la quiétude
> des gens et d'agiter des existences trop calmes, ça te jouera un mauvais
> tour.

> [Claudine, old girl, you will never fix this need to poke your nose into
> things that are none of your business, this slightly contemptible desire
> to show that, wily and in the know, you are aware of lots of things be-
> yond your age! The need to astonish, the thirst to disrupt people's tran-
> quility and to agitate too-calm lives, all that will get you into trouble.]
> (203)

Not only does Claudine recognize that she has made a mistake, she
knows *why*. She capably and maturely attributes her misstep to her
desire to appear precocious: a delicious paradox. Yet despite her moments of lucid energy, Claudine has moments of inexplicable lassitude,
like the decadent adolescents: "Etendue sur mon lit, l'après-midi, je
songe à trop de choses. . . . Qu'ai-je? . . . Mon cœur souffre de nos-
talgie. . . . Comme j'ai déchu de moi-même depuis l'an dernier! J'ai
perdu l'innocent bonheur de remuer, de grimper, de bondir. . . . Je
lis, je lis, je lis. Tout. N'importe quoi. Je n'ai que ça pour m'occuper,
pour me tirer d'ici et de moi" [Lying on my bed, in the afternoon,
I think about too many things. . . . What's wrong with me? . . . My
heart suffers from nostalgia. . . . How I have fallen since last year! I

have lost the innocent joy of moving around, climbing, jumping . . . I read, I read, I read. Everything. Anything. I have only that to occupy me, to get me out of here and out of myself] (259–60). Here, reading replaces more physical activities, which she views as belonging to her past. It allows her to escape from her daily life and to forget herself. Her mental state, one of extreme nervousness, recalls the mental fragility associated with decadence. She claims that her frame of mind lacks precision, like that of someone about to experience a blow on the head (269). In a passage that develops this idea of impending disaster, Claudine succeeds in giving a micro-explanation of adolescent angst: "Il serait puéril de le nier, mon existence se corse. . . . Je n'éprouve aucun besoin de confier mon état à qui que ce soit au monde" [It would be childish to deny it; my existence is getting complicated (. . .) I feel no need to confide my state to anyone in the world]. She decides not to write to her friend Claire to tell her of the approaching "moment fatal" [fatal moment], nor to ask her father, who would only answer that he has never studied "cette espèce-là" [that species] (271). The "espèce" [species] in question is of course the female adolescent, and the "fatal moment" she awaits with mixed fear and anticipation is the coming of adulthood, probably in the form of marriage. Notable here is the utter lack of people in whom she can confide. She seems to know instinctively that her closest friends and relatives would fail to provide her with the support and assistance she craves. This feeling of isolation expressed by Claudine characterizes many of the novels studied, both at the turn of the century and earlier. The adolescent often feels oppressed by her emotions and thoughts, and at the same time completely alone, unable or unwilling to seek the advice of others. To a greater extent than the other adolescents considered here, and partially due to the journal format, Claudine can both experience and analyze her emotions, predicting her own reactions and criticizing what she feels to be her weaknesses. The complexity of her mind's meanderings is well suited to the form of the narrative.

Anna de Noailles' character, a young nun, suffers from similar confusion prompted not by madness, a tragic epistolary relationship, or the certitude of coming catastrophe, but by the conflict between her emotional and physical attachment to her male visitor and the dictates of her religious commitment. Like Claudine, she experiences nervous upset, getting a special dispensation from the doctor to miss communion due to sickness (Noailles 1904, 70). Her feelings for Julien haunt her and become a threat to her mental space; she finds the idea of death preferable to the "déshonneur" [dishonor] associated with seduction (72, 84). She begins to perceive her attraction to him as a maddening ailment that alienates her from the other nuns: "Je ne suis plus, ici, pareille aux autres, je suis différente de mes sœurs. C'est cela qui me donne cet accablement, cette lente et calme folie" [I am no longer like the others here; I am different from my sisters. That is what gives me this despondency, this slow and calm madness] (90). The nun's "madness" comes from feeling radically different in a place where fitting in, resembling the others, is key.

The nun perceives her mind as an instrument of seduction (Noailles 1904, 108), and tries to fight her desire with her mind by thinking of her sensuality as a form of "folie," which she refuses rationally (98). Her sexually charged nocturnal meetings with Julien become instant memories, far removed from the mental purity of her days (104). The nun uses her mind to create a clear separation between her night and day selves that protects her sense of purity and commitment to God. Finally, the young protagonist manages to compare her dreams of Julien with reality, choosing the dream over life: "Il y avait dans ce rêve Julien. . . . Et c'était mieux que la vie, plus petit, plus étroit, plus clair. . . . La vraie vie est trop large, elle a trop de degrés. Ce petit rêve, c'était l'essentiel" [Julien was in the dream . . . And it was better than life, smaller, narrower, clearer. . . . Real life is too big; it has too many degrees. This little dream was the essential] (135). This dream has a special significance, for dreams in novels of female adolescence of the end of the nineteenth century tend to correspond to an unhealthy desire to escape from reality.[28] Yet in *Le Visage émerveillé*, since "reality" is in fact the convent, and "escape" corresponds to the nun's relationship with Julien, the fact that she chooses a dream version of her meetings with Julien over actual meetings signifies a distancing from the false reality of her new sexual life. Therefore, the dream actually corresponds to a move back toward the "truth" of her life at the convent, where she is protected from "la vraie vie" that she finds overwhelming. A life outside with Julien doesn't interest her; the dream of him, interestingly juxtaposed with images of childhood joy and security, is "better than life." Though the nun's sources of concern differ from Claudine's, she uses her mind in equally complex ways, to negotiate between mystical and sensual seduction.

Like Colette and Noailles, Marcelle Tinayre portrays the mental processes of the female adolescent. In Jules Bertaut's enthusiastic review of the contributions made by female novelists to the literary study of the female adolescent, Marcelle Tinayre receives special attention:[29]

> Reread the first fifty pages of one of the boldest novels by Madame Tinayre, *Avant l'amour*, and you will find almost in each line these "found" things that were not imagined after the fact, but are a kind of confession, direct or indirect. [30] Listen to her heroine analyze herself at this both happy and critical period of the woman's life. (Bertaut 1909, 33)

Bertaut goes on to say that Tinayre's perceptive portrait of the young female mind revealed a near-documentary aspect that male novelists could never hope to achieve. Indeed, Tinayre succeeds in capturing in a few lines the paradoxical nature of the adolescent mind:

> Impatiente de tout connnaître, avide de sentir, j'aurais voulu embrasser à la fois toutes les formes de la vie. Je sentais en moi une flamme sans aliment, des impulsions sans but, des vouloirs sans objet, toute une force inemployée qui se dépensait en agitations vaines. J'avais perdu l'insouciance joyeuse de l'enfant avant d'avoir conquis la libre responsabilité de la femme.

> [Impatient to know everything, greedy to feel, I would have liked to embrace all forms of life at once. I felt in myself a flame without fuel, impulses without goals, desires without objects, an entire unused force that was spent in vain agitations. I had lost the joyful carelessness of the child before having conquered the free responsibility of the woman.] (Tinayre 1897, 38–39)

In this passage, Tinayre's narrator conveys the paradoxical nature of the adolescent mind, marked by curiosity, openness, desire, and impatience. The narrator conceives of adolescence as an intermediate phase between childhood and adulthood, without the principal qualities of either. The transitional mental space of the adolescent is distinguished by passionate enthusiasm for nothing in particular. The adolescent hasn't yet found a goal or project that will enable her to employ her enthusiasm and energy effectively. She spends her time on "agitations vaines" while waiting for some meaningful purpose in life.

In another passage, Marianne describes the new worlds that open to her through the discovery of books. Her room becomes a space propitious to the mental wanderings that such books facilitate (Tinayre 1897, 39–40). Poetry and novels offer more sensual pleasure than the dry classics provided by her tutor, and allow her imagination to take flight. Marianne describes her temporary interest in religion (48).[31] Soon she abandons religion in favor of life, realizing that her need for something to cling to would be better served by a real-life love than by the "mystical love" offered by religion (43).

Marianne resembles the nun and Claudine in her use of her mind both as a means of escape and as a tool to combat unhealthy escapes from reality. Her mental space is equally complex; she observes her own behavior and can analyze it and influence it through the use of her mind. As opposed to the novels by male authors, which portray the adolescent mental space as one of disorder (if they refer to it at all), these novels evoke (albeit in addition to an element of confusion) its richness and flexibility.

EDUCATION FOR THE NEW WOMAN

By the end of the nineteenth century, writers of both sexes had begun to consider the need for a new feminine ideal. Certain feminist writers proposed what they called the "New Woman," an image of femininity that would break down worn-out stereotypes of mannish single women and change society for the better.[32] Jennifer Waelti-Walters writes of the lukewarm welcome the New Woman received from readers and writers alike. Though we as modern readers find the New Woman as literary heroine interesting, she writes, such a character was far too subversive to be appreciated at the time: "The popular view propagated by the press was that new women were man-hating, man-imitating, cig-arette-smoking shrews who were fighting for rights that no real women either wanted or needed" (Waelti-Walters 1990, 174). Indeed, writers of both sexes condemned the New Woman: in Camille Pert's novel *Les Florifères*, female characters undergo sterilizing operations to be able to enjoy sex without fear of pregnancy. The consequences of such action were undeniably threatening for a French society still fighting under-population and embracing "une conception ultra-traditionaliste du rôle de la femme."[33] By playing on societal fears and prejudices, Pert exploits and condemns the idea of the New Woman by revealing her to be an "unnatural" being who disrupts the laws of nature and society. Carroll Smith-Rosenberg evokes this debate over the "naturalness" of gender roles: "By defining [the New Woman] as physiologically 'unnatural,' those whom she threatened reaffirmed the legitimacy and the 'naturalness' of the bourgeois order. By insisting on their own social and sexual legitimacy in words formed out of a century of women's reform rhetoric, the New Women repudiated that order" (Smith-Rosenberg 1989, 265).[34] The New Women had the rhetorical tools to defend their rights, but were battling a large group that clung to bourgeois values and traditional gender roles as the only natural order.

Many viewed educational reform as the chief impetus behind the New Woman phenomenon. Such reform frightened those who viewed it as a threat to domestic life. In a book from 1894 in which he analyzes the changes in women's lives and roles since the advent of female education, social critic Octave Uzanne voices the anti-reform stance by lauding the education of the early to mid-nineteenth century that initiated a young girl "in a fair and sure way to her future duties of mistress of the house, wife, and mother" (Uzanne 1894, 470).[35] He bewails the fact that "increasingly, girls receive cumbersome instruction, heavy with a thousand superfluous if not harmful notions, and their education, following the same pace, is becoming more and more boyish" (471). For Uzanne, women's education should be minimal, for most ideas taught to young men are superfluous to women's existence and can actually be dangerous for them. According to Uzanne, receiving the same education as young men had dangerous consequences: "Their nature is distorted, their bodies and their minds become more awkward along with it; they become less feminine without being virilized, thus inaugurating a third sex" (472). Here again is the notion of "nature": for Uzanne, women who are too educated are unnatural. They become a third sex, neither men nor women. Uzanne counsels young men to choose their wives carefully:

> Here's some good advice to follow when you marry: over a girl who solves problems at the blackboard, who is familiar with the Sassanid Empire, who has an opinion on the Investiture Controversy and who knows anatomy, choose a humble young lady who doesn't scorn crocheting, who is interested in weaving and who likes to embroider. But hurry, for it can be feared that soon there won't be any of them left. (473)

Though he doesn't explain why, it is clear that Uzanne values domestic skills over the ability to reason and reflect. He even suggests that the two are mutually exclusive, and that education deprives a woman of her ability to run a home. For Uzanne, the domestic maternal instinct is the only thing protecting young Parisiennes from the dangers of virilizing education (477). He instills fear in the reader that real, natural women are on the path to extinction. Uzanne's text is a strong example of the sort of argument used against educational reform, an argument that was well received by those who feared the adverse effects of new educational opportunities for women.

While most male writers and some female writers such as Camille Pert were critical of the New Woman, some male writer-critics such as Jules Bois welcomed her with enthusiasm. In his *Eve nouvelle* of 1895, Bois writes in support of a new understanding of women as completely independent of men. One of his most interesting arguments is that men writing about women tend to make lapdogs of them. Women should be free, writes Bois. He then proceeds to trace their role through history, outlining the images and archetypes associated with femininity at each period. Bois has an unusual style that combines his own ideas, examples from writers, stereotypes, and pseudo-monologues of young girls. His writing is dramatic and grand: "The era of the woman, truly woman, is finally beginning," he proclaims (Bois 1895, 157). Education will provide society with this new independent woman, Bois posits, citing England and America as models for France in this respect. He writes that reform of the educational system will help the feminist cause more than suppressing the dowry system, which was cited by some as an oppressive weight on women. Moreover, Bois gives a surprisingly modern argument for the necessary contributions of women in the workforce, denying that home and family would be neglected by working women. "The society of the future is the child of woman," Bois announces, and "The new society won't be the new society unless it becomes feminist" (354).[36] In the eyes of Bois, society will not and cannot change for the better unless France eliminates its antiquated notions about gender roles.

In his book on the girl's place in literature, Jules Bertaut contends that the most important result of educational reform was that it distinguished "education," which was the responsibility of the girl's family, and "instruction," the job of the school. The fact that the girl left home for several hours a day gave her the opportunity to develop an individual identity in a daily struggle with her schoolmates and teachers (Bertaut 1910, 168). The basic solitude of the schoolgirl forces her to consider herself and her place in society, without the religious screens in place before the turn of the century. The new doors opening to the girl cause her to rebel in the face of different forms of authority, and to know things that before she would learn only after adolescence (170).

Bertaut considers that modern education and the rise of feminism led
to revolt on the part of young women: "Prevailing feminist ideas come
to the rescue and finish by making the young girl realize how deplor-
able her situation is and how easy it would be to remedy such slavery"
(247). Feminist ideas revealed to young women the possibilities within
their reach, but access to feminist thought was limited. One excellent
source was the novel. According to Jennifer Waelti-Walters, the best
models for the new woman were the Belle Epoque female novelists who
helped to promote her: "The real new women are independent, critical,
and endowed with a social conscience: as they are presented within the
novels of the period, so they were in reality, if we consider the lives
of the authors themselves" (Waelti-Walters 1990, 175). Waelti-Walters further characterizes the New Woman, based on feminist Belle
Epoque novels:

> She is, above all, a woman determined to escape from the constraints of
> home life, who looks askance at marriage because it represents another
> set of restrictions. Above all, she believes that education can provide
> the way for a woman to become psychologically and financially self-
> sufficient, freeing her to claim her place as man's equal in the home
> and in the workplace. She demands freedom of movement, freedom to
> dispose of her body and affections as she sees fit, and economic eman-
> cipation, too. (177)

As the above vocabulary demonstrates, the most significant aspect of
New Womanhood, as depicted in the novels, was *freedom*—intellectual,
professional, economic, and sexual.

In her article on French novels of female education at the Belle
Epoque, Juliette Rogers considers the popularity of the literary phenomenon at the time, as well as its disappearance from the canon today.[37] According to Rogers, the *Erziehungsromane* failed because wom-
en's writing was disdained, while men writing for and about women
were looked down upon for having "sold out" for commercial purposes.
Despite the forces working against it, the female novel managed to
survive with the help of literary journals and prizes, Rogers points
out, and it benefited as well from educational reform, which created
a female reading public. In their novels, women writers both criticize
the current state of the educational system and suggest possibilities for
change (Rogers 1994, 323–24).

Some of the most vocal opponents of the traditional system of educating girls were not women. Marcel Prévost was an active critic of the

traditional educational system still in place at the turn of the century, which he viewed as endorsing hypocrisy. He explores the links between the new woman, education, and marriage in the preface to his novel entitled *Les Demi-Vierges*. These "half-virgins" are young women who explore to the extreme limits the possibilities of romantic and sexual play before marriage. In his preface, Prévost displays an awareness of the religious community's objection to his novel, defends the novel on the grounds of its basis in truth, and warns his readers of the danger- ous trend in the education of girls: "Entre la conception chrétienne du mariage et le type de la demi-vierge, il y a . . . antinomie irréduct- ible. Or, l'éducation moderne des jeunes filles tend de plus en plus à développer le type demi-vierge. Il faut donc changer l'éducation de la jeune fille—cela presse!—ou bien le mariage chrétien périra" [Between the Christian conception of marriage and the half-virgin type, there is . . . diehard antinomy. And yet, modern education of girls tends increasingly to develop the half-virgin type. The education of girls must therefore be changed—this is urgent!—or Christian marriage will perish] (Prévost 1901, iv). Without stating outright his convic- tions regarding feminist education, Prévost warns conservatives of the dangers involved in failing to modify educational practices to suit the needs of modern young women.

The idea of the New Woman contains an altruistic element. The New Woman does not merely claim educational rights for herself; she then passes her knowledge on to the next generation. Having attained a certain level of confidence and autonomy, she then works to prepare girls to participate in society and effect positive change:

> In the novels written around 1900 the characters presented as new women are educated already and tend therefore to belong to the bour- geoisie, while the younger characters are sometimes girls from poorer families who grow into independent women in the novels. This pattern occurs more frequently as teaching becomes recognized as a way for a girl with no dowry to earn a decent living. (Waelti-Walters 1990, 178)

Yet the new social obligations of women involved more than the edu- cation of young girls. In her article entitled "Sortir," Michelle Perrot writes of the female tendency toward movement out of the home, which saw a marked increase at this time. Aware of increasing social problems, women volunteered for charity work in hospitals, "residences" for low- income workers, and other social work organizations. Their biggest concern remained the well-being of women. Perrot summarizes their mindset in the following: "First and foremost, women must be known, educated, and defended" (Perrot 1991, 470). Their efforts were spurred on both by nascent feminism and by a sincere desire for amelioration of societal conditions.

It is at the time of the New Woman debate that Madeleine Pelletier was writing her book on the feminist education of girls, first published in 1914. Pelletier was one of the first successful female doctors. She firmly believed in educational reform, arguing that women were capable of playing key roles in society if their education prepared them for critical thought and action. Her radical method of education was based on equality between boys and girls. She felt, for example, that boys should do household chores, while girls should have male teachers and physical education classes, including instruction in firing guns, so that they might walk alone in the countryside without fear. Pelletier advocates the reduction of signs of sexual difference at an early age: girls should dress like boys to enjoy freedom of movement and have short hair to discourage vanity (Pelletier 1978, 80).

As for the intellectual education of the young girl, Pelletier lauds its progress in comparison with the convent instruction offered to girls decades before, yet bemoans the lack of materials in girls' *lycées*. She objects most to the feminine image girls glean from the reading material given them, an image of worth based on sexual or maternal love:

> The young woman gets from them ideas on what woman is, what she must be, on her role with regard to men and in society; and heroines that spring from the imagination of authors who, it can be said, all consider woman an inferior being are the least likely to make the student who studies them feminist. (Pelletier 1978, 99)

 Pelletier feels strongly that reading material matters greatly in the development of the young mind. In her eyes, all novelists portray women as fundamentally inferior. She considers that social structures and gender roles are internalized based on what a young person reads. Her view of education calls for the teacher to try to establish parallels between books and life. She also argues that Latin should not be the major focus of study, and that education should match social status, that is to say, people from the lower classes ought not to educate their daughters (105).[38] Structured education should continue as long as possible, until the girl is capable of earning a living (107). Though Pelletier's impassioned, and perhaps embittered, appeal for revolution in the education of young women was first published after the novels considered in this section, the causes for her protest were much the same as those pushing novelists to rethink the role of the adolescent.

In the section of this study devoted to the body, we have seen the supposed effect on the female body (and mind) of postponing or refusing marriage and reproduction. The detractors of the New Woman argued that education would have a virilizing effect on the female body. Carroll Smith-Rosenberg makes reference to this belief in her article: "The woman who favored her mind at the expense of her ovaries . . . would disorder a delicate physiological balance. . . . No longer reproductive, she would begin to look like a man" (Smith-Rosenberg 1989, 267). Whether or not the author of the *Vierges fortes* books, Marcel Prévost, intended to support this argument, his description of Romaine Pirnitz would seem to corroborate the theory. The female characters who fight to create new educational opportunities for girls in Paris are prime examples of dangerous elements of society: according to Smith-Rosenberg, turn-of-the-century physicians in the United States viewed the New Woman's lack of enthusiasm for motherhood as "sociosexual deviance" (267). Though Prévost felt strongly about the need to change educational methods for girls, by creating unfeminine instructors he merely fed into the stereotypes about single, educated women that were prevalent at the time.

Here is the goal of the feminist group in Prévost's *Vierges fortes* books, as stated by its fictional leader, Romaine Pirnitz, in *Léa*: "Il s'agissait de fonder l'éducation intégrale de la femme par la femme; de créer un séminaire de jeunes filles qui fussent des personnes morales, capables de suffire elles-mêmes à leurs besoins, sans l'obligation de recourir aux hommes—à une époque où . . . le célibat devenait, pour beaucoup d'entre elles, une cruelle nécessité sociale" [The idea was to found integral education of woman by woman; creating a seminar of young girls who would be moral people, capable of satisfying their own needs, without being obliged to resort to men—at a time when . . . celibacy was becoming a cruel social necessity for many of them] (Prévost 1900, 16). In her book, Madeleine Pelletier refers briefly to the novel, directly criticizing the methods used by Pirnitz and her comrades to further the cause of feminist education: "Female emancipation reform speaks to the general population, a school only addresses a small number of people, and as her effort is thwarted by all of society, the result is nil or almost; it is a drop of water in the ocean" (Pelletier 1978, 65). Traveling and lecturing would have enabled the characters to reach a much wider audience, according to Pelletier. Though she may be right about the more immediate effects of lectures, Pelletier disregards both the difficulties involved in travel and public presentations for young women of the time, and the clear intention of Pirnitz's group to reach as young an audience as possible, something that lectures would render difficult. Pelletier's criticism of the novel reveals her personal convictions regarding female education and employment, but also creates an interesting dialogue between literature and life. These moments of parallel between the two, albeit rare, tend to confirm the contention of this study that the novels both reflected and influenced social roles.

The reasons for the failure of the girls' school in Prévost's novel are more financial than anything else, despite one murder scandal that concretizes the school's already dubious moral reputation. Prévost may have been influenced by ideas such as those of Rémy de Gourmont, expressed in "la jeune fille d'aujourd'hui" [the young girl today] (1901) from *Le Chemin de velours*. The author claims that the turn-of-the-century adolescent does not want emancipation, and that she should remain faithful to traditional principles and become a housewife (Gourmont 1923, 292–93). For Gourmont, the modern girl merely wants to love and be loved (294). Any intelligence she may possess is a "gift that is fatal to her freedom" (295). The idea that intelligence was a threat to young women was hardly new, but calling it a threat to their freedom is. The implication is that intelligence will limit the girl's choice of husbands. Jules Bertaut takes a more moderate view: "It seems that the immense feminist agitation . . . has barely crossed the young girl's mind; she may retain a more or less deep trace of it, but has not drawn from it a life principle sufficient to transform her entire being" (Bertaut 1910, 291–92). Bertaut conceives of change according to feminist principles as a distinct, and even welcome, possibility, whereas Gourmont views it as a concrete threat.

In the novels written by women, social spaces such as the school and the convent appear to be sources of physical and mental escape from would-be confinement at home, an idea that echoes the earlier section on spaces. The adolescent girl, often orphaned either literally or figuratively, finds in these social and educational spaces replacement family structures and emotional bonds. Yet these bonds may prove to be illusory and the closed spaces potential prisons.

For Marianne in Marcelle Tinayre's *Avant l'amour*, education means the possibility of leaving the confines of her home and of interacting socially with other girls. Her "serious" education begins at twelve years of age, at which point she has had only a few history and geography lessons from her godfather and no religious instruction (Tinayre 1897, 16). Marianne attends all-girl classes with an older female teacher, yet fails to make much progress, learning more on her own and through discussions with her stepbrother Maxime. In her article on the early novels of Marcelle Tinayre, Elisabeth Ceaux observes that Marianne's education was of poor quality, prompting her to read her stepbrother's books clandestinely (Ceaux 1984, 209). Ceaux claims that Tinayre contributed to female emancipation by revealing that the religious instruction intended to inspire devotional fervor in young girls was an obstacle to self-actualization.[39] According to Ceaux, Tinayre promoted a pagan conception of life, rejecting the false comfort of religion (213). Marianne explains her indifference to the technical and unemotional religious instruction she receives that fails to engage her imagination or her heart (21). Marianne notes how the sensual language used in the first communion rites links them to marriage (25–26).[40] Here, religious fervor is for the adolescent but a temporary replacement for greater joys to come through love and marriage.

In *Hellé* (1899), Tinayre explores in greater detail the theme of female education, revealing the aforementioned two-part conception thereof: book learning, or "instruction," which takes place in isolation, and social education, or "éducation," which involves circulation in an urban landscape.[41] Hellé's early education takes place in her own home, thanks to an uncle both highly educated and unusually liberal, who feels that girls' schools are "usines d'abêtissement" [factories of stupidity]. Her uncle points out the differences between the education of girls and boys: "Si notre frère m'avait laissé un garçon, celui-ci n'aurait pas d'autre précepteur que moi-même. A notre petite nièce, un minimum de connaissances suffira, à moins qu'elle ne révèle des aptitudes extraordinaires" [If our brother had left me a boy, he would have had no other tutor than myself. For our little niece, minimal knowledge will suffice, unless she reveals extraordinary aptitude] (Tinayre 1926, 6–7). Hellé does reveal such "extraordinary aptitude," thereby escaping from the limited spheres normally open to the female student. Her awakening to the world of books is a revelation, a rebirth, a sensorial epiphany: "Les mots même, par le hasard de leur assemblage, s'animèrent d'une vie que je ne soupçonnais pas. Ils furent la couleur, la musique, le parfum" [Even words, by the coincidence of their assembly, were animated with a life that I hadn't suspected. They were color, music, perfume] (11). Fortunately for Hellé, her uncle prefers unusual teaching methods, based on reflection and experience, to the book-based traditional ones

(16–17). She studies subjects long considered inappropriate for girls, such as philosophical systems and the evolution of religious dogma (18). Nineteenth-century girls were expected to learn and to accept dogma, not to understand its evolution and to think critically about it. In this sense, Hellé's education is quite subversive.

Her education does prevent Hellé from behaving like other adolescent girls; the narrator dismisses the sudden burst of feeling provoked by religiosity and puberty in most adolescent girls as unnatural and unhealthy (Tinayre 1926, 19). Indeed, Hellé's uncle reacts with rage and scorn to the fundamentally religious forms of female education proposed by his wife: "Que je ne trouve plus ici ces montruosités barbares! Il ne manquerait plus que de voir Hellé porter des scapulaires, réciter des chapelets et croire aux démons. Une fille que j'ai élevée comme mon propre fils! on voudrait en faire une sournoise, une abêtie, un gibier de confessionnal!" [I had better not find these barbarous monstrosities here again! The last straw would be to see Hellé wear scapulars, recite rosaries and believe in demons. A girl that I raised like my own son! They want to make her sneaky, stupid confessional quarry!] (19–20). Clearly, the uncle opposes his secular methods to what he views as the less rational methods of religious study. His reference to raising Hellé "like my own son" suggests the still-existing gulf between educational practices for boys and for girls. As he explains to Hellé: "Il fallait, pour achever mon œuvre, écarter de toi les contagions morbides, les puérilités mondaines, un mysticisme néfaste à la raison. Je t'ai modelée sur l'immortelle et gracieuse image d'Hypathie" [In order to complete my work, I had to keep away from you morbid contagion, worldly childishness and mysticism dangerous to reason. I modeled you on the immortal and graceful image of Hypatia] (25).[42] Hellé's education breaks the traditional mold in several ways. She learns at home, with a male relative as teacher, untraditional subjects and teaching methods are part of her curriculum, and religion and sentiment have no place in her education. The system succeeds in creating a young woman capable of logical thought, both abstract and concrete.

Hellé receives two different types of social education. Antoine Genesvrier, a family friend, shows her the value of charity work, warning her of the trap of intellectual egotism that is the "vice unique" [sole vice] of her education (Tinayre 1926, 146). His message is that Hellé must use her ability to reason for a greater good, and not just for her own pleasure and gratification. Another sort of social education comes from Parisian ladies who try to make up for gaps in her education before she confronts married life. Mme Marboy claims that marriage demands of women self-sacrifice and surrender and suggests that Hellé will not be able to lower herself and swallow her pride for marriage (288). This lesson encourages Hellé to follow tradition by sacrificing herself to her husband's will. These two lessons echo one another in interesting ways: they both encourage the woman to think of others, but Genesvrier means society in general, whereas the women mean a husband. His lesson suggests an opening of the self toward others, while theirs proposes a closing of the self in the interest of another. Hellé's answer reveals her untraditional conception of marriage: "Je ne veux ni me sacrifier, ni sacrifier mon mari. Nous devons nous efforcer de réaliser ensemble une vie harmonieuse en nous respectant, en nous aidant, en nous complétant" [I don't want to sacrifice either myself or my husband. We must try to achieve a harmonious life together while respecting, helping and completing each other] (289). Mme Marboy responds with scorn that Hellé is a truly modern woman (289). Hellé indeed represents the New Woman, educated for intellectual and moral autonomy, yet possessing a social conscience that allows her to teach and learn from those less fortunate than herself. Her untraditional education allows her to challenge social values and to break paths in territory from which "respectable" girls were previously excluded.

Colette's *Claudine à l'école* differs somewhat from *Hellé* in that it shows the joys and struggles of a provincial schoolgirl in a more traditional academic setting. The educational space, despite its positive aspects revealed in Claudine's declaration at the end of the novel (Colette 1989a, 170), is fraught with problems of many sorts. Claudine, the observant and sharp-tongued narrator, spends her time criticizing the environment of the school and the mental and physical weaknesses of her schoolmates. She is quick to point out the inadequacy of the school buildings and of the teaching staff, not to mention the academic exercises and rituals in which the girls participate. The classrooms are described as incredibly filthy, poorly equipped, and foul-smelling (11).[43] Joan Hinde Stewart also notes Claudine's basic loneliness, her lack of "authentic bonds" with parents or friends (Stewart 1981, 262). Yet despite these isolating factors, Claudine thrives at school. In one passage, Claudine establishes the hierarchy of educational options, suggesting that her school is one of the worst, but that she enjoys herself much more there than she would in a stricter academic setting (11). Claudine expresses a surprisingly lucid opinion of her social and familial situation, yet remains unfazed by the inappropriateness of her education to her class. Juliette Rogers insists on Claudine's novelty: "The prim (but definitely not proper) Claudine gives a new image of the twentieth-century teenager—an independent and modern heroine" (Rogers 1994, 325). Rogers cites Claudine's spunk in doing extra forbidden reading that allows her to criticize the school's curriculum during an oral exam (325). Claudine represents what Rogers calls "a new type of critical reader who, through analysis, contemplation, and group discussion, uses reading as a tool to inform herself and to establish a conscious position for herself in her own culture" (330).[44] By continually seeking information beyond that which she is expected to know, Claudine keeps herself intellectually stimulated and maintains her superior social role.

Despite the obvious flaws of her school, Claudine enjoys being in a place where she savors intellectual and socioeconomic superiority over her classmates. Her nostalgia when the buildings are renovated reveals her deep emotional attachment to the original school: "Je n'ai plus les "rabicoins" où on se mussait dans la poussière, ni les couloirs de ce vieux bâtiment compliqué dans lequel on ne savait jamais si on se trouvait chez les instituteurs ou bien chez nous, et où on débouchait si naturellement dans une chambre de sous-maître qu'on avait à peine besoin de s'excuser en rentrant à la classe" [I don't have the "crannies" anymore where we hid in the dust, nor the corridors of that old complicated building where we never knew if we were in the teachers' rooms or in ours, and where you popped so naturally into a teacher assistant's room that you barely needed to excuse yourself when going back to class] (87). Claudine misses the labyrinthine space of the former school building, with its corridors connecting the various zones of activity in unexpected ways. She thrives in spaces open to circulation. The thought of being locked into her hotel room by the headmistress the night before the final exams drives her mad (100). Perhaps because she is accustomed to complete control over her movements at home, Claudine cannot bear the thought of being confined either physically or figuratively. Despite the negative aspects of the school and of the educational system in general, Claudine does well there. It is a space in which she can push boundaries, challenge rules, and violate codes, thereby winning the admiration and envy of her classmates. It is a theater she knows by heart, where she chooses her roles and regulates her own entrances and exits.

In the second novel in Colette's Claudine series, the heroine discovers a new educational space in Paris. The city temporarily destabilizes her, but Claudine soon learns to navigate its more complex nooks and crannies. Paris poses new social challenges, and Claudine is equal to them all. She rapidly develops friendships and a sense of Parisian style, and learns how to handle unwelcome male attention, including marriage proposals. In one passage, Claudine deftly sweeps through several social spaces, initiating each displacement. First, she attends an opera with her cousin and love interest Renaud, a man several decades her senior. Second, she proposes a move to a new level of familiarity by calling him by his first name rather than "uncle" (275). After the show, she proposes that they take a walk rather than go home immediately (277). Then she proposes that they have a drink together, and overrides Renaud's veto of a loud *brasserie* (277). Claudine dominates the food and beverage order, as well as the conversation, and on the way home declares to Renaud her adoration of him (282). To describe her inebriated seduction of Renaud, she divides herself into a "sage" [good] Claudine and a "folle" [wild] Claudine. The spatial element of her conquest becomes evident in the interplay between these two halves of herself:

> Elle . . . monte, rêveuse éveillée, les trois étages, et se couche, la folle Claudine, rejointe—il est bien temps—par la sage Claudine dans son lit bateau. Mais la Claudine sage s'efface timidement, admirative et respectueuse, devant l'autre, qui est allée droit où le Destin la poussait, sans se retourner, comme une conquérante ou une condamnée.

> [The awakened dreamer, the wild Claudine, climbs the three floors and gets into bed, joined—finally—by the good Claudine in her sleigh bed. But the good Claudine steps aside timidly, admiring and respectful, for the other, who went straight where Destiny was pushing her, without turning back, like a conqueror or a convict.](283)

Claudine's social education involves not only mastering the spaces through which she passes, but also learning how to modify her behavior to fit a space. The doubling of this scene concretizes a typical adolescent ambivalence toward adult experiences that one's conscience (the "sage" Claudine) deems inappropriate or immoral. Claudine's ability to mentally divide herself to allow her to savor experiences, as well as her quick recognition that such a process has occurred, indicate a certain level of maturity and an adult ability to negotiate both physical and mental spaces.

In Anna de Noailles' *Le Visage émerveillé*, because educational and social spaces are not part of the equation, the central tension is that between a closed, familiar world, here a convent, and the seemingly limitless outside one. This outer world is tempting for its mystery and exoticism, as suggested by certain symbolic objects. The nun recalls a fan once belonging to her mother, printed with an Italian scene. The fan's words and pictures incite in the young girl a mental development of the scene. Her imagination creates an entire exotic place, "tout un pays," from one tiny memory (Noailles 1904, 67). The Italian water-colors that her secret visitor Julien offers her have a similar effect (77). Julien's discussion of his travels allows her to imagine the exotic places that had seemed unreal to her as a little girl (118). The Haitian sister Bénédicta provides another source of inspiration for exotic reverie (148). All that is foreign, exterior to the convent walls, exerts a powerful attraction for the protagonist's imaginative nature.

Yet for all the largely positive but unreal images the narrator associates with the outside world, the idea of leaving her shelter stirs up bitter memories and triggers moral fears. Her aunt's worldly salons always left her feeling bored and sad (Noailles 1904, 34). She is disturbed by the strangely changing costumes of her mother and sister, who come for a monthly visit (144). Julien, who represents the outside world, reads Baudelaire, whose writing frightens her, and has thoughts that seem similarly worrisome and impure (109, 118). He describes her as a precious, sacred object shut away and enslaved in a secret place, a combination of images that shocks her (119). Another worrisome thought is the novelty that Julien insists she will hold for society men after having been so unattainable (158–59). She acknowledges the tantalizing challenge of seducing a nun—"Une religieuse, on la désire, parce que, chaque fois, elle dit: 'On ne peut pas s'habituer, c'est trop mal'" [A nun is desirable because she says each time: "We can't get used to this; this is wrong"] (Noailles 1904, 164)—as well as the absurdity and awkwardness of a former nun rejoining the outside world (165). The nun perceives the outside world as an artificial and threatening space, whose lessons she does not wish to know.

At the novel's end, the narrator chooses the dream world she has created within the convent over a move back into the reality of the outside world, no matter how idyllic or romantic such a voyage may appear. As we saw in the last section, she chooses her protected dream life over the reality outside (135). She prefers to continue her life at the convent, where her flights of fancy distinguish her from the other sisters: "Moi seule ici je suis la reine, je suis oisive et langoureuse et les autres sont des esclaves qui travaillent" [Here alone I am queen; I am idle and languid and the others are slaves that work] (133). At the convent, she is free to imagine Julien finding happiness and forgetting his cares with another woman (211). At the end of the novel, the nun remains in the *huis clos* of the convent, yet is free once again to paint, at her leisure, idealized mental landscapes of love and of exotic places far away. She has opted against opening her horizons to the lessons available outside the convent walls, choosing instead the safer and, for her, more agreeable combination of religious dogma and imagination.

Juliette Rogers suggests that, for many young Belle Epoque heroines, the dearth of female role models capable of challenging them mentally and nurturing them physically and emotionally pushed them to create and become "la femme nouvelle" [new woman] (Rogers 1994, 326). For the young girl of the early twentieth century, doors were opening besides those of the school. New opportunities for social movement presented themselves to young women, who then began to play increasingly important roles in French society. In *Féministes à la Belle Epoque*, Jean Rabaut points out that the young heroine often "se flatte . . . de mener une existence beaucoup plus intelligente que celle de ses contemporaines polarisées vers la pêche au mari" [prides herself . . . on the fact that she leads a much more intelligent life than her contemporaries who are all focused on fishing for husbands] (Rabaut 1985, 214). Yet characters in the novels, like actual women, left careers, often in the field of education, to marry and have families. Rogers explains this unexpected choice of traditional roles by evoking the new liberal republican feminism of the late nineteenth century, which encouraged emancipated, educated wives and mothers (329). Moreover, these novels read by working and middle-class women were intended as a diversion, not as a call to revolution (330).

Rogers claims that, in fact, the novels add to the concept of the heroine "by offering independent and intelligent working female protagonists who simultaneously acted in a way that assured their readership that the role of wife and mother was not unheroic or unworthy" (Rogers 1994, 331). Educated heroines gain a freshly critical eye along with expanding freedom and independence. As Rabaut states, "Without a doubt, the New Woman is on the move. Already the woman exists who wants not only to live her life, but also to do it of her own accord, and for whom this is both a principle and a necessity" (Rabaut 1985, 215). This advancement sheds new light on the French women's culture of the Belle Epoque (331–32). Period novels trace this unprecedented movement by outlining the spaces, educational and other, that the girls learn to master, including the often unfamiliar urban landscape. Slowly but surely, young women in these novels are learning to define their own terms, choose their own destinies. No matter how liberated they become in certain arenas, however, one of the key forces maintaining boundaries for young women is the ubiquitous and omnipotent power of love.

Love and Marriage: Escape or Return?

At the turn of the century, adolescent girls were expected to find good husbands who were financially capable of supporting a family. Love and sexual compatibility were far from being primary values for the parents and mentors of young women. However, growing concerns for the adverse effects of marriage on an uneducated and unprepared adolescent, including the contraction of various sexually transmitted diseases, incited some writers and members of the medical profession to argue for increased sexual education of adolescent girls. As Yvonne Knibiehler points out in her article entitled "Corps et cœurs" [Bodies and Hearts], theirs was a difficult task. At the end of the nineteenth century, Knibiehler writes, doctors strongly recommended that girls receive sexual education in order to reduce the incidence of syphilis:

> A forewarned young girl could better resist seduction; she could de-mand that her fiancé show proof of intact health. Information manuals appeared. But that women had acquired the right to monitor their own bodies already represented a revolution. How could they be granted the right to check on the man's body? (Knibiehler 1991, 363)

Most girls did not have access to such manuals, and therefore approached marriage with extremely limited knowledge of their own physiological functions, not to mention those of their suitors. Portrayals of these girls' thoughts about young men in the novel are therefore stripped of eroticism or understanding of their physical responses. Characters describe feeling weak, ill at ease, or blushing uncontrollably. Most of-ten, the issue of sexual attraction is buried under romantic daydreams centered on the desire to see and talk with the object of affection. Love therefore becomes a metaphor for sex, emotional attraction replacing physical attraction, and the heroines' ignorance of sexuality leads to some occasionally humorous, and sometimes hazardous, situations.

In her book, feminist doctor Madeleine Pelletier presents her ar-guments for sexual education for girls. She proposes that parents tell their daughters the truth about sexuality at the age of seven, explaining "relations intersexuelles" [intersexual relations] at twelve years of age and warning them about the possible dangers associated with strangers (Pelletier 1978, 112). More detailed explanations come later: "It is around fifteen years of age that all of reality will be revealed without any special consideration; physical and sentimental, normal and pathological love will be explained as it is. Of course, the greatest detail will be given on love from a social perspective!" (113). Pelletier proposes showing the girl social reality by taking her for walks in the city and indicating various levels of prostitution, sexual activity, and gambling, watching over her until twenty years of age, when she is able to think clearly:

> From fifteen to sixteen years of age, a girl's ability to reason is still weak; despite all advice, even examples, she might yield to the natural attraction that youth has for youth and slowly lose all of her good habits of study or of regular work. At twenty, the girl has all of her reason, therefore she will have complete freedom despite risks and perils. (114)

As for sexual activity and marriage, Pelletier argues that girls choosing to avoid sexuality should be encouraged: "Laws and customs enslave woman and she can barely find a bit of freedom by depriving herself of love" (114). Though a woman can live a long happy life without sex, Pelletier proposes that, if she does desire physical love, she should get married, but that she should make sure to protect herself financially (115). Even for radical feminist Madeleine Pelletier, love is an option, as long as women protect themselves as much as possible from negative outcomes.

The male novelists' portrayals of love reveal the absence of such instruction as that proposed by Pelletier. Their female adolescents fall in love only with impossible suitors or reject love out of irrational fear. The only adolescent to marry is Léa, Marcel Prévost's heroine, whose conjugal happiness fails to prevent her death. For these novelists, love leads to impasse, both emotionally and physically. They suggest that lack of education leads girls to choose inappropriate spouses, or leaves them incapable of choosing at all. In each case, romance and eventual marriage appear to be the ideal goals, both for the novelist and for the characters, but for a number of reasons, the characters fail to achieve them. These writers do not argue for celibacy; they merely observe the many psychological and sociological obstacles separating young girls from marital bliss. The adolescents they portray fail to negotiate effectively between their own needs and desires and the societal demands imposed upon them.

Despite their sheltered innocence, the adolescent characters of Francis Jammes find ample encounters to fuel romantic dreams, but their lack of education and social contact complicate or doom their romantic attempts. They may deny the appeal of love, as is the case of Pomme d'Anis, who is convinced of her undesirability. Most of the heroine's misfortune in *Clara d'Ellébeuse* is caused by her sexual ignorance, which allows her to replace reality with partial truths and romantic imaginings. When she reads her great-uncle's letter in which he refers to his beloved's pregnancy, she decides that she too must be pregnant because of having hugged Roger (136). Clara's naïveté, which causes her to misunderstand the letter and to misread the signs communicated by her body, encourages both her romantic dreams and the amalgam she makes of her own experience and that of her unfortunate relative. Out of love for Roger, she decides to keep the horrible "truth" of her condition a secret from her parents, and it is probably in imitation of Laure, her romantic role model, that she decides to take her life. Illusions about love, both that which Clara experiences herself and that about which she reads in her great-uncle's letters, prevent her from seeking help or explanations that might have saved her life. Clara's passionate nature and lack of instruction, as well as a possible dose of hereditary madness at which the novel hints repeatedly, cause her to distance herself from reality to the point of suicide. Clara's emotional and mental space is so filled with romantic illusions that she cannot think clearly and logically. As in the case of so many other characters, a good dose of sexual education may have averted disaster.

Francis Jammes' novels are filled with female adolescents who suffer from their utter lack of effective education and social contact. Almaïde d'Etremont is another Jammes character, a lonely adolescent who is prevented from pursuing a social life by a cruel uncle, and who begs God to provide her with an object of affection: "O mon Dieu! se dit Almaïde d'Etremont . . . mon Dieu, écoutez-moi, je veux aimer, je suis si triste . . . si malheureuse. . . . Mon Dieu, j'ai le besoin d'aimer quelqu'un. . . . Je crie vers Vous" [O my God! Almaïde d'Etremont says to herself . . . my God, listen to me, I want to love, I am so sad . . . so unhappy. . . . My God, I need to love someone. . . . I cry out to You] (172). Almaïde's desire for love causes her to pursue companionship and physical contact with a young goatherd, by whom she becomes pregnant just before his death. These sexual encounters make Almaïde an atypical example of a female adolescent.[45] Yet Almaïde's naïve joy at experiencing first love, as stated by the narrator, reveals her emotional adolescence: "Qu'il est bon que se dissipe enfin la tristesse d'Almaïde! Oh! l'écœurante vie que, jusqu'à présent, elle a traînée! Elles s'enfuient maintenant, les nausées de l'existence ancienne, l'âcre et monotone douleur qui gonflait son âme de dégoût, l'iniquité de n'être aimé de personne" [How good it is that Almaïde's sadness is finally vanishing! Oh! What a sickening life she has dragged along until now! Now it is all flying away, the nausea of her old life, the sharp, monotonous pain that swelled her soul with disgust, the iniquity of being loved by no one] (183).[46] Because she has been so sheltered and victimized for her entire life, Almaïde functions emotionally like a much younger person. Like Clara, Almaïde lives in an isolated world marked by sexual ignorance. In both novels, the unfortunate outcome can be traced to the characters' obliviousness to even the most basic biological truths. Jammes describes an innocent, isolated space of female adolescence, where minor collisions with the facts of life create a violent disequilibrium in the characters' lives.

Romain Rolland's novel portrays a dreamy adolescent, lost in her illusions of love. At the same time, Antoinette has a more realistic view of the economic element of marriage than do certain other characters. She is aware that, given her financial circumstances and her looks, she can afford to be choosy about her mate, and wants to make the choice herself: "Elle entendait bien faire son choix, elle-même. Elle savait qu'elle était, ou qu'elle serait très riche—elle était un 'beau parti'. . . . [E]lle voulait bien se faire prendre; mais elle ne voulait pas qu'on la prît. Dans sa petite tête, elle avait déjà décidé qui elle épouserait" [She intended to make her own choice. She knew that she was, or would be, very rich—she was a "good match" . . . She was willing to have herself be taken, but didn't want someone to take her. In her little head, she had already decided whom she would marry] (24). Antoinette is strong and independent and intends to choose her spouse. Her "love" keeps her from worrying about her father's financial difficulties: "Elle était toute au plaisir de son amour naissant: elle ne voulait pas penser aux choses inquiétantes; elle se persuadait que les nuages se dissiperaient d'eux-mêmes—ou qu'il serait assez temps pour les voir, quand on ne pourrait plus faire autrement" [She gave in completely to the pleasure of her nascent love; she didn't want to think about worrisome things; she persuaded herself that the clouds would dissipate of their own accord—or that it would be time to see them when one couldn't do otherwise] (30).

Despite her concrete awareness of marriage as a contract, Antoinette's vision is clouded by romantic reverie. It is not until the family begins to fall apart financially that Antoinette loses her illusions about ideal marriage in her future.

After her father's suicide and her mother's death, Antoinette sacrifices the possibility of romantic love in order to nurture her brother: "Cette petite fille de dix-sept à dix-huit ans, frivole et tendre, fut transformée par sa résolution héroïque: il y avait en elle une ardeur de dévouement et un orgueil de la lutte, que personne n'eût soupçonnés, elle-même moins que tout autre" [This little girl of seventeen to eighteen years old, frivolous and tender, was transformed by her heroic resolution: there was in her a devoted ardor and a pride in struggle, that no one would have guessed, she herself less than anyone] (Rolland 1908, 55). Her love for her brother is such that she refuses a marriage proposal because to accept would mean moving away from Olivier. Fraternal affection satisfies her until a meeting with musician Jean-Christophe kindles a new romantic flame. They share magical and seemingly impossible coincidental moments, first sitting in the same *loge* during a concert, then staring at one another from two different trains that happen to stop in the same station at the same time, and finally encountering each other on the street one day for just a moment before traffic separates them. Antoinette's attraction to Jean-Christophe, born of the randomness of their encounters, is only communicated to him through her brother Olivier after her death, when a letter helps Olivier put together the pieces of the story and find Jean-Christophe. Though Antoinette's life has love as its central theme, she never experiences a fully realized, mutual love apart from that which she shares with her brother. Her constant sacrifice and selflessness deprive her of her own life and her own love. In the name of fraternal devotion, she refuses to devote any time to herself or to take on any new social roles.

Jammes, Rolland, and Prévost suggest in these novels that love and marriage rarely coexist for young females. Their adolescent characters live in worlds of illusion, denial and missed opportunity. More than anything, their naiveté and/or social status deprive them of the possibility of finding happiness in love and marriage.

In the female novelists' works, love nearly always plays a central role. As Jennifer Waelti-Walters observes in her book on Belle Epoque feminist writers: "Whatever their age, station, and aims in life, the major problem to be faced by the women characters, be it at the theoretical or practical level, is always love" (Waelti-Walters 1990, 178). For

Waelti-Walters, this preoccupation with love can be linked to French culture.[47] Love is undeniably of utmost importance for these characters, even if it temporarily disappears as the narrative pursues other concerns. Waelti-Walters also writes that the female character at this time believes that "romantic love would be her reward for a youth of self-control, self-effacement, and self-denial" (8). Indeed, in the novels that describe difficult youths where the girl feels misunderstood by all those around her, the final scene is often one of romantic connection, as in *Hellé*, *Avant l'amour*, and *Claudine à Paris*.

Of the novelists presented here, Marcelle Tinayre is the most lauded for her uncanny ability to portray the young female mind as it experiences love. References have already been made to the enthusiasm of male critics such as André Billy and Jules Bertaut for the novels of Marcelle Tinayre. Elisabeth Ceaux shares their enthusiasm, calling Tinayre a "novelist of love" who deftly penetrates female psychology and attributes to heroines the aspirations and vindications that were fermenting at the time (Ceaux 1984, 210). In Marcelle Tinayre's *Avant l'amour*, a passage at the beginning of the novel expresses the need for instruction about sex such as that proposed by Madeleine Pelletier. A narratorial voice recounts memories of the lack of instruction given to her classmates, and their vain and damaging attempts to learn the truth about sexuality from various sources (Tinayre 1897, 18). The narrator remembers "ce souci inévitable et constant des choses de l'amour qui naît avec l'adolescence" [that inevitable and constant worry about love that is born with adolescence]; she writes, "Quand j'évoque la terreur, le dégoût, la tristesse que je reçus de certaines confidences, je me demande si la délicate et prudente révélation de la vérité ne vaudrait pas mieux que l'hypocrisie obligatoire" [When I evoke the terror, the disgust, the sadness that I received from certain secrets, I wonder whether delicate and prudent revelation of truth wouldn't be better than obligatory hypocrisy] (18). Such "revelation of truth" would demand a rare maternal candor, which the narrator claims to be an unrealistic expectation for women themselves raised in ignorance (19). Without such honesty from an older female relative, the girl stays ignorant and necessarily devious:

> Soumise au respect des convenances, modelée sur le type conventionnel de la demoiselle comme il faut, préparée pour donner des garanties apparentes aux futurs épouseurs, la jeune fille apprend, dès la première robe longue, cet art de dissimulation qu'elle exercera plus tard, contre

ces mêmes épouseurs devenus des maris. Si par hasard les livres trop
éloquents, les amitiés trop curieuses sont écartés du gynécée, la vierge
conservée jusqu'à dix-huit ans dans cet état de candeur idéale arrive au
mariage dépourvue de tout recours contre la conspiration des familles
et des jeunes gens.

[Submissive to respect of conventions, modeled on the conventional
type of the respectable young lady, prepared to give apparent guarantees to future suitors, the young girl learns, from her first long dress,
that art of dissimulation that she will practice later, against those same
suitors who have become husbands. If by chance too eloquent books
or too curious friends are kept away from the gynaeceum, the virgin
preserved until the age of eighteen in this state of ideal candor arrives
at marriage devoid of any recourse against the conspiring of families
and young men.] (18–19)

Because of her "conspiring" family, the young girl has no hope to learn
the truth unless she comes across pieces of it in books or from friends.
In any case, Tinayre feels that French girls should no longer remain ignorant up until the day of their marriage. Her narrator goes on to give
a vivid picture of the horror and potential danger of the uninformed
bride after her wedding night: "Le lendemain des noces, brutalisée,
écœurée, elle se soumet comme un animal passif ou médite déjà des
revanches dont seront seuls responsables les parents, le mari, les ab-
surdes mœurs qui ont tendu le piège légal, patenté et fleuri, où tombe
la vierge pour s'y réveiller femme" [The day after the wedding, brutal-
ized, sickened, she submits like a passive animal or already meditates
revenge for which the only responsible parties are the parents, the
husband, the absurd mores that set the legal, licensed and flowery trap
where the virgin falls and wakes up a woman] (20). Of the novels considered here, these passages contain the most blatant criticism of the
social system in place at the turn of the century, which seemed to make
female ignorance a prerequisite for marriage. Tinayre feels that "prudent revelation of truth" would allow the girl to avoid this horror on
her wedding night. This notion of revealing truth in order to facilitate
the young woman's rites of passage can be extended to include other
things besides sexuality. Education in general would help prevent many
of the misunderstandings and painful experiences that were considered
to be natural rites of passage for young women.

Tinayre's character Marianne in *Avant l'amour* passes through
three phases in love, which vaguely correspond to her relationships

with men, and which clearly demonstrate her sexual and social education. Her first phase is one of ignorant naïveté, where the glimpse of
a decidedly sexual relationship shocks her due to the religious teachings she has internalized (Tinayre 1897, 32). Because of her romantic
ideals, Marianne finds other girls her age tedious, with their "chasse
aux maris" [husband hunt] (37). Marianne herself realizes early the
economic component of marriage when her adoptive mother explains
to her that her lack of beauty or money will most likely turn away any
would-be suitors (38). Yet Marianne's romantic dreams are encouraged
by her reading material, which consists mainly of "dangerous" novels
about love: "Le désir de l'amour, imprécis et hallucinant, entra soudain
dans ma jeunesse. Il se manifesta d'abord par une vive douleur de me
sentir laide, incapable peut-être d'inspirer ces passions admirables dont
la flamme m'avait brûlée, à travers les mensonges de l'art . . . " [The desire for love, imprecise and hallucinatory, suddenly entered my youth.
It appeared first as a sharp pain at feeling ugly, possibly incapable of inspiring those admirable passions whose flames had burned me through
the lies of art . . .] (40). For Marianne, the only way to experience the
love of which she dreams is to be beautiful and to inspire passion in
men. Her romantic reveries are made manifest in nightly languorous
scenes where mental and physical phenomena meet in "une angoisse
triste et délicieuse" [a sad and delicious anxiety] where she longs for
a mysterious man (41). Like Claudine, Marianne dreams of a faceless
lover who will one day make himself known to her. It is during this
period of romantic daydream that Marianne meets her first "love,"
Francis, whom she idealizes without realizing that she does not feel
"cette secousse au cœur, cette émotion lancinante qu'il me semblait
nécessaire d'éprouver" [that jolt to the heart, that throbbing emotion
that it seemed to me necessary to feel] (45–46).

The second phase of Marianne's romantic education corresponds to
a dashing man named Jacques Rambert, who seduces her with music,
dance, and other sensual delights. When Marianne discovers her illegitimacy, she naïvely assumes that such news will not affect Rambert's
passion. Her rude awakening relieves her of many of her illusions and
leads her to consider her right to love even in the absence of marriage
(Tinayre 1897, 92). These experiences instruct Marianne in the danger
of precociously embellishing a love object and convince her that she
may need to seek amorous fulfillment outside of marriage. Marianne's
decision to pursue love with or without the benediction of the church
is most subversive for the time. She formulates her decision in terms of

rights, saying that she has a right to love in whatever form it happens to present itself to her.

The third and final phase of Marianne's lessons in love comes from Maxime, her stepbrother. Together they discuss such topics as societal expectations and whether or not marriage is linked to love (Tinayre 1897, 118). Maxime rapidly falls in unrequited love with Marianne, and for the sake of their friendship, she decides to accept his displays of affection: "Goûtant le plaisir d'être aimée, plus que le bonheur d'aimer, j'étais tendre pourtant par instinct, par besoin, par reconnaissance" [Tasting the pleasure of being loved, more than the joy of loving, I was tender by instinct, by need, by gratitude] (126). With Maxime, she experiences the sensuality she longs for, yet without love for him in particular: "J'oubliai la bouche qui me donnait ces baisers pour savourer les baisers mêmes" [I forgot the mouth that was giving me those kisses to savor the kisses themselves] (149). She describes her purely physical responses as "fièvre," "douceur," "volupté," and "vertige" [fever, sweetness, sensuality, dizziness] (166). Yet Marianne reaches her breaking point, feeling ashamed for letting her sensuality lead her into dangerous territory when she awakens after a torrid meeting with Maxime, "brisée, fiévreuse, avec un cri de honte et de douleur" [broken, feverish, with a cry of shame and pain] (167). After briefly toying with the idea of marrying a rich older man who disgusts her (174), Marianne decides to struggle to preserve her physical relationship with Maxime, criticizing the "hypocrite chasteté" [hypocritical chastity] imposed on young women (210).

Marianne's discoveries about Maxime's sexual experiences make her nostalgic for her former innocence, when love seemed easier and simpler (Tinayre 1897, 251–52). When Maxime, her social superior, proposes marriage, Marianne's refusal, which she views as an "escape" from his "domination," gives her a "triomphale sensation de pureté reconquise" [triumphant sensation of recovered purity] (262). She renounces marriage, but when Maxime fights in a duel then decides to go abroad, she realizes that her feelings may resemble love more closely than she thought (280–81). When she sees Maxime just before his departure, she succumbs to his physical advances: "Je ne songeais pas à fuir, pas plus qu'à me donner, pas plus qu'à me défendre. . . . Il m'avait prise . . ." [I didn't think of fleeing, of giving myself, or of defending myself. . . . He had taken me . . .] (289). Marianne's neutral attitude here deserves comment. She is not terrified, nor is she particularly aroused—it is almost as though she separates herself from the experience mentally. Such a distant perspective may be attributed to the last vestiges of her religious education. This is the only novel in this study that evokes the pain of a first sexual experience: "L'épouvante physique de la virginité perdue m'arrachèrent une plainte" [The physical horror of lost virginity tore a moan from me] (290). This scene marks the culmination of Marianne's sexual and romantic education. She has accepted the love of a man who, like her, has learned about love through successive experiences. Their union confirms Marianne's conception of love as necessarily fulfilling physically, emotionally, and intellectually. At the end of the novel, Marianne describes her existence two years after Maxime's departure. Despite the bleak setting, the novel ends on an optimistic, triumphant note: "J'ai revendiqué ma part de bonheur sur la fatalité, sur les conventions, sur la misère de ma destinée de femme, sur l'impureté et la brutalité d'un homme. J'ai fait ma vie et conquis mon compagnon . . . " [I claimed my share of happiness over fate, over conventions, over the misery of my destiny as a woman, over the impurity and the brutality of a man. I made my life and conquered my companion . . .] (299). Through the three phases of Marianne's romantic education, she learns how to pursue love on her own terms. Each step eliminates certain romantic illusions and strengthens her ability to decide for herself what sort of love and/or marriage she will accept. Her solitude at the novel's end merely reinforces the impression of Marianne as an autonomous, truly "new" woman.

In Tinayre's *Hellé*, love is inextricably linked with education. Elisabeth Ceaux remarks in her study of the novelist's early works that Tinayre presents a new idea of love in this novel, one based on admiration before love, on intellectual equality with a male partner, and on an interest in social problems that does not entail a loss of feminity (Ceaux 1984, 214). Her uncle decides to move to Paris so that Hellé can learn of life and of men and pick a man she admires as her life companion (Tinayre 1926, 28). Hellé is confronted with two possible mates: a worldly poet, Maurice Clairmont, and an idealistic, hermit-like philosopher, Antoine Genesvrier. Hellé first falls for Maurice, who seduces her with his poetry. With Antoine Genesvrier, Hellé shares vigorous debates on the nature of marriage and the roles of husband and wife (144). Her uncle's dying wish that she find in a husband "un guide et un ami" [a guide and a friend] (197–98) is reflected in the proposal she receives from Antoine: "Nous serions ce couple dont je vous parlais autrefois, non plus le maître et l'esclave, mais les époux égaux et différents, associés pour le bien et le bonheur, fortifiés, meilleurs l'un par l'autre" [We would be that couple that I told you about once, not a master and a slave, but equal and different spouses, associated for good and for happiness, fortified, each made better by the other] (214). Like Marianne, Hellé must learn to shed her romantic illusions (215). Despite her extensive and rigorous education, Hellé responds more easily to the younger, glossy Maurice than to the older intellectual.

After a long period of confusion during which Hellé nearly marries Maurice, she chooses the deep intellectual and emotional connection she enjoys with Antoine. The description of their joyful embrace at the novel's end suggests a disturbing element that contradicts the egalitarian idyll proposed by Antoine: "Et j'étais dans les bras d'Antoine. Il tenait, sur sa poitrine soulevée d'un grand souffle palpitant, la belle proie virginale enfin soumise et vaincue" [And I was in Antoine's arms. On his chest lifted by a great palpitating breath, he held the beautiful virginal prey, at last submissive and overcome] (Tinayre 1926, 358). Hellé is the narrator, and it is she who rejects the notion of marriage as subjugation. Why, then, this unexpected vocabulary of domination and defeat? Perhaps the author added this to calm conservative readers, but it is more likely that she intends to show that what matters is the woman's agency. In other words, Hellé chooses the role she will play with Antoine, and momentarily enjoys the role of "beautiful prey." Despite this ambiguous image, Hellé claims to have found her ideal partner (358). She has realized her uncle's dream of a balanced marriage based on mutual admiration and intellectual compatibility.

For Colette's Claudine, heterosexual love comes toward the end of the second novel in the saga, *Claudine à Paris*. Her earliest loves are intense affairs with her schoolmates and/or teachers.[48] In an article on English boarding school friendships, Martha Vicinus traces the patterns of such passionate friendships, facilitated by the creation of new boarding schools at the end of the nineteenth century.[49] For Vicinus, such schools affected girls by granting them increased independence and by creating in them the desire for special closeness with a friend (Vicinus 1989, 215). According to Vicinus, relationships between women of differing age and social status were common. "Questions of public power, authority, and control were central to relationships between women of differing ages, just as they were central to the new schools' ideology" (215). Though Vicinus concentrates her attention on England and on lesbian relationships, her observations find an echo in Colette's novel of the same period, as there is always, in all of Claudine's relationships, an unequal power dynamic. Claudine's first love, or "crush," as Vicinus terms such emotional links, is Aimée, her English teacher.[50] As Vicinus observes, "Emotions were concentrated on a distant, inaccessible, but admired student or teacher; differences in age and authority encouraged and intensified desire" (215). Claudine clearly expresses both the attraction she feels toward Aimée and her awareness of the irrational nature of her love, blaming it on her "cœur déraisonnable" [unrealistic heart] (Colette 1989a, 18). When Claudine loses Aimée to the headmistress, Mademoiselle Sergent, she expresses typical feelings of betrayal, jealousy, and anger (35). She misses most the complicity she had with Aimée, the fact that she knew the "depths of her thoughts." In this respect, early relationships between women may have been more intense than youthful heterosexual ones, due to the element of profound communication.

The attention of men, at least that of the men who frequent the school, means less to Claudine, unless it can gain her some measure of notoriety among her classmates. The young teacher Antonin Rabastens' affection leaves her cold and scornful; he is only good for amusing her and making her friends jealous (Colette 1989a, 76). When Dutertre, the school inspector, kisses her in the hallway, Colette's reaction shows a precocious awareness of psychology and intimate power dynamics, surprising for a girl of her age and inexperience. She feels "humiliating" pride, realizing that attention from Dutertre means that she is not physically unpleasant, and that she has been chosen over her classmates for this dubious honor of his attention. Furthermore, she loves having secrets from her friends (94–95). Claudine's ability to gauge and analyze her emotions is rather unique. Temporal distance from the event only clarifies her vision and perspective. She concludes that the incident is of no interest because his attempt at seduction failed, moving quickly to more pressing matters like her dress for the prize distribution (136). Yet despite Claudine's seeming nonchalance about her first awkward romantic steps, she remains a typical adolescent, dreaming of her ideal companion, who remains interestingly genderless: "J'aimerais danser avec quelqu'un que j'adorerais de tout mon cœur, j'aurais voulu avoir là ce quelqu'un, pour me détendre à lui dire tout ce que je ne confie qu'à Fanchette ou à mon oreiller (et même pas à mon journal)" [I would like to dance with someone that I adore with all my heart, because I would like to have him here, to relax by telling him everything that I only tell Fanchette or my pillow (not even my diary)] (166). Claudine manages to fool many of her schoolmates and teachers by establishing a convincing façade of calm and disinterest in romantic conquest. Yet her passionate affair with Aimée and the romantic vision cited above reveal a deep interest in affairs of the heart and in finding happiness with another.

It is not until *Claudine à Paris* that Claudine gains the maturity to engage in a serious romantic relationship. Yet again, her choice reveals an unequal balance of power. Her attraction to her uncle/cousin Renaud is almost immediate.[51] When he kisses her hand, she notices the shape of his mouth (Colette 1989b, 222), and notes that Renaud "m'attire et me réchauffe" [attracts me and warms me] (225). At the end of the novel, she decides quite rationally to sleep with Renaud, knowing that she can no longer refuse her desires: "Dame, puisque c'est aujourd'hui que je me donne, il peut bien me prendre aujourd'hui s'il veut, tout ça est à lui . . . " [Of course, since I'm giving myself today, he can take me today if he wants, all of this is his . . .] (289). Though she recognizes her powerlessness in the face of Renaud's charms, she hopes that he will not be brutal or move too quickly. He holds all the power, due to his extensive experience, his age, and her inability to control herself. Claudine actually proposes to Renaud that she be his mistress, fearing that marrying him would deprive her nephew Marcel of his inheritance. This potentially dangerous situation is resolved when Renaud insists on marrying Claudine. To the modern reader, Claudine seems to be a relatively well-adjusted young girl who accepts both her romantic visions and her body and its impulses, not without self-critical laughter, of course. Joan Hinde Stewart writes of Claudine that she "seeks a sexual identity; in her day she was one of the rare female protagonists in fiction to embark on such a search" (Stewart 1981, 264).[52] Of the heroines considered here, Claudine is the most vocal about her romantic and sexual thoughts, displaying a modern conception of relationships that Renaud binds into more traditional form. Like Hellé and Marianne, Claudine goes through a period of romantic *apprentissage*, learning how to express herself and to participate fully in her relationships, both romantic and otherwise.

In the Countess de Noaille's novel *Le Visage émerveillé*, the protagonist's physical awakening brings with it a shift in perception and in objects of desire. The arrival of a young man into the nun's bucolic milieu leads her to confuse divine inspiration and sexual interest. At first, she convinces herself of Julien's inferiority in comparison to God: "Vous êtes plus beau que lui, Seigneur!" [You are more handsome than he is, Lord!] (16). Eventually, however, this certitude changes to doubt: "Seigneur! Pourquoi y a-t-il des hommes qui vous ressemblent . . . j'ai peur" [Lord! Why are there men who resemble you . . . I am afraid]

(30). The nun conflates her desire with her faith and with other forms of love, such as the familial; she justifies Julien's kisses by stating that her mother kissed her brother in the same way (52). As her faith comes to be partially replaced by romantic love, Julien rivals God's place in her life: "Vous ne parlez pas. Lui me parle. Je le crois comme je vous croyais, quand vous me parliez autrefois, dans mon cœur. Lui, c'est vous, vivant. Je l'écoute" [You don't speak. He talks to me. I believe him as I believed you, when you spoke to me in the past, in my heart. He is you, but alive. I listen to him] (85). This time her excuse is slightly more complex: her violation of her vows is pardonable because Julien represents God himself. She insists on the resemblance between love and faith: "L'amour, c'est un doux, involontaire mécanisme du cœur, comme la foi la plus vive, comme l'extase que les saintes nous souhaitent" [Love is a sweet, involuntary mechanism of the heart, like the sharpest faith, like the ecstasy that the saints wish for us] (100). The nun understands romantic love in terms of spiritual conviction, as this is the only way that she can rationalize her experience.

Though the nun differs somewhat from the other heroines, she undergoes a learning process through which she discovers her own needs and a source of inner strength. Early entries in her journal reveal a fear of men and of love (Noailles 1904, 35, 53), and her first physical contact with Julien leaves her feeling "malheureuse" [unhappy] (64). Gradually, however, she gains confidence, realizing that she can decide her future. When she refuses to leave the convent with Julien, his suffering gives her a feeling of superiority and of power (65). The nun learns through her experiences with Julien that, despite the sensual appeal of contact with him, her relationship with God and with her fellow sisters means most to her. After a difficult period of self-doubt and experimentation, she gains the self-awareness to choose one life and form of love over another.

The heroine's obsession with love often provides the central impetus in these novels. As critic Jean Larnac observes, "cerebral activity" is no substitute for love for these "poor strays" who "feel so alone" and are so vulnerable to temptation (Larnac 1929, 230). Larnac suggests that, no matter how the novelist chooses to paint the young heroine, she is always a slave to love: "Basically, all of them are slaves to their senses, their nerves or their hearts, according to the temperament of the novelist who creates them. No attempt is possible if it contradicts the law of their nature, which is to love" (231). Because of the time at which they were writing, these novelists, whether male or female, felt most comfortable depicting the search for love with marriage as a shadowy yet undeniable presence. Yet none of the male novelists presented here portray actual marriages; death always prevents the happy event, or at least precludes marital bliss (in the case of Léa). For the female novelists, marriage is always projected at the end of the novel, never portrayed. Why this discomfort with facing the reality of marriage within the literary work, if it was expected by both reader and writer?

One possible explanation may come from Waelti-Walters' discussion of the fin-de-siècle/Belle Epoque conception of marriage, including the unrealistic expectation that a woman give everything to her husband. Female characters wrestle to achieve "the right to exist as people without denying their lives as daughters, lovers, wives, or mothers, and then to achieve that right without losing all sense of themselves as normal, loving, and lovable women" (Waelti-Walters 1990, 179). Unlike Jules Bois, who felt that woman's natural liberation would bring with it a reformation of the couple and the man's role within that couple, Waelti-Walters suggests that change needed to come from both sides. Jean Larnac has a different perspective, and notes an interesting paradox in these Belle Epoque novels. While girls were gaining more freedom and educational opportunities, the impersonal system, combined with their delicate natures, led them constantly back to love as a source of happiness. Yet Larnac sees the male characters in these novels as incapable of understanding and providing these New Women with the affection and support they need: "Their enthusiasm, sensitivity, and fine intuition conflict with the heavy masculine temperament so deeply embedded in matter that it is powerless to understand them and each of its words and gestures makes them suffer. Renaud is too fashionable, too 'female' for Claudine's . . . simple nature" (229). Larnac even suggests that the incomprehension of men pushes women toward independence: "It's because man is powerless to sense them that they free themselves" (229–30). This perspective would tend to place most of the blame for unhappy and nonexistent marriages on men. In any case, the novelists considered here, male and female, display in their works an awareness of shifting social boundaries and the ensuing need for transformation of marriage; they balked when it came to proposing in their works new models for marital equilibrium and egalitarian bliss.

Of the many men and women writing novels about adolescent heroines at the turn of the century, the male writers' works are little known and read today, except perhaps for Rolland's *Jean-Christophe*, of which *Antoinette* is but a small part. The novels by women, but for a few exceptions, have disappeared entirely. Even at the time they were written, the latter were not welcomed to the literary scene nor much appreciated. Those critics known to defend female writers on occasion were equally apt to denigrate them in other works. In his *Paris d'avant guerre*,[53] Jules Bertaut sharply criticizes female writers, saying they lack talent and remain too thoroughly *femme*. Paul Flat, who wrote *Nos femmes de lettres* in 1909, is a reader and critic who considers the subject matter of women writers to be of principal concern to men. Emile Faguet, who wrote an article called "Femmes auteurs,"[54] serves as an example of a man whose patronizing attitude clouds his appreciation of women's writing.[55] The novels in question often sold many copies and enjoyed considerable popularity, yet were rapidly forgotten. Yet as Waelti-Walters points out, certain novels deserve a closer look despite their occasionally "topical" subject matter (Waelti-Walters 1990, 176). She defends the seeming superficiality of women's writing of the time as a faithful expression of their lives: "One of the major reasons why the women wrote the way they did is that women's experience was changing substantially in the Belle Epoque, and the authors were observing, recording, analyzing, and encouraging the shifts. They had little time for introspection and none for problems of writing for its own sake" (176). Waelti-Walters views period novels as near-journalistic attempts to portray social reality rather than vehicles for literary effusion.

One can argue that such societal shifts are no excuse for lack of literary prowess, as all authors experience them. Yet it is true that women experienced a particularly rich time of social and political turbulence at the end of the nineteenth century. Moreover, they had merely begun to enjoy the sort of education from which male authors had always benefited. Female writers of the Belle Epoque did not have access to the literary study open to most male writers.[56] Christine Planté writes of the tension experienced by the woman writer at the mercy of male critics and of her reading public, both for what she writes and for who she is as a writer. Planté observes the striking "continuity of the gazes directed at women writers, the talk about them, the fantastical constructions that they inspire" and the resulting "continuity of contradictions" suffered by women writers, "their difficulties in their relationships with men, with literature, in their representations of themselves, born of this gap between what they seek, what they wish to be, and what is said about them" (Planté 1989, 47). Despite the situation described by Planté and other phenomena working against women writers, they continued to write, to document their experiences, and to use their own

gifts and lessons to prepare their readership for the slow transformation
of French society.

The unique contributions of Belle Epoque female writers have
gained respect in recent criticism. Anne Sauvy writes of the particular
ability of turn-of-the-century women writers to focus on personal experience in a relatively enclosed space. For Sauvy, these writers "mainly
wrote novels, voluntarily intimist, that very often reflected the field
of personal experience and of one milieu, women not seeming to be
tempted by vast frescoes where multiple characters intersect" (Sauvy
1986, 247). In another article, she further explains this phenomenon:

> A genre develops and imposes itself, that of the novel of attitudes, the
> novel of daily life, the psychological novel, very appreciated by women
> who like to find in it a world close to their own, that carries them at
> most into a different social sphere or into a foreign country not too far
> away; there they seek life models that they understand and thanks to
> the novel, they can hope, cry or dream about a love story. (448)

The novelists Sauvy refers to were women writing for women.
Waelti-Walters observes the "careful subversion" of their novels, which
contain both overt and covert arguments for reform (Waelti-Walters
1990, 177). She gives much credit to these novelists for promoting
change: "Within the movement for reform it was the feminist novelists of the period who analyzed women's problems in the private sphere;
charted the public advances; and encouraged, informed, and subverted
their readers so that there was a gradual but visible adjustment of roles
in French society before 1914" (179). The power of this writing, she
claims, comes from its documentary weight (180–81). Like Waelti-
Walters, Sauvy regrets the disappearance of these novels, calling them
a "mine" unfortunately "scorned."[57]

Though these critics do not focus in particular on the adolescent
heroine, their enthusiastic praise of these novels and commentary on
their underestimated importance apply to those novels specifically
about female adolescence as well. Jules Bertaut, most likely the only
man of his time to write a book-length work on the significance of
the young female character, writes of the characteristics of the "young
girl of today," and his description confirms the commentary of more
recent critics on the novels. For Bertaut, the new young woman is liberated, has a complete personality, and is a real woman, with her own
life, ideas, and passions (Bertaut 1910, 299). At the turn of the century,
being a woman still means playing the roles society dictates, those of

wife and mother, yet these young girls have more say in when and how they take on those roles.[58]

The diversity of these heroines and their ability to make decisions and to adapt to their environment distinguish them from the adolescent female characters preceding them, who all seemed to be at odds with their environment, albeit in different ways. The novels display the differences in opinion among turn-of-the-century writers about just what the adolescent girl is or should be and how characters representing her ought to behave. Yet parallels may be drawn between these young heroines; though they may express frustration with certain constricting social structures or with expectations placed upon them, in the end they choose to respect the broadest societal guidelines while making personal decisions that may violate the finer points of traditional female behavior. Plausible explanations for such studied subversion are several. The literary consumers of the Belle Epoque may not have been ready for heroines acting without any regard for accepted mores. It is also possible that the novelists themselves were unprepared to advocate in their writings a social reality the realization of which they were loath to confront. Both men and women writers were treading a fine line between observation of social trends and prediction thereof. Depicting a vibrant and willful heroine who, despite her potential for complete intellectual and financial autonomy, opts for the traditional roles of wife and mother may have been a good way of subtly skirting the issue of dynamic social roles without alarming the reading public or the representatives of political power who were reluctantly allowing the slow process of emancipation. The heroines may be thinking audacious thoughts, but in the end, they choose to think them within the confines of traditional relationships. The modifications in portrayals of female adolescents in the years to follow may spring from this very tension between the psychological and social reality of adolescent characters at the turn of the century.

3
Beneath the Surface
(1910–1930)

In a 1911 work entitled *Evolution actuelle du roman*, literary critic André Billy published the thoughts of a group of French writers on the state of the novel, the reasons for its transformation, and its future. Many of the respondents pointed to the increasingly important role of women in novelistic production and consumption. They suggested that changing societal attitudes led to new literary preoccupations, and that novels were becoming "life lessons" (Billy 1911, 84). One female respondent, Aurel, expressed the hope that women novelists would change the novel, in particular by portraying what gender "inflicts on the mind" (11). Aurel thus signaled what she thought to be one of the primary aspects of the future novel: the relationship between the mind and gender. Indeed, in the years following the publication of Billy's book, thought about gender and the mind influenced the novel like never before. This chapter explores the ways in which the intersection of these elements contributed to French literary understanding of female adolescence in the second and third decades of the century. It shows the progress made in representations of adolescence from static to dynamic, from ideological to socially realistic. These portrayals reflect a richer, more developed and nuanced conception of adolescent subjectivity, enhanced by a new focus on the life of the mind. Perhaps because of this new focus, women began to dominate the novel of female adolescence at this time.

During the period from 1910 to 1930, psychoanalysis and surrealism reached their height in France.[1] Though of different natures—one being scientific, the other aesthetic—these two movements reflected one another, informing thought in many domains. In her book on the representation of woman in surrealism, Katherine Conley historically links the two movements. "In a sense," she writes, "both surrealism and psychoanalysis were the result of the major changes that took place in nineteenth-century Europe after the Industrial Revolution. The surrealists wanted to accomplish in art what psychoanalysis had achieved in science" (Conley 1996, 5). Both movements have been criticized for their disservice to women.[2] The purpose of this study is not to criticize either, nor is it to apply psychoanalytic or surrealist theory to a certain number of primary texts. Rather, my goal is to examine the ways in which the same forces that fueled psychoanalysis and surrealism may have affected novelistic portrayals of female adolescence. In his 1939 work entitled *The Civilizing Process*, Norbert Elias argues that "the structure of psychological functions, the particular standard of behavioural controls at a given period, is connected to the structure of social functions and the change in relationships between people" (Elias 1982, 324). Society and the individual mind are thus intimately linked. An examination of the parallels between psychological inquiry, society, and literature will therefore contextualize this study of female adolescent subjectivity in the novel of the period.

Psychoanalysis and surrealism focus on the inner reaches of the mind, on that which exists beneath the surface of conscious thought. Conley outlines the essential doctrines of surrealism as the following: "the importance of openness to the unconscious; the rejection of any kind of censorship; the privileged place of collaboration, of the collective experience; the role of chance in surprising us into seeing the marvelous in everyday objects and occurrences; and acknowledgement of the significance of associating art with political and social life" (Conley 1996, xv). This last idea is of interest in the context of my study, which seeks to reveal the system of influences linking literary representation and sociopolitical reality. Conley acknowledges that both surrealism and psychoanalysis sprang from the same source, yet draws a distinction between the ways in which each deals with shock and trauma: psychoanalysis medically, surrealism through examination "in an effort to mine the unconscious for its full, at times disquieting, poetic potential, and to explore fully the recently acquired awareness of alternative modes of perceiving reality" (6). This new awareness will gain significance in the context of the following discussion.

Conley evokes other parallels between the two movements. Dreams played an important role in both psychoanalysis and surrealism, largely due perhaps to André Breton's fascination with Freud:

> In describing the origins of surrealism and the purpose of *écriture au-*
> *tomatique*, not only does Breton invoke Freud and the desire to explore
> the riches of the unconscious, but he also specifically expresses the
> desire to examine dream states for the sense of disorientation from
> rational reality that they produce. . . . He too sought to give voice to
> that which had been "marginalized, silenced, and repressed" in French
> post-Enlightenment thought. (Conley 1996, 139)

Moreover, Conley claims that Breton's project anticipated feminism
in its "explicit desire to think of the unsaid and repressed within society as crucial wellsprings for artistic expression" (139). Again, this
notion will come into play in the course of my discussion of female
adolescence. More recent writers and psychoanalysts such as Hélène
Cixous and Jacques Lacan, Conley suggests, "add the perspective of
gender to Breton's view of the unconscious as an essential element to
the understanding of humanity and also as a potentially powerful tool
of subversion to the patriarchal order" (144). Such a tool of subversion
lends itself naturally to writing about a marginalized and appropriated
group, and hence to this discussion. Though Breton's vision of woman
is problematic for many critics, some aspects of the surrealist project
have reappeared in more recent work with an eye to gender issues.[3]

Certainly, regardless of their possible parallels, feminism, psychoanalysis, and surrealism were all, to varying degrees, key elements of
literary and intellectual inquiry from 1910 to 1930. In her *Histoire de*
la psychanalyse en France, Elisabeth Roudinesco points out that surrealist thought about the feminine corresponded at least temporally to
developments in psychiatric thought and to the rise of feminism: "The
representation of femininity in surrealism is contemporary with the
rise of feminism and renovation of the psychiatric gaze begun in the
first quarter of the century" (Roudinesco 1994, 36). I include these
observations from experts on surrealism and psychoanalysis in order
to demonstrate that the early decades of the century were a particularly rich time for thought about the inner workings of the mind, the
psychological formation of adult identity, and woman's place in society.
Though psychoanalysis, surrealism, and feminism can by no means be
conflated, I wish to suggest that, during the period in question, they
provided French novelists with an array of notions that they could
exploit for their psychological portraits of young female characters.
The female adolescent, an inchoate being both mentally and sexually,
provided an ideal medium for novelistic exploration of psychological
formation and the development of adult female identity. Just as it al-

lowed decadent and Belle Epoque novelists to explore the prevailing literary themes of their day, female adolescence enables writers from 1910 to 1930 to consider the life of the mind and to create complex young female subjects instead of ideological models.

Psychoanalytic thought is then an appropriate frame for a study of female adolescent subjectivity in the early twentieth century. In Volume 4 of his *Bourgeois Experience*, Peter Gay gives an outline of the basic notions of psychoanalytic theory:

> The impression that so much of mental life is beyond understanding is an intelligible misperception springing from an unwillingness to delve beneath surfaces. The connections we fail to see have been driven into a realm of the mind, the unconscious, to which the investigator has at best indirect access. . . . It is first the society of the child—its parents, siblings, teachers, priests—and internalized prohibitions acquired from a wider world that sets limits on passions. . . . [T]he individual's imperious desires and the needs of civilization are usually at odds. All education, whatever else it might be, is also a stringent imposition of unwelcome boundaries. (Gay 1984, 9)

In this brief passage, Gay indicates various *leitmotifs* of the novel of female adolescence from 1910 to 1930: the importance of the unconscious, societal entities that impose limits on youth, the conflict between the individual and his milieu, and the role of formal education. In the introduction to a book on female development fictions, Elizabeth Abel writes of the *Bildungsroman* as a series of "clashes with an inimical milieu" that often culminate in "withdrawal, rebellion or suicide," social integration being possible only through extreme compromise (6). The female coming-of-age novel, Abel argues, has its own set of narrative tensions, "between autonomy and relationship, separation and community, loyalty to women and attraction to men." Indeed, these themes recur in the novels examined here. According to Abel:

> The female protagonist or Bildungsheld must chart a treacherous course between the penalties of expressing sexuality and suppressing it, between the costs of inner concentration and of direct confrontation of society, between the price of succumbing to madness and of grasping a repressive "normality." (Abel 1983, 12–13)

The female *Bildungsroman* allowed writers to discuss nascent adulthood and the many challenges of defining individual identity (upon which psychoanalysis had begun to shed some light).

Karen Horney's writings on feminine psychology focus on adolescence as a time of personality change based on anxiety and guilt
regarding female roles (Horney 1967, 237).[4] Horney notes that disturbing symptoms of female adolescence such as mistrust, aggression, and
defensiveness could be avoided through education and treatment beginning during early childhood, when girls could be educated "in cour-
age and endurance" instead of being filled with fears (244). Writings
about surrealism and about psychoanalysis reveal a similar interest in
adolescence as a formative period. Moreover, the two movements were
intimately linked in their attention to what lay beneath the surface of
conscious perception, and facilitated revolutionary thinking about the
impact such hidden thought processes could have on artistic production and other areas of human experience.

If, as the preceding chapters suggest, the decadent optic character-
ized female adolescence in extremely physiological terms, and the Belle
Epoque witnessed a shift to spatial terms, the two decades in question
here inspired literary portrayals of adolescence that were heavily influenced by the psychological explorations taking place at the time. In the
previous chapters, I have referred to the increasing numbers of female
readers at the end of the nineteenth century. Peter Gay notes the role
of inner life, represented by the unconscious, in the significant rise of
female and adolescent readership:

> Female readers with some time on their hands and money in their
> pockets became the preferred prey of the publishing industry. . . . So
> did adolescents hungry for models to emulate, and consumers of news-
> papers, whether male or female, commanding just enough leisure to
> absorb the day's dose of fiction. . . . In the work of nineteenth-century
> imaginative writers, the producers were likely to meet the consumers'
> daydreams. Unconscious spoke to unconscious. (Gay 1984, 225–26)

This phenomenon, true of the relationship between writer and reader
in the late nineteenth century, develops in intensity from 1910 to 1930,
when the unconscious is on the mind of the reading and writing public. Elizabeth Roudinesco links the rise of Freudian theory to French
society's worship of the writer: "The permeability of the literary milieu
to Freudian thought can be explained by the importance that French
society between the two wars accorded to the status of writer" (Roudinesco 1994, 20). Whether the popularity of movements like surrealism
and psychoanalysis can be linked to the status of writer, to the growing
reading public, or to some other historical or social condition, a study

of the novel of adolescence cannot ignore their undeniable presence and influence from 1910 to 1930.

Like the previous chapters, this one will consider various aspects of adolescence such as the body, family relationships, nature, education, and sexuality within the context of psychological portraiture. I wish to show the ways in which thinking about the mind and its functioning shaped portrayals of female adolescence by female writers. As was the case in the periods covered by the preceding chapters, male writers dominated the canon from 1910 to 1930. Diana Holmes has suggested that women were both deprived of the possibility of writing and written out of the canon (Holmes 1996, xii). This project is, in part, an attempt to illuminate areas of literature that failed to become part of French literary memory. Predictably, portrayals of young women by women differ, and these differences will be analyzed here. Finally, I wish to demonstrate the ways in which novels of female adolescence from 1910 to 1930 reflect and promote social and political change.

Novels of female adolescence written by men exist, but they are certainly far from common. Female adolescents can of course be found in their writings, but one can argue that their portrayals of young women lack the psychological depth found in novels of the same period written by women. One may contend that a male writer cannot be expected to delve into the adolescent female psyche with the same degree of comfort as a woman.[5] What interests me more than questions of whether writers can only depict what they know personally is just how male writers attempted to show female consciousness at this time, or simply rejected it in favor of a surface portrayal of the female adolescent character. Novels by Proust, Cocteau, Larbaud, Gide, and Alain-Fournier could be used to demonstrate the narrative techniques employed by male writers to reveal/conceal the female adolescent mind. Male writers do not attribute to the young female character an identity of her own; rather, they appropriate her consciousness to their own ends. A study of portrayals of female adolescence by male authors demands separate treatment, as it is beyond the scope of my primary concerns here. Therefore, I will merely indicate some of the ways in which each male writer avoids plunging deeply into the female adolescent psyche, such psychological probing being a key element of works by female novelists.

Though Marcel Proust deals at length with adolescence, his portraits of girls lack psychological depth. In *A l'ombre des jeunes filles en fleurs*, the young girls of the title are a plural entity, where individual identity is erased in the interest of the whole. In her book on women, writing, and psychoanalysis, Rachel Bowlby writes about the "mutilated, fragmentary" nature of Proust's *passantes*, likening them to those of Baudelaire in the latter half of the nineteenth century (Bowlby 1992, 11). Bowlby writes that "one passante is like another in that she can be replaced, that another and another will figure in the same way, without there being any single, constitutive event, even in retrospect" (11). With few exceptions, Proust's young women are all *passantes*, in that they are interchangeable, expendable, unremarkable.[6]

Other male-penned novels of the early decades of the century reveal a similar avoidance of female psychology. *Fermina Marquez* by Valéry Larbaud bears a misleading title: it presents the perspective of lustful adolescent male characters without so much as scratching the surface of the title character, their collective obsession. *Le Grand Meaulnes*, one of the classic novels of male adolescence, presents female characters that serve as love objects to the male characters but do little else. Their existence, their thoughts, even their words do not figure in the novel, apart from occasional comments reported by the narrator. Indeed, their presence in the novel is twice filtered through a male adolescent perspective, which renders problematic anything that is reported of them. Their desire is not explored; their lives command little interest and fail to reveal the complex emotional and intellectual makeup of adolescence. Indeed, writers of male adolescence have been criticized for misrepresenting the separate world of youth.[7] If male writers did not succeed in portraying realistic male adolescents, how could they write accurate psychological descriptions of female ones? This chapter deals with the inner life of the female adolescent character; it is clear that none of these novels provides sufficient material for consideration. The female characters as portrayed in the novels have little outer life to speak of, let alone innerlife.

As for the female writers—Marguerite Audoux, Rachilde, Camille Pert, Lucie Delarue-Mardrus, and Colette—this chapter will discuss their key works of female adolescence from the period in question. Diana Holmes has pointed out the inferior status of women's writing at the time, despite an explosion of female writers and advances in female education:

> From the last decade of the century, there was a marked increase in the numbers of women writers published and acknowledged in the contemporary press. This confirms the connection between education, civil rights and writing, for this was the generation of women born in the

1870s who had benefited from the Third Republic's reform of female education and from some minor advances in social freedom. The critical reception accorded to their works maintained the identification of great art with masculinity, for if they were not condemned, as Sand was, for trying to be like men, they were consistently relegated (as were Tinayre, Reval, Yver, and Colette) to a minor feminine sphere, and read in terms of the available feminine stereotypes. (Holmes 1996, 18)

Yet it was just those stereotypes that female writers tended to attack. Female novelists of the early twentieth century, as Jean Rabaut has observed, "strike out at the reigning hypocrisy, in particular at the conventional type of the girl."[8] Lucie Delarue-Mardrus saw the jeune fille, Rabaut claims, as a " hybrid being, monster subject to the laws of physiology, neither child nor woman" (Rabaut 1985, 162). Female novelists invented new ways of perceiving adolescence, some less than flattering, that challenged flat portrayals of the past. There is a clear sense of competition here, with each new crop of writers claiming to get things "right" about female adolescence. Certainly, with the category of adolescence changing shape constantly as society evolved, it seems logical for novelists to want to keep up with those changes, and, as we have said before, to predict, and even to influence, them.

These novels reveal a new understanding of the young female protagonist that entails a shift away from traditional loci of authority, such as the patriarchal family, the school, and marriage according to societal dictates (body, family, nature, school, love). The novel form in particular, Holmes suggests, provided the woman author with independent income and offered more scope for the discussion of social issues than did other genres such as poetry: "Around the turn of the century the number of women-authored texts which deal more or less explicitly with the question of female identity and experience suggests a significant circulation and negotiation of women's issues through literature" (Holmes 1996, 19–20). Holmes's comments confirm the dialogue between life and literature that has been postulated throughout this study. What is different here is the emphasis placed on personal experience, on individual psychology. As we saw in Chapter 2, Anne Sauvy writes that women tended to write novels that reflected personal experience (Sauvy 1986, 247). This focus on one person's experience naturally facilitates the exploration of individual perspective and psychological makeup. The adolescent characters challenge authority in subtle ways, developing individual forms of self-reliance that come from within.

It is important to mention here that these novels represent evolving notions of adolescence in that they include a wide variety of female protagonists, both in age and in milieu. Several of the narratives present part of the protagonist's childhood as well as her adolescence, an appropriate innovation at a time marked by the thought of Freud on developmental psychology. It is helpful to realize that readers and writers from 1910 to 1930, whether or not they had access to Freud, began to think about the effects of the experiences and trauma of early life on the development of adult personality. All of the heroines discussed here experience some form of trauma in early life. They cope with emotional, and sometimes physical, trauma in very different ways, but all reveal the lasting effects thereof. The novels forming the basis for this analysis are Marguerite Audoux's *Marie-Claire* (1910), Rachilde's *Son Printemps* (1912), Camille Pert's *La Petite Cady* (1914), Colette's *Le Blé en herbe* (1923), and Lucie Delarue-Mardrus's *L'Ex-voto* (1920), *Graine au vent* (1926), and *Le Pain blanc* (1923). I have chosen several novels by Delarue-Mardrus because, though all are novels of female adolescence, they portray different aspects of adolescence and protagonists of varying milieu, age, and lifestyle.

The Family in Question

Novels of female adolescence by Audoux, Rachilde, Pert, Colette, and Delarue-Mardrus challenge the traditional family in various ways. Yet they acknowledge the monumental role that the family played in the girl's developing identity and in her eventual internalization of social order. As Jessica Benjamin writes in *The Bonds of Love*: "Obedience to the laws of civilization is first inspired, not by fear or prudence, Freud tells us, but by love, love for those early powerful figures who first demand obedience" (Benjamin 1988, 5). In the case of the female adolescent protagonist as seen here, this love is called into question: she may have no living family members, be temporarily abandoned by her family, or have conflictual familial relationships. In these novels, mother-daughter relationships are among the most fraught with strife. Psychoanalytic theory postulates that such conflict arises from the girl's need to destroy her mother inwardly in order to assert her difference (79). Yet the girl's subsequent passive identification to her father is a necessary part of her development and leads her to idealize both her father and love (87, 117).[9] In only two of the novels considered here (both by Lucie Delarue-Mardrus) does the adolescent girl develop a close relationship with her father at the expense of her mother. In all other novels, both parents are either literally absent or figuratively so.[10] The absence or problematic presence of family leads the adolescent to seek out nurturing relationships with people to whom she is not related. Unlike the Belle Epoque novels, where the surrogate family proves to be a stable source of love and support, these novels present no totally dependable relationships, and emotional structures can constantly shift and leave the girl protagonist feeling alone and unloved. In response to her feelings of abandonment or isolation, the adolescent develops a new self-reliance and an ability to take responsibility. Norbert Elias has noted the role parents play in imparting to children the structure of societal values and taboos around which they order their lives (Elias 1982, 328–330). Yet, in several novels, the adolescent characters circumvent the civilizing process, creating their own codes of conduct without, or in spite of, their parents.

In the opening pages of Marguerite Audoux's *Marie-Claire*, the orphaned heroine is sent from a convent school to a farm where she spends the better part of her adolescence, from age twelve to around eighteen. Her existence is not an easy one, but Marie-Claire develops mental and visual games to survive the slings and arrows of daily life. She transforms her simple and austere surroundings through her imaginative faculty, which is used less to create images of worlds she does not know (as in Noailles' *Le Visage émerveillé*, for example) and more to embellish the rather harsh one she inhabits. The night before her departure from the convent, she envisions her new life on the farm (Audoux 1987, 83). Peaceful and friendly elements such as flowered plains, handsome white sheep, and obedient dogs calm the protagonist's fears as she heads toward her new life. As discussed in the last chapter, the natural space is a positive and soothing one. She imagines a friendly farewell from the lime trees near the convent (84). Marie-Claire uses her imagination to lighten difficult situations, to keep her distracted when she is afraid or bored, and to people her solitude with surrogate friends.

Parents are also replaced with substitutes, including Sister Marie-Aimée at the convent, the farmers at her foster home, and a deaf family who lives near the farm. Marie-Claire has developed the ability to survive on her own, but still needs support and love. When her longing to see a beloved friend becomes unbearable, she attempts an impossible nocturnal trip on foot through unfamiliar territory. After she falls in love with Henri Deslois, a rich relative of the farm owners, her roman-

tic reverie involves an attempt to create a family idyll in the abandoned
house formerly inhabited by the deaf family. Her new relationship with
Henri allows Marie-Claire to mature, slowly abandoning some of her
former sources of security. As Bernard-Marie Garreau suggests in his
book entitled *Marguerite Audoux: La Famille réinventée*, Marie-Claire
becomes a woman during her time with Henri and is able to shake off
the nostalgic bonds of prolonged childhood, symbolized by her attachment to a surrogate mother figure, Sister Marie-Aimée: "The new
relationship with Henri, whether physical or not, a relationship that
conforms to the aspirations of a young girl of seventeen, transforms
the omnipresence of the nun to the past, the prolonged childhood to a
childhood completed, nostalgia to memory" (Garreau 1997, 147). Developing an adult romantic attachment enables the heroine to put aside
her childhood sources of reassurance and to begin to mature and to
look toward a future family rather than replacing her lost one with
surrogates.

In Rachilde's novel *Son Printemps*, family relations are reduced to
stressful interactions with the protagonist's grandmother, a demanding
and increasingly senile woman who fails to understand her grandaugh-
ter and keeps her all but prisoner on their estate. Miane has no siblings,
and her only friends are below her in social rank, and therefore spurned
by her grandmother. Much of Miane's evening time is spent feeling like
an orphan, alone and abandoned: "Comme elle est seule! Comme elle
est abandonnée! Où sont ceux qui l'aiment? Où sont ses parents?" [How
alone she is! How abandoned she is! Where are those who love her?
Where are her parents?] (Rachilde 1920, 46). Miane feels just as lonely
as if her grandmother were not with her. In some ways, her situation is
more painful than Marie-Claire's, as she has no kind surrogate parent
figures. For Miane, the domestic space is marked by tension; certain
rooms are closed to her due to her grandmother's irrational fears (203).
Her education has been based on snobbish isolation, where the luxury
of her surroundings is insufficient compensation for the absence of any
social life. In her home, where she is spied on by her grandmother and
punished for being honest, Miane feels like a "prisonnier de guerre"
[prisoner of war] (275, 309). It is only when she is outside that she experiences some peace of mind. Due to her social superiority as the
only "demoiselle" [young lady] in a rural village, Miane rules over her
group of friends. Her domination comes both from her fortune and
from the powerful potential of her youth (7). Yet dawning knowledge
of her worth, games with friends, and walks through the countryside

prove insufficient to counterbalance the trauma of her life with her grandmother. Miane's lack of family structure and support makes her vulnerable to "les tentations des grands crepuscules moraux" [the temptations of the great moral shadows], according to her priest (184). More than the fear of moral corruption, though, Miane is haunted by her desire for company and love.

Apart from occasional lapses into loneliness, Miane succeeds in peopling her environment with animals, working-class acquaintances, and even an imagined lover who embodies her religious fervor by representing God incarnate. Miane's downfall comes when her grandmother finds and destroys the engraving of Cupid that was the archetype for Miane's dream lover (Rachilde 1920, 313). Soon after the loss of her most prized possession, Miane ends her life. Though her grandmother's act cannot be considered the only impetus for the heroine's suicide, it is clear that, given her emotionally fragile state due to the successive deaths of her friend Marie and her beloved cat Moute, she clings to her vision of love as the only source of solace. The destruction of the symbol of that vision ends her hope for future happiness and with it the will to live. Miane's suicide has larger significance. She and her grandmother are the sole remaining members of an upper-class family. The tragic end of the family line can be read as an ominous sign for upper-class illusions. Living in cold, opulent isolation, the novel suggests, leads to an unbearably lonely existence that fosters an unhealthy separation from reality. Of course, the novel can also be read in terms of the decadent movement that so colored Rachilde's earlier novels, as discussed in the first chapter.

Like those of Marie-Claire and Miane, Cady's family relationship (in Camille Pert's *La Petite Cady*) leaves her with unsatisfied emotional needs. She and her mother rarely see each other and do not communicate well with one another. Cady's little sister, her mother's clear favorite, irritates Cady with her lack of intelligence and superficiality. The sisters have a strange relationship and barely know one another. Cady becomes jealous when her mother gives special attention to her sister, neglecting Cady. There remains only a lascivious stepfather whose wife Cady pretends to be on Sunday drives. In one episode, Cady sees mysterious photos of a young man who resembles her. Unsatisfied with her mother's vague explanation, Cady attempts in vain to find out who the man is and how he is related to her. This curious episode can be read as a sign of destructive lack of family communication, as Cady's mother avoids making contact with her daughter. It also suggests the existence of at least one other family member who might be a positive presence in Cady's life.

Faced with an unhealthy and cold family atmosphere, Cady attempts to amuse herself and to seek affection outside of her family. Her precocious knowledge of sexual relationships leads her to use her looks to seduce those around her, especially older men whom she meets when her stepfather gives dinners in her home. Cady reveals hints of premature femininity, as when she hides her face in her hands (Pert 1914, 8). Her governess immediately notices her strange and precocious sensuality (23). Cady delights in the all-male space of her stepfather's smoking room, where she occupies a privileged place, enjoying certain "jouissances obscures et aiguës" [obscure and acute pleasures] in the company of men who treat her like a "jouet vivant" [living toy] (39). Cady willingly plays the role of the dressed-up doll, enjoying the affection and admiration of her stepfather's guests.

Unlike a simple plaything, however, Cady actively attempts to seduce men. In one scene, she tries to disturb a storyteller by pressing her young body against him with "un étrange instinct de la séduction sensuelle que la femme porte en soi" [a strange instinct of sensual seduction that the woman carries within] that is inappropriate for her age (Pert 1914, 49). She seeks out physical contact with men in a precocious display of seductive power, wanting to bite, scream, and be squeezed by cruel arms until she faints (50). This masochistic impulse distinguishes Cady from the other adolescents in this study. Her surprisingly adult behavior can be partially attributed to her unsatisfied need for love. Ignored by her family members, Cady imitates her only female role models, including flirtatious governesses and a promiscuous neighbor, and attempts to gain attention and love through seduction. Her precocious physical and mental development can thus be linked to her desire for the affection lacking in her home.

In Colette's *Le Blé en herbe*, though Phil and Vinca's parents do not treat them cruelly, they are exterior to the majority of the plot, floating on the perimeter of each scene like extras on a movie set. At least in the context of vacation, the adolescents live with their parents yet seem to exist separately from parental authority, with minimal structures and rules and near-total freedom. Parents exist for Vinca only as "shadows," as largely inconsequential obstacles around which, or despite which, real life takes place. Vinca "vivait, parmi ces parents-fantômes qu'elle distinguait mal et entendait peu, une vie étrange" [lived a strange life among these parent-ghosts that she could barely see and rarely heard]

(Colette 1974, 32–33). The narrator characterizes Vinca and Phil's parents as "Ombres familières, devenues presque invisibles" [familiar shadows that had become almost invisible] (63). Vinca and Phil do not dislike their parents, but they simply do not pay much attention to them. In *L'Ame de l'adolescente*, adolescent psychologist Philippe Mendousse writes of this tendency, especially in the infatuated adolescent, to reduce parents to shadowy figures:

> Most adolescents, especially when they are cultivating a real or imaginary crush, move inward and, while attending to their daily tasks, while acting even considerate and affectionate, have the impression of moving around shadows, in the home of ghost parents whose image is less evident in their thought than that of people and fictions to which their nascent feelings go. (Mendousse 1963, 110)

Indeed, Vinca mentally ejects all figures of authority, especially the "pales Ombres . . . du cercle de famille" [pale family circle shadows] from the world in which only she and Phil count (39). As Mendousse suggests, only the couple matters in the adolescent mind, and all others are simply dismissed from her field of perception. Each time their parents speak, the adolescents banish the "êtres vagues" [vague beings] from their presence (40). One of the reasons for this gap between Vinca and her parents is that she cannot imagine her parents having the painful feelings of love that she is experiencing (41). Like many children, Vinca cannot imagine parallels between her experiences and those of her parents. Diana Holmes makes the compelling argument that their parents have a childish optimism that Phil and Vinca, "in their adolescent wisdom, envy" (Holmes 1991, 106). Certainly the parental figures in the novel appear to live in a vacuum of cheerfulness and faith. Not blatantly conflictual as is often the case in the male novel of adolescence, Vinca's relationship with her parents does not seem to affect her vacation or her maturation, positively or negatively. Her parents simply play minor roles in Vinca's daily life.

Colette's narrative strategies contribute to Vinca's portrait in unexpected ways. Holmes has pointed out that "despite the central concern with female identity, Colette partially adopts the perspective of the male protagonist" (Holmes 1991, 5). This shifting perspective allows the author to create a multifaceted portrait of the novel's heroine, revealing both her childish and mature sides, her paradoxical attitude, at once nostalgic, as when she expresses the desire to return to childhood (Colette 1974, 71) and precocious, as when she chooses silence as a weapon (71). She wishes for a simple transition from childish forms of love to more adult ones, and welcomes moments of peaceful enjoyment, such as the calm, daily swim that restores their threatened childhood (10). Adolescence is a space of turbulence and torment, while childhood is associated with the peace and innocence of swimming in the sea. Vinca's adult fears and desires are reflected in, and communicated through, her eyes (11): she has a "regard de femme sagace" [gaze of an astute woman] (82), and her long-endured jealousy has given her a sheen that is seen only "aux paupières des femmes contraintes de souffrir en secret" [on the eyelids of women forced to suffer secretly] (99). Colette's narrative shifts in perspective, depicting Vinca as she sees herself, from Phil's perspective, and from that of an outside observer.

Such shifting characterization appropriately reveals both childish and mature aspects of Vinca's behavior, traits common to literary adolescence. As Holmes notes, "Vinca is situated at the juncture between child and adult identity. . . . In this dual characterization dignity is a quality of childhood and Vinca's more 'womanly' words and gestures are associated with humiliation" (Holmes 1991, 62–63).[11] Vinca seems more than willing to accept Phil's superiority in terms of age and sexual experience. For him, she remains stubbornly and belatedly childlike, though he hopes that next year she'll behave like a woman, throwing herself at his feet (Colette 1974, 6–7). As Holmes observes, dignity is associated here with childhood, whereas humiliation (throwing herself at his feet) is a sign of womanhood. Phil resents what he sees as Vinca's prolonged phase of childish dignity, yet the narrator observes that they are both prematurely aged by love, silence, and separation (32). The strange pattern of meeting only during vacations has created an oddly adult love between them, heavy with misunderstanding that has matured them early. Both inhabit the ambiguous space of adolescence, which ironically becomes a source of conflict as they struggle toward adulthood. For Vinca, the prematurely adult love she shares with Phil is the only family structure she wants or needs; thus, she willingly sacrifices her innocence in hopes of ensuring the long life of their relationship.

In Delarue-Mardrus's *Graine au vent*, the family unit, intact at the beginning of the novel, undergoes dramatic restructuring. The twelve-year-old protagonist and her mother have a strained relationship, based largely on Alexandra's close bond with her father. Alexandra's mother wonders whether she really loves her daughter, who seems to have sto-

len her place (Delarue-Mardrus 1928b, 14). Enraged at the close relationship between her husband and her daughter and at her daughter's
unstructured lifestyle dominated by hunting, Alexandra's mother announces that her next child, truly hers, will be raised differently (74).
The tension with her mother does not seem to affect Alexandra, who
appears almost glad to avoid her.

When her mother dies in childbirth, however, Alexandra's life changes
abruptly. Her father withdraws into a shell, giving the new baby to a
wet-nurse and leaving his eldest daughter to fend for herself. Initially
she looks forward to a life without her mother, where she will be able
to do whatever she likes and to have her father to herself (Delarue-
Mardrus 1928b, 113). Soon, however, she feels abandoned by her father,
who takes to drinking excessively, and comes to think of her mother
as a worse enemy dead than alive (115). Alexandra justifies her lack of
responsibility as a function of her youth without thinking of the repercussions of her lifestyle in terms of her social role (134, 138).

It is not until she sees her sickly and abused sister at a nurse's home
that Alexandra decides to change her life and assume responsibility
for herself and for those she loves. She cleans the house, demands that
her father stop drinking, and begins taking care of her little sister. Her
new responsibilities cause Alexandra to regret her tense relationship
with her mother (Delarue-Mardrus 1928b, 177). Alexandra gains a new
perspective on responsibility and parenting that enables her to criticize
her immature behavior of the past. Her little sister provides her with
some much-needed human company and gives her existence meaning
because she now has someone to love (187). She has learned to value
family stability over egotism, and has realized that placing the comfort
and well-being of others before her own gives her greater satisfaction
than did living only for herself.

Reconciliation in the novel comes when Alexandra realizes the importance of her mother's role in her life and takes over the nurturing
role for her little sister, then shows signs of taking her father's place as
artist and family breadwinner. The protagonist's coming-of-age entails
the sacrifice of her superficial freedom for the good of a weaker, innocent person. She single-handedly fights to save her family and succeeds.
The novel presents the superiority of one model over another, of domesticity over a wilder, less structured lifestyle. The heroine learns, in
effect, to accept responsibility at home—one of the principal causes of
tension with her mother. Yet rather than fighting her mother's lessons,
Alexandra learns to incorporate them, to appreciate their differences

while forging her own path. In effect, Alexandra combines elements of her mother and father's roles, becoming a responsible adult and capable parent figure to her younger sister.

In *L'Ex-voto*, also by Delarue-Mardrus, the heroine, Ludivine, resembles Alexandra in her wildness and love of the outdoors. Ludivine has a household built on tension: her father's heavy drinking causes him to be abusive. To escape her unhappy home life, Ludivine creates a family of children of which she is the head. Like Alexandra, Ludivine must in the face of crisis accept responsibility for the good of the family. She is fundamentally pessimistic about her future, assuming that she will become a drunken criminal, like so many others (Delarue-Mardrus 1928a, 73). This statement on the part of the protagonist reveals the precarious social role of young working-class women of the early century, whose difficult lives were typically haunted by poverty, alcoholism, and violence. Having no other options, Ludivine is prepared to accept the fate of her mother and of so many other women around her.[12]

Only when they take in Delphin, an orphaned neighbor, do things change at the house. Like Alexandra, Ludivine instigates a thorough cleaning and takes the helm at her home (Delarue-Mardrus 1928a, 93). As is the case for Alexandra, taking on adult responsibility faciliates Ludivine's maturation process (95). When her father continues to drink and to act agressively toward his family, Ludivine, in her new role as "chef de famille" [head of the household], confronts him (107). Afterward, the protagonist knows that her father, like everyone else, fears her (111). Something in Ludivine gives her the power to control others, even those who are technically her superiors. The move of an adolescent daughter to the center of the family was not uncommon or shocking in society or in literature. In his book on the girl in French literature, Jules Bertaut wrote that, after 1880, thanks in part to new educational opportunities, in part to changing paternal roles, the girl was increasingly important to the functioning of the family, gaining a new power through her nascent womanhood: "As an adolescent, she imposed herself by the grace of her already clairvoyant and crafty being. On the verge of becoming a woman, she commands with the will of her smile, by the happiness that others want to make shine in her eyes" (Bertaut 1910, 173). Though Bertaut was referring to a slightly earlier period, and no doubt meant a more figurative reworking of familial roles, Delarue-Mardrus's novel nonetheless provides a concrete example of the trend he signaled.

Other characters, both male and female, young and old, obey Ludivine, not to make her happy, as Bertaut suggests, but rather out of fear. Norbert Elias analyzes in his book *The Civilizing Process* the role of fear in the family relationship (Elias 1982, 328–30). However, Elias suggests that fears are transferred from parents to children, while in *L'Ex-voto*, the opposite is true. Rather than reproducing her parents' fears, conveyed to her through a series of societal pressures, Ludivine instills fear in the rest of the family. If, as Elias contends, the transmission of such codes within the family reveals the civilizing process, Delarue-Mardrus's novel confirms Bertaut's observations by providing a model of behavior in which adolescent daughters take a place of new power in the family.

In Delarue-Mardrus's *Le Pain blanc*, Elise adopts, and is adopted by, several surrogate families during the course of the novel in an attempt to find the love she longs for. She has a close relationship with her father, who leaves the family when she is ten, but poor relations with the rest of her biological family. Her mother, who prefers her sons and who is, according to the father, a terribly sick and unhappy woman (Delarue-Mardrus 1923, 21), promptly sends Elise away to a convent school, at which point her already conflictual relationship with her brothers weakens (Delarue-Mardrus 1923, 104). The tense relationship she shares with her mother worsens after an unpleasant visit, soon after which Elise learns of her mother's suicide. At home for the funeral, Elise discovers newfound sympathy for her mother, just before realizing that her mother has disinherited her (125). Elise thinks of herself as alone in life, despite the presence of her brothers and father (140). Like Miane, Elise fails to find the love and support she needs in her family members, and feels essentially orphaned.

When her father comes to take her to live with him, Elise is temporarily charmed by the love she has been missing for so long, as well as the exotic nature of her exciting automobile trip toward the unknown (Delarue-Mardrus 1923, 148). Elise's hesitations and anxieties regarding her stepmother, long maligned by her mother, are assuaged when she observes her stepmother's cultured tastes. Yet Elise never finds a real family in her new home, and feels more alone than ever (197–98). Even in her father's home, Elise finds little outlet for her emotions and nothing resembling the family structure she so ardently desires.

When her father dies suddenly after discovering his new wife's adultery, Elise realizes that she is living with her parents' killer and feels abandoned and completely, hopelessly alone (Delarue-Mardrus 1923,

226, 234). The narrator observes that young women are destined to be
unhappy: "Guettées par le mariage ou le célibat, les passions ou la ma-
ternité, leur sort ne peut être que tragique" [Vulnerable to marriage or
celibacy, passions or maternity, their destiny can only be tragic] (105).
All of the options available to young women lead, according to the narrator, to a tragic destiny. Elise's various family replacements do disap-
point her in some way. Yet through her difficult experiences, she gains
new confidence in herself and in her ability to make decisions about her
life. Because of the failure of her various family structures, Elise has in
some ways escaped from these categories, and has created an unusual
space in which she alone makes decisions about her future.

The shifting shapes of the family in these novels demand of the
adolescent character a solid self-reliance. Difficult lessons come early in
life, and the girl cannot depend on her family for protection and love.
She must learn to provide for herself through the choices she makes
the nurturing and support she needs. Because of this necessity, the
adolescent heroine is stronger and more autonomous than ever before,
using her mind to soften the blow of apparent or real abandonment, to
create friends, to break noxious emotional bonds, and to seek to fill a
necessary social role.

Experiencing the Body

Though the body plays a lesser role from 1910 to 1930 than in novels
from the turn of the century, body awareness is a universal element of
the novel of female adolescence, and indeed of female adolescence in
general. Despite the minimal space accorded to the body in many of
these texts, from 1910 to 1930 the female body occupied social consciousness in France and elsewhere like never before. As Joan Jacobs
Brumberg writes in her book entitled *The Body Project*, "Every girl suffers some kind of adolescent angst about her body; it is the historical
moment that defines how she reacts to her changing flesh" (Brumberg
1997, xviii). Yet as Brumberg points out, Margaret Mead's landmark
work *Coming of Age in Samoa* (1928) suggested that, in certain cultures,
girls do not experience self-consciousness during puberty in the same
way Western girls do. As in the earlier novels, rites of passage marking
puberty appear here, but the markers of puberty have changed since the
Belle Epoque. Whereas before 1910 reaching puberty meant putting
up the hair and lengthening the skirts (xix), after 1910, and especially
after 1920, physical maturity is increasingly marked by shorter skirts

and by bobbing the hair. The "garçonne" look made popular by Victor Margueritte's 1922 novel of the same name dictated the new fashion. Yet there were other causes. Christine Bard refers in her book to the debate over the length of women's skirts caused by an elevated number of accidents due to heavy, cumbersome skirts (Bard 1995, 192). Bard also discusses feminists who penned tracts against the corset and high heels, and in support of gymnastics and the practice of safe sex (192). Doctor and radical feminist Madeleine Pelletier argued in 1912 for male garb for young girls, citing ease of movement and equality in socialization as reasons (196–97). Medically speaking, the abolition of the corset and the new trend toward shorter skirts greatly modified women's physical experience. In an article on menstruation and nineteenth-century medicine, Vern Bullough and Martha Voght note that the fifteen-pound skirts and corsets of the latter half of the nineteenth century caused prolonged and painful menstrual periods. By 1910, when skirts were short and the corset a thing of the past, such symptoms had been alleviated in most women (Brumberg 1997, 80). This wave of androgyny in fashion ended by 1929, when skirt length and hair began to grow again, a phenomenon that Bard calls a "return to femininity" (Bard 1995, 207). Its influence carried over from aesthetics to ideology, changing permanently the way young women looked and behaved.

The changes in the aesthetics of femininity during the 1920s were accompanied by modifications in attitude and behavior. By the 1920s, Brumberg claims, girls' lives were rapidly changing.[13] She notes that, after World War I, girls cut loose from community and church ties. Clubs for girls like the Girl Scouts, established in the late nineteenth century to provide chaperoned activity for the increasing numbers of sexually maturing young women, began to see a decline in membership, partially due to new entertainment options and to the young girl's increasing independence from her mother and from other figures of authority. Self-esteem began to be based on external qualities, rather than on immaterial concepts such as goodness and morality (Brumberg 1997, 101).[14] Girls began to enjoy frequent and increasingly intimate interactions with boys, developed their sexual allure through clothing and cosmetics, and tried "slimming": a body project tied to the scientific discovery of the calorie.[15] Also in the 1920s, Edgar Allen, a professor at Washington University in St. Louis, demonstrated the existence and effects of estrogen. Over the next fifteen years, the role of hormones in the menstrual cycle was established. Speculation on the relationship between hormones and mood appeared, linking physical and mental aspects of female experience. Age at menarche has continued to decline internationally; in the 1920s, European girls menstruated at an average age of fourteen to fifteen (Laslett 1971, 222). Like Brumberg, historian Peter Laslett observes that nutrition can affect age at menarche and, in turn, population size. It can also affect the physiological relationships between classes, and therefore the "internal balance of the domestic group" (236). Menstruation always has a profound effect on society, but this was perhaps more true at the time of the first steps toward understanding the female body's functions.

The 1920s witnessed an unveiling of the female body, with arms and legs displayed like never before. This led to new beauty and dietary regimes, and a new body aesthetic with specific demands.[16] Also relatively new was the attempt to lower one's weight through food restriction and exercise, dictated by the new silhouette introduced in 1908 by Parisian designer Paul Poiret. He replaced the voluptuous Victorian hourglass by shifting visual interest to the legs. The slender, long-limbed, and relatively flat-chested Poiret archetype, associated with the chemise dress of the American "flapper" and the "garçonne" in France, demanded constant dieting that led to widespread eating disorders (Brumberg 1997, 99–100). Historian Mary Louise Roberts points out that the changing shape of femininity that blurred sexual difference raised questions about gender roles: new minimalist fashions and androgynous styles were even blamed for the falling birth rate in France (Roberts 1994, 73). The new look promoted youth as never before: "The ideal body type was no longer the fully mature woman, but a child whose body was not yet marked by her sex" (76). The emphasis on a youthful appearance gave rise to myriad beauty products and the creation of the *salon de beauté* in the 1920s, Roberts notes (82). Kathy Peiss writes of the marketing strategies used to sell rouge and powders in the early decades of the century: such products were said to help women achieve the "bloom of youth" (Peiss 1990, 151).[17] Women aimed for a slim, young, and most of all, free appearance. Ironically, as Roberts observes, such an illusion of effortless freedom often required many hours of strain and virtual starvation (Roberts 1994, 83–84). The 1920s were then the beginning of today's trend where girls seek to control their bodies from within, through diet and exercise, rather than from without, through corsets and girdles (Brumberg 1997, 123).[18]

From 1910 to 1930, the body was undeniably transformed through dress and external trappings, but new theories of the body from the inside increased as well, largely due to the writings of Sigmund Freud on female sexuality. Critic Jacques André writes that Freud called attention to the various female body parts and their role in nascent sexuality, claiming that, at adolescence, sexuality moves from the clitoris to the vagina (André 1995, 47). André points out that this new internally directed focus on the female body leads to "inwardness" in literature (133). He thus links thinking about the internal female body to writing about the psychological aspect of feminity. He also writes that the physical changes at puberty have inevitable mental echoes:

> Puberty for a girl means the body opening (or reopening) to the point of blood, summoning particularly urgently narcissistic defences against the ensuing breach. It is inside, unbeknownst to her and engendering archaic anxiety, that puberty confronts the feminine psyche, overcoming fantasy with too much reality. (153)

This switch from an external to an internal gauge of sexuality at adolescence mirrors similar developments at the same time in social history, according to Joan Brumberg's book. Freud referred to female sexuality as a "dark continent," a phrase that had already been used to refer to the rainforest, "so as to signify what part of femininity remains inaccessible to him" (André 1995, 47). The phrase suggests that the female inner world, at least for the male observer, is a mysterious, impenetrable space.

No discussion of the relationship between the inner and outer aspects of the female body in the early twentieth century can avoid some mention of the discourse surrounding hysteria. Already a *leitmotif* of medical and literary discourse in the nineteenth century, Freud's attention to it may have contributed to its weight. In her book on hysteria and narrative, Claire Kahane observes that, for Freud, hysteria was the "somatic representation of a repressed bisexual conflict, an unconscious refusal to accept a single and defined subject position in the oedipal structuration of desire and identity," the struggle between masculine and feminine sexual identities (Kahane 1995, xi). Hysteria tends to be played out, according to Kahane, in areas of the body other than the genitals, leading to disturbance in voice, vision, and hearing, "the earliest bodily zones of exchange between inside and outside" (xi). Hysteria can also cause confusion between body and language.[19] In *Le Deuxième sexe*, Simone de Beauvoir contributes to this notion of hysteria as a confusion between the inner and outer body, or more specifically, as a communion between the body and the mind. She writes that the reciprocal

action between endocrine secretions and nervous regulation characterizes female psychology. The female body, in particular that of a young
girl, is hysterical in that psychic life and its physiological realization
are so closely tied (Beauvoir 1949, 332). This confusion between mental
and physical phenomena, between outer and inner impulses, is not new
in literature in the twentieth century,[20] but the detailed extraliterary
discourse surrounding it reflects a fresh perspective on female psychic
life and its link to the body.

The female body was then, from 1910 to 1930, an object of much
scrutiny, a cause of much concern. Though knowledge of its most intimate functions had become widespread, the translation of scientific
wisdom into an understanding of female physical and mental experience
proved to be an arduous and yet stimulating task. Fashion designers,
medical doctors, educators, parents, politicians, psychoanalysts, and
artists turned their attention to the freshly fathomable female body and
provided their own templates for the ordering of women's experience.
Female novelists paid varying degrees of attention to the girl's changing body in their novels, but their portraits of young heroines reveal
myriad other concerns in circulation in post-Belle Epoque France.

Their writings, however, did not necessarily reflect their lives. Rachilde, a prolific novelist and journalist of the late nineteenth and early
twentieth centuries, often irritated feminists of the early twentieth century due to her contradictory behavior and writings. Though she had a
penchant for male garb before her marriage to Alfred Vallette, thereafter she buried her tomboy existence for a more sedate and feminine
wifely role (Bard 1995, 203). Rachilde was often compared to feminist
Madeleine Pelletier for her cross-dressing, but the novelist's anti-fem-
inism set her well apart from those who championed Pelletier's ideas
on female physical education.[21] In her novels of female adolescence,
Rachilde presents heroines who bend societal dictates in more subtle
ways than transvestism. Descriptions of the body reveal an outsider's
perspective, and female protagonists lack the sort of physical education
that Pelletier deemed so vital.

Miane in Rachilde's *Son Printemps* (1912) undergoes a physical transformation at the age of fifteen, and physical hints at the woman she
will become are present already. Her eyes are "profonds pour son âge"
[penetrating for her age] and she is a "vierge femme" [woman virgin]
(Rachilde 1920, 141). Yet Miane remains unaware of her own body and
its functions. It is the narrator who enlightens the reader about the
power of the young woman's physical presence. The narrator, however,

has a near-misogynistic view of female puberty: the reader discovers that "jeunes filles" suffer from annoying tendencies, laughing or crying without cause and suffering from dangerous, often incurable, neurosis (50). The narrator views with some suspicion the neurotic tendencies of the young woman. For her, adolescents belong to an intermediary category, being neither children nor adults: "La vierge de quinze ans est encore un enfant par ses impuretés et n'est pas encore une femme par son intelligence. Trop pure ou trop intelligente, elle serait sans doute une anomalie, elle ferait, comme on dit, le désespoir de ses parents . . . " [The fifteen-year-old virgin is still a child in her impurities and is not yet a woman in intelligence. Too pure or too intelligent, she would no doubt be an anomaly, she would be, as they say, the despair of her parents . . .] (51). It is unclear why girls who are too pure or too intelligent would be more likely to drive their parents to despair, but clearly the narrator feels that the safest kind of female adolescent is the average kind. Miane's principal "névrose" [neurosis], excessive purity, reveals her naïveté: she has a basic "horreur du mariage" [horror of marriage] (52). Moreover, the narrator reveals that she has a misplaced sense of pride and a conviction that early death is a source of grandeur (53). The narrator avoids delving deeper into Miane's reasons for fearing marriage, or her fascination with death. The only physical detail given of Miane's maturing body is a passing reference to her experience of menstruation as a time of melancholy and taste for death (57). Yet the narrator never discloses Miane's own feelings about her changing body. Only her basic ignorance of the principles of reproduction and her obsession with death are repeatedly mentioned (57–58, 73), ominous signs pointing to the inevitable outcome of the novel.

Camille Pert's character Cady, despite her relative youth, appreciates and manipulates her body to gain attention and affection, though not necessarily to seduce a husband, as was the case with adolescents of the Belle Epoque. The novel rarely reveals Cady's impression of her own body: instead, her perception is usually filtered through the appreciation of others. On one occasion, though, Cady puts on makeup and appreciates what she sees, which the narrator describes as an "étrange et séduisante miniature de femme, à l'inquiétante flamme du regard à la fois innocent et averti; curieuse fleur précoce de civilisation, adorable et troublant petit monstre" [strange and seductive miniature woman, with a worrisome flame in her gaze at once both innocent and aware; curious precocious flower of civilisation, adorable and unsettling little monster] (Pert 1914, 38–39). This scene suggests that she revels in her premature

ability to manipulate her appearance in order to resemble a woman.
The only scene where the author may suggest the heroine's exploration
of her body is one where her governess wakes to strange sounds coming from Cady's bed (Chapter 15). This scene may be read as one of
masturbation, but it is the only example of its kind. Otherwise, Cady's
body is revealed through the eyes of others, most often men.

When Cady poses nude for an artist friend, the narrator signals
the impact of Cady's body on the viewer, underlining her youthful
slimness and her body's interestingly and compellingly androgynous
quality (Pert 1914, 100). Though these comments suggest an exterior
gaze on Cady, she herself realizes the impact of her body on the artist:
"D'un coup d'œil rapide, elle mesura le trouble éperdu de l'homme et
sentit s'épandre en elle la conscience de sa suprême force tranquille de
femme" [In one rapid glance, she measured the man's overwhelming
emotion and felt the awareness of her supreme calm woman's strength
spread in her] (100). Her "corps inachevé" [unfinished body], not quite
that of a child nor that of a woman, possesses a rare beauty that the artist attempts to capture before womanhood replaces it (102). The artist
is confused but entranced by the curious and "enigmatic" combination
of woman and child in Cady (104), what the narrator calls the "femme-
enfant" [woman-child] (157). The hybrid quality of Cady's body, half
woman, half child, makes it irresistibly seductive.

Cady slowly learns to contextualize the display of the body, distinguishing between what she deems acceptable and inappropriate uses
of it. When her mother goes away for two days, the servants hold a
party at which an intoxicated English governess performs a nude jig.
When Cady's little sister attempts the same, Cady realizes the awful
incongruity of such behavior on the part of a little girl. Another lesson
about the body comes when she is the victim of an attempted sexual
assault in her friend's home, which ends when she stabs her attacker.
Through these and other traumatic lessons, Cady begins to understand
the possible dangers of precociously manipulating the body to provoke
desire. She comes to understand, without formal sexual education, the
power of sexuality and the role of the body therein. More specifically,
she learns to associate certain behaviors with certain ages, and to disap-
prove of age-inappropriate displays.

Of the novels considered here, Colette's *Le Blé en herbe* gives the
most detailed description of the heroine's body. Due perhaps to the setting, which entails bathing attire and light dresses, Vinca's slim, tanned
form appears in many scenes. Again, Vinca's perception of her own

body is revealed only indirectly. In *Le Deuxième sexe*, Simone de Beauvoir claims that Vinca represents a common archetype of the young girl: a "half-wild, half-tamed creature" (Beauvoir 1949, 351). I propose that these two halves in fact correspond to the two life phases for which adolescence serves as an intermediary: childhood and adulthood. Diana Holmes has observed that Colette's heroine is "long-legged, gawky and graceful at the turning point between childhood and womanhood" (Holmes 1991, 71). Vinca experiences a typical adolescent conflict between her childlike interest in the world and her more adult romantic desire for Phil. She is torn between her desire to become an adult and her reluctance to do so, leaving her in a paradoxical position of constant denial of the very adult trappings with which she occasionally experiments, including makeup and fancy dresses. Female adolescence as portrayed by Colette is thus a complex intermediary phase where the adolescent girl is destined to suffer from her conflicting desires, traceable to her rapidly changing body.

In *L' Ex-voto* by Lucie Delarue-Mardrus, much power is attributed to the hypnotic, unusually pale eyes and hair of the heroine, Ludivine, which often attract the attention of various male and female admirers. Yet the heroine remains unfazed by the gaze of others: "Elle-même restait sans opinion sur sa propre personne. Tout comme les pêcheurs parlant de la mer, elle eût, avec toute l'ironie normande, déclaré volontiers en parlant de sa figure: 'J'y fais point seulement attention'" [She herself had no opinion about her own looks. Just as fishermen speak of the sea, she readily declared of her face, with all the irony of Normandy, "I just don't pay any attention to it"] (Delarue-Mardrus 1928a, 5). Ludivine's source of pride is being the feisty "maître" of a ragtag band of children (6–7). In the first chapters of the novel, Ludivine's chief source of authority is her strong personality, and she seems unaware of her seductive power.

When her appearance inspires her wealthy suitor Lauderin to shower her with gifts, including stylish clothes, Ludivine is transformed physically. The unexpected luxury of her new outfits contrasts sharply with her simple home: "[L]a silhouette nouvelle de Ludivine jurait avec le modeste intérieur où elle continuait à s'activer en bonne ménagère" [Ludivine's new silhouette clashed with the modest interior where she continued to bustle about like a good housewife] (Delarue-Mardrus 1928a, 212). In fact, her attachment to her home dominates her value system. When she travels, she attracts a great deal of attention, but the admiration of strangers means nothing to her: "Ce n'était pas son

monde. Ces gens-là ne connaissaient ni son nom ni son histoire. Ils
la trouvaient jolie, et c'est tout" [This wasn't her world. These people
didn't know her name or her story. They found her pretty, that's all]
(224). For Ludivine, superficial appreciation of her physical form means
nothing; only the interest and respect of those who know her life have
any value for her.

Slowly, Ludivine begins to protest against certain trappings of the
chic world represented by her fiancé and his fashionable sister, like pow-
der and perfume, finding her new clothes "comic" enough (Delarue-
Mardrus 1928a, 261). When Ludivine eventually rejects the superficial
world they represent, she returns to more familiar garb, wearing a
simple, plain outfit on the day of her wedding to Delphin, a poor fisherman. Ludivine is temporarily seduced by the luxury Lauderin can
offer her, but she soon prefers the simple pleasures of her youth, embellished by her honest, emotional attachment to her fishing village.
The novel offers two body images to the reader: that of a Ludivine
simply dressed, strong, active, and natural, and that of the transformed
Ludivine, fancily dressed but uncomfortable in her original milieu.
The reader is led to believe, like Ludivine herself, that her original,
unaffected appearance is far preferable to her fancy new dresses. The
seduction of physical transformation is temporary—Ludivine prefers
an untreated version of herself, one better suited to her environment
and to her personality.

In *Le Pain blanc*, also by Delarue-Mardrus, the narrator describes
Elise Arnaud's physical transformation at puberty as a time of discomfort and emotional upheaval:

> Un peu d'anémie, quelques malaises la retardaient dans son élan
> studieux. La puberté tourmentait son corps puéril. Elle changeait.
> Gênée par les nouveautés de son être physique et comme honteuse
> de n'être plus tout à fait une enfant, Elysée avait alternativement, sans
> cause apparente, des crises de larmes et des rires godiches, giboulées
> humaines. Et ce fut dans la même quinzaine qu'elle changea de cours
> et recourba sa natte dans le cou.

> [A little anemia and a few fainting spells slowed her studious momen-
> tum. Puberty tormented her young body. She was changing. Bothered
> by the newness of her physical being and almost ashamed of no longer
> being completely a child, Elysée had alternatively, without apparent
> cause, crying fits and silly laughter, human showers. And in the same
> two-week period she changed classes and put her braid up.] (Delarue-
> Mardrus 1923, 107–8)

A change of hairstyle and class are the rites of passage associated with a new post-pubescent social status. The narrator gives a sense of Elise's adolescent awkwardness at school; her arms are "too long" and her bun is "too tight" (112).

It is not until Elise comes to live with her father and his new wife that she discovers herself as a physical being. Indeed, her new urban setting focuses attention on appearance. During her shopping trip with her stepmother, she discovers the marvels of physical transformation, made possible in fashionable Parisian boutiques. Elise admires her new self in the mirror: "Elle se vit, dans les glaces à trois pans, changer de silhouette, devenir un autre être" [She saw herself change shape in the three-panel mirrors, become another being] (Delarue-Mardrus 1923, 171). Like Ludivine, Elise experiences a change of identity when she tries on luxurious clothing, as though she has become someone else. Here, however, the transformation is not stigmatized as it is in *L'Ex-voto*. The narrator links Elise's late discovery of stylish clothing to her nascent femininity, suggesting that dressing up is a natural feminine taste of which Elise has been heretofore deprived (171). The attention of the salesgirls who laud her beauty and figure, and the appreciative glances she attracts after her purchases, make her feel awkward, insecure, and ridiculous (173). Such description of self-doubt is rare in the novel of female adolescence, and suggests that the adolescent may not be comfortable with putting on the costume of an unfamiliar role. As in *L'Ex-voto*, attire is linked to identity, yet unlike Ludivine, Elise does not relish the change in identity brought on by new clothing.

Elise soon learns that Parisian society values seduction, and that elegant clothing and beauty play important roles in the seduction game. She doubts her femininity and seductive powers, wondering why a young count would come to her home to see her (Delarue-Mardrus 1923, 177). Elise remains unfamiliar with her new form, yet slowly becomes aware of the status achieved with attractiveness. At her first party, she experiences her beauty with great joy, feeling like a queen: "Ce fut peut-être la première fois qu'elle se comprit belle, tant les regards des filles et des garçons l'admiraient" [It was perhaps the first time that she understood how beautiful she was, with so many admiring gazes from girls and boys] (192). The approving gaze of others is what enables Elise to acknowledge her beauty. Unsurprisingly, when she decides to withdraw from the fashionable world into which she has been inducted, her interest in her physical appearance and personal seduction disappear as well. She becomes aware of the hypocrisy and the prurient nature of Parisian society, and the possible dangers associated with being a young pretty girl (242). Suddenly beauty becomes a potential liability, and innocent illusions disappear. For Elise, body awareness is born with her departure from the convent and fades away when she leaves the superficial world of appearances for one that places less emphasis on the material. In this context, adolescent body consciousness would seem to be a function of milieu: Elise must distance herself from the *monde* in order to gain perspective on the high value it places on physical appearance and on a certain kind of beauty dictated by fashion. Her withdrawal from Parisian high society indicates a refusal to judge worth according to allegiance to fashion, and a privileging of artistic and mental forms of expression over purely physical ones.

The writers considered in this chapter handle descriptions of the body and its accoutrements in different ways, from complete avoidance to detailed descriptions of the adolescent's own perception of her body. Attitudes toward attention to the body's changing shape vary: thinking about appearance can suggest an unhealthy emphasis on shallow values, or it can be a natural sign of the physical and mental changes taking place during adolescence. In either case, the body's presence in novels from the period discussed here differs from that which one can observe earlier in the century, when the physical processes in motion during adolescence were still a new and exciting topic.[22] Rather than detailing the rites of passage associated with physical maturation, novels from 1910 to 1930 focus on the adolescent's changing identity as reflected in her physical appearance. The appearance is not in itself significant except as an external sign of mental and emotional transformation.

NATURAL ENLIGHTENMENT

In John Neubauer's book on the *Fin-de-siècle Culture of Adolescence*, he observes that nature is one of the key spaces of youth. Yet the natural world as it appears in the novel of adolescence is a complex one, perhaps more so for young women than for young men. In *Le Deuxième sexe*, Simone de Beauvoir observes that natural realms play a paradoxical role in novels written by women. Nature is at once the woman's kingdom and place of exile, and it represents both the woman herself and her negation. Though few contemporary critics conceive of literature as direct representation, certain early twentieth-century portrayals of young girls and their relationship to nature caused critic Jean Larnac to assume that female novelists were in fact presenting their own early lives. As we saw in Chapter 2, Larnac saw contemporary novels of female adolescence as depicting a lamentable lack of education, as evidenced by the characters' wild roaming through nature. Indeed, in earlier novels of female adolescence, the natural realm tends to be a self-sufficient retreat where the adolescent is soothed by the sheer power of nature. Yet I would argue that, after 1910, nature facilitates without replacing the kind of rumination that helps each adolescent character search to identify her place, her identity. Rather than running to the country to hide from her problems, the adolescent confronts them there, using the natural retreat as a backdrop for her personal development.

Without resorting to mawkish sentiment, *Marie-Claire* by Marguerite Audoux gives a simple portrayal of farm life, revealing through the young narrator's eyes the simple moments of happiness she experiences in a rural setting. The novel was greeted with nearly unanimous praise when it appeared in 1910. Much of the criticism centered on Audoux's ability to imbue simple scenes and people with grandeur. Critic André Billy praises Audoux for her "very perceptive and purified feeling for nature" (Billy 1937, 123). Billy was not alone in appreciating Audoux's novel. The writer Alain-Fournier wrote a review of *Marie-Claire* in the year of its publication. In it, he praises the simplicity and greatness of the work, especially the author's rendering of the soulfully silent communication between peasants at the farm in Sologne. Alain-Fournier lauds Audoux for her ability to render in one word or phrase "the private tragedy of an existence" (Alain-Fournier 1910, 618). He calls her work totally original and refers to it as "the first novel written by a woman" (618). Audoux places Marie-Claire's path toward self-awareness in a natural realm.

Marie-Claire's move to the farm at thirteen years of age begins a new era of necessary autonomy and self-development. The descriptions of farm life reveal the narrator's vivid imagination, which reassures her in a new environment. She finds resemblances between people and animals (Audoux 1987, 94), and begins to look to the sheep themselves for friendship, seeing their resemblances with girls she has known (111). Marie-Claire also imagines comfort in moments of trauma. When she witnesses a grim battle between a wolf and a shepherdess, she calms herself by imagining the part in the latter's hair as a safe path (118). Imaginative transformation of reality has the power both to distract her in times of sadness and to reassure her at frightening moments.

Yet Marie-Claire's imagination is not always comforting, though it always reveals a strong creative capacity. The warnings she hears from others about potential dangers on the farm contribute to her less agreeable imaginings (Audoux 1987, 97). Her perceptions can also be misleading. When she loses her way during a snowstorm, she mistakenly perceives the tree trunks lining the walk as columns in a church (111–12). The introduction of new elements into a familiar scene (lanterns, snow) completely changes her perception thereof. When one of the sheep is bitten by a snake, his swollen head frightens her excessively, and her imagination transforms the ailing sheep into a monster (127–28). Marie-Claire's imaginative mind can thus interpret elements of her everyday life on the farm as disorienting, even frightening.

The novel establishes a clear link between Marie-Claire's mental state and her environment. When Marie-Claire meets and falls in love with Henri Deslois, nature becomes a mirror that reflects her emotions. The lovers meet in her secret hiding spot outdoors. Henri's sudden invasion of her secret hideout can be read, in addition to the intrinsic sexual imagery, as the eruption of adult romantic feelings into her hitherto childlike mind. She conflates her growing feelings for Henri with the natural settings where their subsequent meetings take place, and those settings become embellished and personified by her thoughts (Audoux 1987, 171, 176). She often wishes to become a part of this magical setting, imagining herself as a tree blown by the wind (173). Her awakening feelings for Henri, encouraged by his willingness to indulge her imaginative nature, transform their meeting sites into utopic fantasy worlds.

For Miane in Rachilde's *Son Printemps*, who belongs to the upper class and therefore enjoys far more leisure time than does Marie-Claire, nature provides a setting for daydreams when she is alone and games when she is accompanied by her young acquaintances. Miane's mind and body can wander at leisure, far from the accusations from her grandmother and priest that she has a tendency toward "dissipation" and an "esprit de révolte" [spirit of revolt] (Rachilde 1920, 31). Her active imagination can be difficult enough for her to deal with alone, creating a kind of vertigo (32). It is as though the whirlwind of thoughts in her head sometimes overwhelms her. At home, Miane feels misunderstood; the outdoors provides welcome escape. She and her best friend Joanille have a favorite place, an isolated thicket that serves as a private social space, "le salon qu'elles se sont choisi" [the lounge that they chose for themselves] (76). This natural meeting place is her

destination of choice when the atmosphere at home becomes unbearable: "Miane, s'échappant de chez elle par la porte du verger, va souvent
rejoindre son amie pour garder les moutons avec elle. C'est l'heure
paisible où, assises côte à côte, les jeunes filles se confient mille choses
puériles et bavardent en se baignant dans l'espace" [Miane often escapes
her house by the orchard door and goes to meet her friend to help her
watch the sheep. This is the peaceful hour where, sitting side by side,
the girls confide a thousand childish things to each other and chat
while bathing in open space] (78). Nature facilitates the only pleasantly
intimate social interaction Miane can enjoy.

The open space of nature soothes Miane when she is with her friend,
but it can also be a powerful panacea when she is alone. Nature becomes a realm where she reigns in youthful glory:

> Elle se sentit reine d'un univers inconnu . . . Miane aimait la solitude
> parce que, seule, elle était la maîtresse du monde, rien ne contrariait
> plus son goût d'innocente domination. Elle commandait à la beauté
> de la nature. . . . Ses prunelles versaient de l'incendie et ses joues re-
> splendissaient, gagnées par le triomphe du printemps qu'elle faisait
> sien. Elle était heureuse et jeune éperdument.

> [She felt like the queen of an unknown universe . . . Miane liked soli-
> tude because alone, she was the mistress of the world; nothing would
> thwart her taste for innocent domination anymore. She commanded
> nature's beauty . . . .Her pupils threw fire and her cheeks glowed, won
> over by the triumph of spring that she made her own. She was madly
> happy and young.] (Rachilde 1920, 118–19)

Youth and beauty are here inextricably linked to the power she experiences in a natural setting. Like Audoux's Marie-Claire, she has
a solitary hideout, a fountain in the garden behind her home where
she can sit and dream. At the fountain, Miane realizes the frustrat-
ing restrictions of class; much like the fountain, her beauty serves no
purpose (122). This is a clear statement about class: Miane's beauty is
of no use because she has no acceptable suitors of her class, no reason
to display herself.

Miane finds comfort and a sense of belonging at her fountain, which
is also the place where she encounters her love interest, Paul, for the
first time (Rachilde 1920, 123). His mysterious appearance at her secret
shrine makes her believe that a divine intervention has taken place, yet
her enthusiasm is rapidly calmed when she realizes the class differences
separating her from Paul. The narrator resorts to images of nature to

describe this separation: "L'Oasis n'existait plus et le désert s'étendait entre eux" [The Oasis no longer existed and the desert spread out between them] (127). Knowing that Paul has come following the river, she reflects on the treacherous potential of nature (125). Despite these ominous feelings, Miane experiences joy when she thinks of Paul, joy that she expresses again through natural metaphors (135, 136). As in Audoux's novel, here natural scenes and emotional states reflect one another.

Yet Miane's joy is short-lived, and she slowly begins to feel detached from her surroundings, even in the natural settings once so soothing to her (Rachilde 1920, 277). The traumatic deaths of her young friend Marie and her beloved cat Moute (304), not to mention her maid/friend's bloody miscarriage, lead her to muse on death. Yet when she considers death, she imagines it as a trip to a new and marvelous country (282). Convinced that death is a positive thing, an exotic trip, Miane drowns herself, calmly and "fièrement" [proudly] killing her "orgueilleux printemps" [arrogant springtime] (314). The spring metaphor, which appears throughout the novel, symbolizes love, youth, and possibility, all of which Miane ends with her life. Despite the powerful and positive force of nature that balances Miane's painful home life, it cannot compensate in the end for her deep-seated feelings of loneliness and despair.[23]

In the novels by Camille Pert, Colette, and Lucie Delarue-Mardrus, nature is a metaphor for emotion. In natural settings, the protagonists feel confident and can express themselves. Cady loves the countryside, comparing it to the city where she lives: "J'aime mieux pleurer là-bas que rire ici" [I prefer to cry there than to laugh here] (Pert 1914, 31). In Colette's *Le Blé en herbe*, nature dominates the narrative, providing a sensual backdrop for the protagonist's developing love affair. Interestingly, the summer setting functions as a temporal and a spatial haven or no man's land, where restrictions and responsibilities are few, and the days blend into a dreamlike blur. Vinca's dream world involves preserving the delicate balance of her relationship with Phil amid the idyll of their vacation spot. In the novel, nature provides a context for the young protagonists, who in turn reflect their surroundings. Diana Holmes observes that the colors of Vinca's hair and eyes link her to nature (Holmes 1991, 74). Any modification of her idealized image of nature, such as unexpectedly poor weather, crushes her (Colette 1974, 26). But Phil's erratic and distant behavior threatens her vacation idyll in much more concrete ways. Like him, she feels the strain of the imposed waiting period before they can act on their love, and at one point, she nearly lets suicide end the tension, allowing herself to slide toward a rocky cliff (30). Nature nearly becomes the scene and the instrument of Vinca's death. Phil prevents her from falling, but Vinca reminds him of the morbid train of her thought, by saying that her sister could replace her, were she to die (33). Rather than reflecting her emotions, the beach setting brings them to the surface.

In Delarue-Mardrus's *Graine au vent*, the outdoors provides a backdrop for Alexandra's hunting expeditions. Her wild ramblings contrast sharply with the calm, domestic interior dominated by her mother. It is not until long after her mother's death that Alexandra learns to mix the two spheres, appreciating elements of both. She takes her sister along on hunting expeditions, skillfully combining her love of nature and her natural maternal impulses, while providing for her family. In *L'Ex-voto*, by the same author, Ludivine realizes that she is happiest when she can commune with nature, and relinquishes all thought of the excitement and chic of the city in favor of her tough but beloved life on the shores of Normandy.

It is then in nature or in relation to nature that many adolescent heroines make decisions, indulge in imaginings, and plan for the future. Larnac observes that, in novels depicting young girls, sweet communion with nature gives way to revolt against society, as we saw in Chapter 2: "As soon as they grow up, most of these girls rebel against the society that refuses them what nature had promised. But education, with its immaterial rules and all of the brakes that it places on temperament, brings them into line despite themselves" (Larnac 1929, 229). Instead of being a key that opens society's doors to the female adolescent, education provides countless obstacles that the protagonist must then circumvent. Her mind now awakened to the existence of lessons to be learned, she must find often untraditional ways of accessing the knowledge for which she so longs.

Intellectual Growth

The debate over the upbringing of young girls that began in the late nineteenth century was raging on in the first two decades of the twentieth century. Whereas the previous chapters dealt with the tension between church and science, as Jules Ferry said in his well-known 1870 speech, by the early twentieth century the church had lost much of its influence over the education of girls.[24] Yet the church adopted some of the arguments espoused by the nationalists in an attempt to link piety and patriotism. Christian activists regarded with horror the secularization of education, claiming that the perfect French woman would be faithful to God's will in efficiently raising a family.[25] In general, though, the debate centered not on religion, but on French family values. As late as 1909, texts arguing for the feminization of education were published; these texts were intended to call women back to their family duties.

The true danger of educating girls, according to such writings, was celibacy, which threatened French society with stagnation (Zaidman 1992, 134). Such a menace was embodied by feminist activists like Madeleine Pelletier, perhaps the most vocal advocate of completely equal education for girls and boys. Historian Karen Offen notes that Pelletier threatened anti-feminists because she devalued marriage and maternity (Offen 1984, 666, 673). Pelletier, like Simone de Beauvoir several decades later, wrote of the "deconstuction work of the social production of the feminine" and of the "accusation made against women, mothers and educators, of being the vehicles of reproduction and of oppression." Zaidman suggests that Pelletier was the first to give the debate over education its full political implication (Zaidman 1992, 128). Opposing specifically feminine education that would cater to girls' supposed needs, Pelletier proposed raising girls like boys to prepare them for the demands of school and of life (134). She decried the creation of what she called "psychological sex" through gender-coded games, dress, and other means of socialization (135). Pelletier would have all children look and act the same in order to give girls an equal chance at education.

Another influential text of the time was that of Margaret Mead, who examined the psychological aspects of female adolescence in "primitive youth," searching for evidence of psychological stress linked to educational rites of passage. Mead suggests that the rise of psychology led to an interest in child/adolescent development, and a desire to better understand the concerns of adolescence (Mead 1928, 1). Explanations for adolescent tribulations were offered by G. Stanley Hall, who, Mead notes, considered adolescence to be a time of inevitable conflict (2). Mead's purpose was to ascertain whether female adolescence was a time of stress and strife for cultures unlike her own. Based on her observation of Samoan girls, she concludes that tension and conflict were not necessary elements of female coming-of-age (196). Educational practices must change, Mead contends, in order for adolescent stress to be reduced and eventually eliminated. Girls must be taught to make their own choices: "how to think, not what to think" (246). Mead's study varies in perspective and in purpose from those of contemporary advocates of female education, yet it raises some of the same issues, such as the importance of socialization in adolescent psychological development. Though the study came at the end of the period in question here, it demonstrates the kind of thought taking place at the time, and adds a new and influential angle to Western understanding of female adolescent psychology and the role of education in adolescence.

In his 1929 *Histoire de la littérature féminine en France*, Jean Larnac infers a link between increasing educational opportunities for women and the high number of French women writers.[26] Yet he also points out that some of the most respected writers, such as Marguerite Audoux and Colette, never benefited from secondary education (Larnac 1929, 223). Indeed, despite the ongoing struggle on the part of feminists such as Madeleine Pelletier to achieve utter equality in terms of the programs of study offered to male and female students, a goal that was achieved in 1924 (Zaidman 1992, 133), the novels do not reveal an obsession with school-based education. Rather, they suggest that the primary lessons in the adolescent girl's development may come from other sources than textbooks and classroom lectures. The heroines are young women with minimal schooling who develop and define their own reality away from the confines of the scholarly space, whereas in the last chapter the women were often if not always defined in terms of school and reading. Larnac observes that, though girls develop intellectually earlier than boys, as they physically mature they give up study for more romantic pursuits:

> One might say that their intelligence disappears suddenly to make way for overactive sensitivity that operates through coquettery, flirtation, music, reading . . . . And though puberty broadens the young man's ideas and leads him to ask great metaphysical questions, it closes the young woman in on herself and forces her with irritating regularity to examine herself, to reflect on her own being, then to see the problems of love and maternity. (Larnac 1929, 265)

Larnac sees puberty as opening the horizons of the young man while closing in those of the young woman on herself and her future as a wife and mother. Indeed, female protagonists spend far more time considering themselves and their place in the world around them than they do learning about history, geography, Latin, or math, or so the novels suggest. For some characters, the importance of school fades during adolescence; for others, school plays no role at all. Learning takes place through mentors or, more frequently, through simple experience, which provides more practical information than does formal education.

In Audoux's novel *Marie-Claire*, more important lessons are learned in nature and from simple farmers than from teachers and learned people. Marie-Claire learns through observation and experimentation, rather than through rote memorization of classroom lectures. Reading offers Marie-Claire another opportunity to create new worlds with her imagination. She prefers the silence and solitude of reading to playing with other children of her age, whom she finds noisy and too boisterous (Audoux 1987, 125–26). Her desire to read is so extreme that she picks up any pieces of paper, hoping to find writing on them (130). A few words at a time are enough to satisfy her insatiable appetite for intellectual stimulation. The farmer's brother gives her a book from which she creates songs; she later steals almanacs to savor secretly in the attic (131). Another book she finds in the attic, *Les Aventures de Télémaque*, keeps her company, and she rereads it in random installments to increase its novelty (134). She enjoys mental journeys with the book's hero (135). When the book suddenly disappears, Marie-Claire misses it as she would a friend (135). Her habit of seeking pleasure and/or solace in books continues during her relationship with Henri Deslois and after her return to the convent (178, 207). Reading allows for solitary stimulation of Marie-Claire's mental faculties, while catering to her desire for company.

Reading appears to be a positive influence for Marie-Claire, yet in his book on the French novel of adolescence, Justin O'Brien notes literature's dangerous influence on the adolescent imagination:

> We have already seen how the adolescent's love of literature feeds his imagination and how large a part his dreams play in his sentimental education. Now, this escape into a dream world, this effort to people one's own spiritual solitude, only serves in the end to increase one's isolation and to retard the process of adaptation; the adolescent, accustomed to the beauty of *his* world, is constantly shocked by reality. (O'Brien 1937b, 184)

Though O'Brien deals only with male adolescents, his observations can be successfully applied to Marie-Claire. While surrounded by books and friends, she is happy, but after her painful separation from the farmers who have become in some sense adoptive parents, her imagination provides a method of escape from painful situations. Her new employer resembles the mother superior from the convent, with yellow skin and gleaming eyes (Audoux 1987, 151). His mother's house makes her think of an ugly old tree stump (161). In this unpleasant place, even the words of the house's owner seem to her to have a disagreeable physical presence: "Ses paroles avaient une odeur insupportable" [Her words had an unbearable odor] (182). As O'Brien notes in the case of male adolescents, Marie-Claire is startled by reality, yet her developed imaginative faculty aids her in surmounting such unexpected moments and in processing the hard lessons of life. Marie-Claire has not learned to value upper-class citizens over those of the lower classes; she simply prefers kind people to cruel ones. Her naïveté reveals a purity of thought and an integrity that she has been able to maintain through her years out of school. She has a kind of wisdom unrelated to the knowledge gained at school.

In Rachilde's *Son Printemps*, Miane's education comes less from books and structured lessons than from her observations. Her teacher is more friend than professor, and they spend more time chatting than learning. After an illness puts an end to the lessons, her grandmother decides that she knows enough "pour faire son salut" [to ensure her salvation] and Miane is left to educate herself as best she can (Rachilde 1920, 45). She makes every effort to behave properly according to her rank (42). Yet her adolescence involves acute emotional states, sadness, worry, and lack of motivation, where studies and games cannot soothe her (44). Her state of mental confusion impels Miane to create order around herself. Books fail to illuminate her in the way nature can: Miane feels that she sees better at night than in books (47). Like Marie-Claire, Miane reads for mental escape, not with the explicit goal of acquiring knowledge.[27]

Many of Miane's lessons come from observing the differences between herself and Fantille, the maid who is exactly her age. Fantille's difficulties, including an unexpected pregnancy, provide Miane with information about the world that she would never get from her grandmother, whose only life lesson for Miane consists of the statement that a young girl is like an unsniffed bouquet on an altar, whose pure perfume rises toward God (Rachilde 1920, 110). This vision of the young woman contrasts sharply with that revealed to Miane during the episode of Fantille's horrific miscarriage. The miscarriage scene reveals Miane's utter ignorance of the workings of the female body and of the realities of marriage. Knowing that she cannot marry the man she thinks she loves, because of their class difference, she dreams of a spiritual union and throws a ring into her fountain as a sign of her engagement to Paul (293). As the narrator points out, Miane's reading has given her little concrete knowledge and in fact has encouraged her tendency to dream: "Miane avait lu beaucoup de livres. Elle savait mal beaucoup de choses, surtout des choses qui n'étaient point à sa portée, et elle vivait dans les légendes" [Miane had read many books. She knew many things badly, especially things that were not within her reach, and she lived in legends] (293). Yet Miane is strangely lucid, knowing that her desires are contradictory and wishing to find a way of resolving her quandary. She curses her interior passion and her need to hide it with an acceptably calm exterior appearance (301). Also, she recognizes her need for solitude, and wonders how to incorporate love into her solitary existence (301). Alone at her fountain, Miane spews forth a long monologue in which she proclaims her hope for the future, and her belief in springtime as a symbol of that hope that cannot be found in books (303). Miane's attitude reveals her disenchantedness with formal or informal education, and her belief in the truth of signs and superstition over that of books.

Miane ends her life because it constantly confronts her with unhappy truths and difficult lessons. She lacks familial or educational structure, and her own efforts to learn leave her traumatized and heartbroken. The tragic ending of the novel merely underscores the tragedy of Miane's existence. Attending lessons of some sort would have provided her with a more realistic conception of the world and of her place in it, and may have counterbalanced her natural propensity for romantic reverie, or at least encouraged her to focus it into creative projects. The adolescent heroine cannot educate herself alone. She must interact with society in order to combine and compare its lessons with those she may find in books.

Some novelists chose to write specifically about the kind of education bourgeois girls tended to receive. In an Avant-Propos to *La Petite Cady*, Camille Pert writes of her goals in writing the novel:

J'ai voulu prendre pour héroïne une enfant vivace, primesautière, énergique, qui dans un milieu sain eût été certainement une femme de valeur et d'action. Et, en la faisant passer par les phases d'une éducation pareille à celle que reçoivent la plupart des jeunes filles bourgeoises, j'ai essayé de rendre les déformations fatales que cette éducation ap-

porterait dans son être, dans ses sens et son intellectualité. Et je suivrai
la répercussion de cette éducation dans la vie tout entière de ce type
choisi . . .

[I wanted to take as heroine a vivacious, spontaneous, energetic child,
who in a healthy milieu would certainly have been a woman of worth
and of action. And in making her go through the phases of an education like that received by most bourgeois girls, I tried to show the fatal
distortions that such an education could bring to her being, her senses
and her intellect. And I will follow the repercussion of that education
in the entire life of this chosen type . . .][28] (Pert 1914, vii–viii)

Pert was disgusted with the state of female education at the time she
wrote her novel, seeing it as "fatally deforming" to the young girl's
senses and intellect. She worried in particular about the decreasing
role of the mother: "La mère moderne ne s'occupe pas de ses enfants,
confie leur être moral et physique à des individus indignes et ignore
absolument le résultat de l'éducation qui leur est donnée ainsi que les
personnalités qui sont modelées, à côté et en dehors d'elle" [The modern mother does not take care of her children, entrusts their moral and
physical education to unworthy individuals and is completely ignorant
of the result of the education they receive or of the personalities that
are molded, next to and outside of her] (vii–ix). This lack of maternal
attention has marked negative consequences, according to Pert. The
novelist quickly insists that her Cady does not represent the modern
girl, because each girl is unique (ix). Pert feels that her young character
represents a societal problem, one that could be partially solved were
mothers to spend more time nurturing and sharing knowledge with
their daughters.

Cady's mother indeed hardly knows her daughter, and spends no
time supervising her education. Her educational goals consist of denying Cady the freedom that other girls enjoy and preserving in her "une
innocence et une ignorance completes" [complete innocence and igno-
rance] so that she can find a good husband (Pert 1914, 58). This passage
proves that the maternal conspiracy of silence about sexual truths that
so traumatized nineteenth-century adolescents is still very much in
place in the early twentieth century. Ignorance is still associated with
innocence, and certain "freedoms" are very dangerous indeed, as the
mother's words suggest. Detailed, thorough education was still considered potentially damaging to the adolescent girl. A politician whom
Cady visits lectures her about the importance of dress and appearance,

rather than wasting time on politics, sciences, law, or the arts. As he says, "La femme . . . doit badiner avec tout ce qu'elle approche, doit tout aborder en riant, sans jamais rien approfondir, sans chercher à se spécialiser et à posséder un réel talent en quoi que ce soit; autrement, elle devient burlesque et odieuse" [Woman . . . must take everything she does lightly, must start everything laughing, without ever getting into too much depth, without trying to specialize or to have a real talent for anything; otherwise, she becomes farcical and odious] (158). For him, women are subjects of study; they do not study themselves. They should know just a tiny bit of many different subjects, but spend most of their time dressing themselves up. Like Cady's mother, he promotes the idea that book learning and freedom ruin a girl's marriage prospects.

In the novel, various characters voice Pert's ideas concerning the dangers of the lax bourgeois education of girls. One of Cady's friends and admirers protests that her education will deprave and ruin her (Pert 1914, 49). Again, the notion developed here is that improper learning can ruin a girl for life. Two teachers speak of the vicious circle of bad mothers who do not educate their daughters properly, saying that domestics teach bourgeois children about passion (75). Miss Armande, shocked by the politician's comments cited above, says that intelligent women could not possibly be content with limiting their interests to appearance and vanity (158). Despite the governess's progressive attitude toward female education, Cady's liberated behavior constantly horrifies her. She says to her charge, "Je comprends que c'est la faute de votre milieu, de votre éducation, la négligence de votre mère, qui en est la cause, mais vous n'êtes pas ce qu'une jeune fille de votre âge devrait être!" [I understand that it's the fault of your milieu, your education, your mother's negligence that has caused this, but you are not what a young girl of your age should be!] (183). Maurice Deber, an admirer of Cady's, agrees. Before leaving on a six-year trip, he says to Cady that he hopes she will change back from an artificial doll to a real girl before his return (221). Maurice promises that, if Cady sheds her ugly shell, he will marry her when he returns.

Neither her mother's model of education nor that of her governess appeals to Cady, probably because neither provides the affection she so craves. Cady develops her mind through reading, which has the advantage of helping her mentally escape from her unhealthy daily life (Pert 1914, 203). Cady's fraternizing with Georges and some of his less innocent friends leads to the death of her governess, and Cady hides her role in the matter. Soon thereafter her stepfather wins a political victory and a new, more-worldly governess is chosen for Cady. These thought-provoking changes in Cady's daily existence lead her to make an important decision. She decides that it is time to stop having fun and to grow up (Pert 1914, 315). This rare passage in Cady's voice at the end reveals that her life until now has been based on amusement, a philosophy with which neither educational school would agree. Like Miane, if Cady had more interaction with girls of her age and class, she would be able to create emotional bonds and perhaps preserve her youthful naïveté. All figures of authority in Cady's life prevent her from freely exploring the world; therefore, she rebels against them and seeks education wherever she can find it. Pert's novel analyzes the educational pitfalls of a particular social class, where the absence of positive and instructive mother/daughter relationships wreaks havoc on the girl's sense of identity and leaves her vulnerable to various social ills.

Another novelist who portrays failed or absent mother/daughter relationships is Lucie Delarue-Mardrus. In his *Histoire de la littérature féminine en France*, Jean Larnac analyzes Lucie Delarue-Mardrus's attitude toward children. He contends that she portrays youth as a time of delicious enchantment, when the "little girl soul, so fresh, so delicious, a sexless soul" experiences the "intoxication of childhood, intoxication without analysis, never found again later . . . " (Larnac 1929, 227). One may argue that, in her novels of adolescence, Delarue-Mardrus portrays both the carefree childhood described by Larnac and a more sedate, responsible lifestyle associated with later adolescence. Her novels trace the process by which young heroines make the transition from one to the other, not without emotional and mental strife, and learn to appreciate the joys, as well as the pains, of both. Hence the novelist's conception of childhood is not entirely rosy, as Larnac would have one believe, nor is adulthood entirely without charm. Adolescence functions as an intermediary period during which the heroine negotiates between the two and sets the stage for her adulthood. Though school in the strictest sense plays a minimal role in the novels, the protagonists constantly evaluate and reevaluate their experiences, learning important lessons that come from a variety of sources.

Class also plays a role in the discussion of education in the Delarue-Mardrus novels. In *Graine au vent*, Alexandra's mother informs her that certain social classes have certain educational standards: "Vous êtes née demoiselle. Est-ce être une demoiselle que de savoir tout juste lire et écrire?" [You were born a young lady. Does being barely able to read and write make one a young lady?] (Delarue-Mardrus 1928b, 64). For her mother, being a "demoiselle" doubtless means mastering reading and writing and gaining some familiarity with music, languages, art, and the fundamentals of domestic skills. The protagonist processes her new responsibility as a member of a certain social group. Soon thereafter she rejects her lower-class friend's amorous advances (70). Alexandra feels that adults cannot understand her problems (72). Alone with her dog, with no one to confide in, she seeks to forget her problems through the distraction of study (73). For the length of the novel, study plays a minor role in Alexandra's life. Her important lessons come from her experiences, not from books.

Perhaps the most important event in Alexandra's mental development is her decision to try her hand at art, having learned through observing her father as a child. This decision comes toward the end of the novel, and represents the culmination of the protagonist's emotional and mental development. As she sculpts, the narrator links her newfound hobby to the growth process that has been taking place throughout the novel (Delarue-Mardrus 1928b, 194). Alexandra enjoys sculpting as much as her previously most beloved pastime, hunting (194). The choice of a nonviolent leisure activity over a violent one is valorized in the novel as a sign of maturity. More important, her father, upon seeing her creation, ends a yearlong silence and embraces his two daughters, both of whom had symbolized for him betrayal of their mother. It is implied that Alexandra will take over and realize her father's dreams of artistic glory (195), thereby saving the family from financial ruin, as well as filling her mother's role as head of the domestic space. Alexandra has sufficiently matured to choose responsibility and artistic creation over personal pleasure and shiftlessness.

In *Le Pain blanc*, also by Delarue-Mardrus, Elise's education can be divided into two parts: the lessons learned at the prestigious school to which her mother sends her, and those learned during her apprenticeship with her worldly stepmother. Faced with new challenges, Elise learns to study, to observe, and to appreciate art and literature. Embarrassed by her initial ignorance, Elise rapidly catches up to the others, and eventually surpasses them. At school she experiences new and invigorating freedom (Delarue-Mardrus 1923, 80). Moreover, she begins to enjoy the challenge of academic work: "Comme les autres, elle subissait l'emprise de cette éducation profondément intelligente qui laissait à chaque esprit . . . l'initiative et l'orgueil du travail" [Like the others, she felt the hold of that profoundly intelligent education that left to each mind . . . the initiative and pride of work] (90). Yet she realizes the impracticality of her education at school when she cannot make a telephone call (125). While school nurtures her sense of liberty and of pride in her work, it fails to provide her with the basic skills necessary for survival in her nonacademic environment.

The major difference between Elise's education at the convent and that which she receives in the *monde* is symbolized by each milieu's attitude toward the Musset verses she had lovingly learned as a child, then forgotten at the convent after being chastised for quoting them. When she moves to Paris, she delightedly rediscovers Musset (Delarue-Mardrus 1923, 179). When Elise realizes that Musset is accepted and appreciated in polite Parisian society, she adopts that society as her guide (180). For Elise, Musset has particular emotional value, because his writing represents for her the only happy moments she spent at home after her father's departure.

The stark contrast between her two "schools" is again underlined when she proudly returns to visit the convent (Delarue-Mardrus 1923, 181). From her new perspective, her former classmates are caged birds who can only admire her freedom and importance from afar. Yet her new lifestyle begins to worry Elise, despite the excitement of her new social activity and the trappings of society life, such as the white bread of the novel's title (189). The snobbery of her new world bothers her, and she betrays its values when she befriends a poor violinist and his group of musicians (191). This rare openness on the part of a member of the upper class distinguishes Elise from the rest of her friends, and serves her well when she comes to detest her worldy environment and its immoral codes of behavior.

Another turning point comes for Elise when she recites her beloved Musset for her friends, who mock her for appreciating such unfashionable verse (Delarue-Mardrus 1923, 195). Elise realizes that she belongs neither in her new world nor at the convent school (207–8). When Elise feels abandoned by all those around her, the poor musician she befriended at the party helps her and offers advice. Her friend's home provides Elise with the warm and loving domestic space lacking in her youth. With his help, Elise learns perhaps the most important lesson of her life: the importance of true friendship, which crosses class boundaries, and the common experience of music. When Elise plays for him, her mind opens as never before (258). Her conversations with his family confirm her convictions about art and give her new interest in learning, teaching, and living. Her new friends help her rediscover love and a zest for life based on the study of music. Elise's various "schools" provide her with different models of education that she uses to define what matters most to her; ultimately, she learns to diregard the opinions of others in finding her own path.

All of these novels reflect a marked absence of, or rethinking of, traditional school scenes. The characters often learn their most important lessons on their own, by observing those around them, rather than through specific instruction based on books. Though this notion is not unusual in fiction, the shift in the novel of adolescence at this time reveals changing perspectives on female education. The novelists propose that young women can become active and productive members of society if they are exposed to life in its many forms. Social interaction, combined with a minimum of formal instruction, provides girls with the information they need to make choices and to prepare for adult life. If, as Juliette Rogers claims, education in the novel creates heroines prepared to function as free adult members of the community (Rogers 1994, 331), then the shift away from the school may indicate an even greater degree of mobility and of autonomy. The long-enduring debate over the best type of education for girls is continued indirectly in period novels; novelists most often depict heroines whose true upbringing takes place outside of the classroom.

Thinking Love, Thinking Sexuality

The First World War further threatened France's already declining population, provoking frantic urging to young women on the part of politicians and various officials to marry and reproduce.[29] As historian Mary Louise Roberts has noted, the drop in the birth rate was seen as an indicator of moral or economic decline in France, and linked to postwar anxieties about industrial ruin, economic chaos, new strength in Germany, and vulnerability to aggression or military attack (Roberts 1994, 97, 107). In order to maintain French power and reputation, it was considered imperative to stabilize the natality rate: legislation was passed in 1920 that was intended to support maternity and do away with contraception and abortion (107, 94). Yet there were those who objected to the means used to marry off young women, specifically their lack of voice in the choice of a husband and the absence of love in most marriages. One such objector was novelist Victor Margueritte, whose 1922 novel *La Garçonne* presented French society with a social type that provoked as much debate as the New Woman heralded by writers and thinkers at the turn of the century. Margueritte's *garçonne* is a young woman named Monique Lherbier, who gradually comes to recognize and rebel against the various traps set for her by her traditional, well-meaning parents. Monique breaks off her engagement to a womanizing but rich and well-bred man and pursues happiness in her own way, shocking readers by sleeping with a random stranger and flirting with homoeroticism before finding the understanding and forgiving man of her dreams and returning to a traditional couple model by the novel's end.

     In her book on gender in postwar France (1917–1927), Mary Louise Roberts outlines three stereotypical female images that developed after the war, and that reflected anxiety about gender roles. The good mother represented patriotism and tradition. The modern woman, or *garçonne*, represented change and sexual liberation. The third category, "la femme seule," was an economically independent but celibate woman who evoked debate on "women's autonomy, status as citizens, and education: the upbringing of their minds, and bodies, and their working competencies" (Roberts 1994, x). The single woman worried many politicians and thinkers who saw in her an undermining of traditional social order (159).[30] Freely elected celibacy appeared incomprehensible and potentially dangerous to the French public. Abstinence and sterility were considered to lead to nervous disorders, nymphomania, cancer, onanism, and sapphism (169–170). Despite initial resistance to the single woman, interest in her and literary portrayals of her revealed French society's gradual acceptance of the female sexual drive, at the time of the arrival of Freudian theory in France (174).

     In her book about French feminism from 1914 to 1940, Christine Bard writes of the influence of Margueritte's novel on the myth of "the roaring twenties." The independent woman was not a new topos, in literature or in life, as our study of the Belle Epoque makes clear. As early as 1904, G. Stanley Hall, who completed the first in-depth study of adolescence, wrote that he shared in "the growing fear that modern woman, at least in more ways and places than one, is in danger of declining from her orbit; that she is coming to lack just confidence and pride in her sex as such, and is just now in danger of lapsing to mannish ways, methods, and ideals, until her original divinity may become obscured" (Hall 1925, 646). Though Hall was referring to the New Woman phenomenon, versions of which appeared more or less si-

multaneously in America, England, and France,[31] the garçonne incited
many of the same fears and concerns as did her earlier counterpart.[32]
More specifically, the garçonne played into anxiety about female sexual
betrayal during the war, portrayed in novels of the period.[33] Readers
of novels about women from the late nineteenth and early twentieth
centuries were familiar with the independent woman figure.[34] The appearance of liberated women had heretofore been limited to marginal
settings, however: Monique Lherbier's revolt hit a bit closer to home.
Yet as Roberts observes, Monique's redemption at the end of the novel
should have appeased the gender and cultural anxieties of those most
attached to traditional social institutions, who feared that the novel
would inspire a new social reality (Roberts 1994, 46–47).

The garçonne stereotype provoked debate even within the feminist
ranks, but the principal demand she represented, woman's basic right
to experience on her own terms love and sex as but a small element
in the larger context of her life, was embraced by many female novelists regardless of their position on feminism. According to Bard, after
the turn of the century, novels increasingly portrayed the independence feminists fought for. Heroines began to seek liberty over love, a
change from the Belle Epoque, when love dominated the narrative.[35]
When they do pursue love, heroines allow themselves the experience
of passion, a violation of traditional sexual morality, and they are newly
critical of their loved ones (Bard 1995, 189). Love is just one experience in many. Also, literature was expected to give a realistic portrait
of women's actual lives: "As for psychological novels, they must offer
models that allow readers to identify easily. Their heroines, politically
seductive, spoke to reason and not to the imaginary. Their Romanesque
consistency mattered little" (189–190). The novel thus began to portray
thinking heroines who spent their time doing other things besides
pining for love.

In this new literary discourse on sexuality that promoted its free
expression, virginity had a paradoxical place. Bard notes that, in Freudian theory, the virgin had an almost phallic power: "Although the conscious discourse presented her generally as an unfinished woman, she
appeared to the unconscious as a self-sufficient power" (Bard 1995,
223). This self-sufficient power contradicts the image of the virgin as
vulnerable to abuse and manipulation. Certainly, Freud's understanding of female sexuality was limited: "Dreams, slips, gestures, symptoms, silences served him as unwitting but, once recognized, informa-
tive guides to the retreats of inner life where sexual desires had taken

refuge" (Gay 1984, 171, 166). Freud insisted on the close observation of clues to the unconscious realm of repressed sexuality, and regarded the virgin with something resembling awe. Yet as Joan Brumberg has observed, by the 1920s to 1930s, virginity had become a social category, not a moral state, and had lost much of its cultural currency (Brumberg 1997, 156). John D'Emilio and Estelle Freedman note the stark contrast between Victorian "absence of information and distorted teaching about sex," which led young girls to assume that touching a boy's hand or eating certain foods led to pregnancy (D'Emilio and Freedman 1988, 177), and the sexual liberty of 1920s society, where girls began to date boys and even engage in premarital sex, which was accepted between fiancés (258).[36] The virgin had no specific power or prestige, nor was she necessarily stigmatized in any way.

The debate over the place and appropriateness of sexual education raged on: those who felt it threatened the sanctity of young minds argued passionately with those who felt that it must exist, and the earlier the better (Bard 1995, 224). Peter Gay observes that, at the time when Freud's writings about female sexuality became available to an international audience, "physicians and educators continued to wrangle over the possible damage that higher education might do to the vulnerable bodies of adolescent girls, and to rehearse, evidently without fear of getting bored, that perennial question of woman's amorousness" (Gay 1984, 166). It was believed that even to speak of sex to young girls would strip them of their innocence (Roberts 1994, 198). Catholic educators believed that sex education should be handled by parents and priests only and be as vague as possible (200). Yet there were increasing voices promoting the development of sexual education and even adolescent sexual activity. Roberts writes of Germaine Montreuil-Straus, who gave lectures to educate young women from 1910 to 1930 (199). Montreuil-Straus opposed Catholics, arguing that sex education should be open, scientific, and neutral, and referring to the female sex drive as described by Havelock Ellis and Freud (199–200).[37] In order to validate her educational project in the eyes of her opponents, Montreuil-Straus defined normative female sexuality as conjugal and reproductive (204). Indeed, mandatory courses for girls on "puériculture," or child-care education, were created in 1923 (207). Other proponents of sex education were more radical: in "Une seule morale pour les deux sexes" [One Moral Code for Both Sexes] (1925), Josette Cornec stated that young girls should be able to experience love and sex as they liked, even outside of marriage, without being censured in any way. In fact, Cornec suggested, virginity is dangerous and can provoke "a halt in intellectual and physical evolution. Repressed desires produce nervous difficulties leading to hysteria and depression. Anemia, so common in adolescent girls, is due most often to deprivation of sexual pleasure" (Bard 1995, 224–25). For Cornec, the expression of sexuality during youth was the best way to ward off physical and mental disorders of all kinds.

Despite such then-shocking proposals on the part of radical feminists, the most successful feminists chose to stick to traditional gender roles: marrying, having children, and extolling the delights of both (Bard 1995, 232). This is not to say that the conjugal couple was a fixed entity. As writer Jules Bois wrote in 1912, the changing experience of women meant that relationships between men and women were evolving, resulting in transformed conceptions of marriage (Bois 1912, 3). Feminists hoped to prove that marriage and love could coexist, signaling a victory of moderate feminism over more radical forms.[38] Appearing at the same time was a new wave of Catholic feminism that similarly supported marriage and maternity. The garçonne, for all the attention she attracted with her first appearance, did not seem to be a viable option for many women. Marrying men they chose and creating happy homes was a goal of which even the staunchest anti-feminists approved.

In the novels, all of the adolescent heroines, with the possible exception of Alexandra, feel the pull of romance and dream of finding happiness with a man. Yet within the typical romance novel structure, they succeed in challenging traditional conceptions of appropriate female behavior, either through class line transgression, flaunting of their assets as sexual merchandise, or reinvention of gender roles. In her book on French women's writing, Diana Holmes suggests that novels provided an appropriate and easy forum for discussion about changing French society and for the calming of anxiety about endangered traditional roles and values (Holmes 1996, 48). Women writers tended to stick to the typical and comfortable romance plot, Holmes writes, while "exploring the social and emotional implications of gendered identity," questioning passive female other-based roles, and pondering the possibility of individual female achievement (49). Romance takes the upper hand over marriage, portrayed by Jean Larnac as a source of infinite suffering for the young woman at the hands of an insensitive husband, as we saw in Chapter 2 (Larnac 1929, 229). He warns that women will never be happy in a loveless marriage (230–31). Larnac's comments, based on his readings of period novels, paint a bleak picture of marriage. Concerned that just such a marriage model might continue to dominate French households, feminists and educators encouraged young women to choose their husbands well, seeking men with whom they communicated well and to whom they felt strong emotional and intellectual attachment.

It is appropriate to point out that, while books on "feminisms" of the period such as Bard's evoke such writers as Colette, Delarue-Mardrus, Noailles, Tinayre, and Rachilde, these writers tended to avoid close association with the feminist struggle and even took anti-feminist stances—Rachilde wrote an essay, ambiguous in some respects, entitled *Pourquoi je ne suis pas féministe* [Why I am Not a Feminist]. Paradoxically, their behavior may have contradicted their writing: Rachilde and Colette were consistently criticized by feminists for emulating the garçonne in their dress and lifestyle while maintaining a more traditional conception of the female role in their novels (Bard 1995, 205).[39] Such a conception is based on the pursuit of love above all else, especially for young women: "Female virginity is marked by a state of permanent sexual and emotional expectation" (Holmes 1996, 59). During this period of expectation, heroines reacted to their need for love in varying ways.

Audoux's character Marie-Claire's chance at love proves to be an impossible one, due to the class differences separating her from Henri Deslois. Yet she falls in love with him honestly and completely, caring little about his financial status, except when it prevents him from telling her the truth. Her attraction to Henri is based on their visual and verbal communication, not on material things. Marie-Claire's heart is temporarily broken when she realizes that the world has other plans for Henri and that their love means nothing in the larger social context. When her relationship with Henri Deslois (who, faithful to his name, obeys his family's "laws" in rejecting Marie-Claire for a woman of his social class) ends abruptly, her perception becomes increasingly lugubrious. Reality appears nightmarish to her (Audoux 1987, 187). The blurred line between dream and reality is a coping mechanism; in her mind, she attempts to erase her pain by considering it a dream (188). Her sleep is interrupted by horrible nightmares, and when she hears of the wedding of Henri Deslois, her imagination construes her pain as a physical presence, a screaming animal attached to her chest (201). During and after her doomed love affair, Marie-Claire's mind provides distractions to numb her emotional agony.

In *Son Printemps* by Rachilde, social class again plays an important role in the impossibility of love, though here the roles are reversed.[40] Though ignorant about the specific implications of marriage, Miane has clearly been taught to think of love and conjugal affairs according to social class, where each class has its preordained role (Rachilde 1920, 65). Yet she also has a typical adolescent romantic vision of being swept away by a dashing prince: "Oh! quand viendra le prince Charmant, dont parlent tous les contes, toutes les chansons, comment la trouvera-t-il? Elle n'a aucune vocation pour le mariage, mais un goût prononcé pour le chevalier Mystère, le bel inconnu qui passera devant sa porte, à minuit, sur un cheval blanc de lune" [Oh! When will Prince Charming come, the one that all tales and songs talk about, and how will he find her? Marriage is absolutely not her calling, but she has a definite taste for the knight Mystery, the handsome stranger who will pass by her door, at midnight, on a horse as white as the moon] (34).[41] Unfortunately for her, the man who catches her eye is the poor son of a church worker. It is not until she sees an engraving of Cupid and recognizes Paul in it that she becomes aware of her attraction to him (88). Miane fabricates a love affair from a variety of elements: her purchased engraving of Cupid, her erotic/romantic religious impulses,[42] and the supposed resemblance between the engraving and the sacristain's son. Gabriella Tegyey has observed that "Miane cannot reconcile her ideal, dreamed love with its real 'double.' The figure of Paul Midal is both the object and the center of the heroine's illusory aspirations and the vulgar incarnation of her dreams" (Tegyey 1995, 69).[43] In a passage reflecting social satire, the narrator insists on the strange character of the adolescent girl, calling her a "bizarre animal" (Rachilde 1920, 90). Miane's romantic reverie is perhaps born of the all too unromantic nature of her daily life. She imagines marriage to be a mystical union, ignoring the more concrete aspects of marriage (185). Again, Miane creates a mental image of marriage based on disparate elements that she chooses to associate with love.

When a series of rude awakenings shatter Miane's romantic illusions, she retreats further into a rosy dream world where love conquers all, even death: "Mon amour est mon bien, ma fortune, mon printemps personnel. Par l'unique puissance de mon amour je peux . . . exalter mon cerveau jusqu'à éloigner les laides grimaces de la mort" [My love is my possession, my fortune, my personal spring. By the unique power of my love I can . . . exalt my brain until I push away the ugly grimaces of death] (Rachilde 1920, 207). Miane fights her feelings of love, trying to convince herself that her heart belongs in fact to Jesus and not to Paul (233). The narrator describes the enjoyment Miane gets from her conviction that God is secretly imprisoned in her heart, attributing such an attitude to the typical naïveté of adolescent girls (251). Religious conviction is used as a way of showing the delightful innocence and "sweet madness" of the adolescent characters regarding love and sex.

As in *Marie-Claire*, class differences provide an important obstacle. Miane's love is vague and based on her basic sheltered ignorance of society and love. Her suicide, prompted by Paul's sudden departure and the destruction of the engraving, can be read as a gesture of despair in the face of the impossibility of realizing her romantic dreams.[44] She cries "Oh! mon Amour! Mes chères Amours!" [Oh! My Love! My dear Loves!] as she drowns without protest in a pond near her home, revealing in her last words the pain of a past and future life without love. Miane's despair can be read in terms of her naïveté surrounding sexuality and her lack of contact with the outside world, most particularly with men. Because she has no viable marriage options and no clear idea of marriage as a social contract and not just a spiritual one, she idealizes the only young man she sees regularly, building him up in her mind as the answer to her prayers. When Paul is no longer a romantic possibility, Miane sees her life as equally hopeless. The future is for her inextricably linked to Paul, who represents her idealized version of love.

Though she is younger than the other protagonists, Camille Pert's Cady has a greater awareness of the social realities of love. She knows that "love" comes in many forms, is aware of the temptations and dangers of sexuality, and uses her charms to manipulate would-be lovers. It is difficult to interpret Cady's constant attempts at seduction, though they can most obviously be read as an attempt to replace the love she does not receive from her parents. Love and seduction are Cady's hobbies; she even helps others with their affairs, dressing her governess seductively before a ride with her stepfather (Chapter 12), then feeling neglected when her plan succeeds (Chapters 13 and 14). Cady's precocious awareness of Eros and Thanatos confuses and bewilders those around her. During one conversation, Renaudin, one of the family's servants, chastises her for knowing of such things at such a young age, to which Cady responds that she already knows many things (Pert 1914, 120). In another scene, a young man struck by Cady's appearance is disappointed to find a child instead of a woman (160). She approaches him in an attempt to "reconquer" him, crazy about "ce jeu de félin qui est l'essence même de la femme . . . Du moins de celle élevée comme la fille de Mme. Darquet" [this feline game that is the very essence of woman . . . at least of one raised like the daughter of Madame Darquet] (163). The narrator thus reminds us that Cady's ineffective education may be to blame for her intense need to flirt and to seduce. Cady provides an excellent example of precocious, and occasionally dangerous, sexual awareness based on absent parents and minimal educational structure. Her intelligence and energy could better be channeled in other ways, were she given a different kind of education.

Colette's *Le Blé en herbe* differs from the other texts in that the female protagonist has already found her love object as the novel opens. The central conflict springs from their precocious relationship. The narrator refers to Vinca as "une adolescente chargée, trop tôt, de l'humilité, des maladresses, de la morne obstination du véritable amour" [an adolescent burdened too early with the humility, the awkwardness, the mournful obstination of true love] (Colette 1974, 14). Despite her youth and relative innocence, Vinca guesses at the sexual feelings aroused in Phil by the older lady in white. Phil makes every attempt to hide his liaison with the stranger from Vinca, but her imagination, coupled with a keen feminine instinct, warns her of danger (54). The first night Phil spends with his lover, Vinca cannot sleep, and checks the time of his return (61). When Phil suddenly bursts into tears in her presence, she knows immediately the cause of his pain (67) and the knowledge causes her to become "froide et douce, comme si son grand amour l'avait quit-tée" [cold and gentle, as though her great love had left her] (70). The events taking place in Phil's life are reflected in Vinca's appearance and behavior.

It becomes clear to the reader and to Phil that Vinca has matured profoundly during the course of the summer. Though she has not experienced the emotional and physical turbulence of a love affair, she is anxious to explore the new impulses plaguing her mind and body. After a summer of frustration created by the disparity between her own feelings and Phil's treatment of her, Vinca takes the initiative in her sexual relationship with him. In her confrontation with Phil over his behavior, she berates him for turning to another for experimentation, insisting that she is not the innocent creature he has imagined. When he assures her that she has no idea of what he has experienced, she cries, "Mais je ne demande qu'à savoir!" [But all I want is to know!] (Colette 1974, 113). Vinca states clearly that Phil's empty excuses render their relationship ridiculous and shallow (111). Here is yet another variation on the theme of the female adolescent imagination. Capable of reading external signs of loss of innocence, the imagination is fueled by those signs, and incites a longing for similar concrete experience and knowledge. Also, Vinca refuses to accept the double standard of behavior offered by Phil to justify his behavior.

Vinca surprises Phil, and perhaps the reader, by initiating a sexual relationship when she feels ready, not when those around her decide it. Vinca decides to act on her passion, taking an active role, rather than allowing others to act for her. Her decision, made when she sees Phil look dreamily toward the place where he lost his innocence, shines in her eyes and worries Phil (Colette 1974, 114). That night, she follows Phil outside and seduces him, arranging every detail, even wearing perfume (119). Vinca's sudden and unexpected maturity and sensual behavior seem strange and jarring to Phil, who conceives of her as a pure, childlike being.

During the course of the novel, Vinca learns to evaluate her imaginary world and to decide which elements are worth a struggle. She makes a bold sexual move, sacrificing her innocence to recover the balance of her relationship with Phil. In her book on adolescent psychology published only five years after *Le Blé en herbe*, Leta Hollingworth writes of the positive consequences of such action: "When daydreams are accompanied by well directed action they lead to constructive attack upon the environment, thus aiding in the establishment of an adequate personality" (Hollingworth 1928, 191). Vinca's behavior can be read as just such an action, necessary to the development of her adult personality. Diana Holmes writes of the end of the novel in terms of its unexpected challenging of gender roles, claiming that, in the novel, "in one sense an account of the formation of a conventional couple, the basis of the relationship is seriously disturbed at the novel's conclusion by Vinca's failure to acknowledge shame or awe at her first experience of sex, and Phil's resulting uncertainty about his masculine role" (Holmes 1991, 3–4). Vinca's decision to sleep with Phil and her nonchalant attitude after doing so both violate well-established codes of female behavior. Though the novel follows a seemingly traditional adolescent pair, it depicts a female character that does not conform to gender expectations and, therefore, a new vision of the couple.

In the novels by Lucie Delarue-Mardrus, love is a theme of varying importance. In *L'Ex-voto*, Ludivine has two suitors, one rich and one poor. She uses her wealthy admirer to obtain money and favors for her family while reserving her love for Delphin, a poor fisherman with whom she is reunited and married at the novel's end. Ludivine's two relationships can be read in terms of sadism and masochism. Her passionate awakening occurs when Delphin's virile and attractive father slaps her after she throws a rock through his window. Though she is angry and humiliated, Ludivine admires the strong, nondrinking man so different from her father, and capable of inspiring in her the first emotion she can remember (Delarue-Mardrus 1928a, 16, 19, 23). Ludivine transfers her passion to Delphin after his father perishes tragically during a storm. Their marriage seems a natural and logical step to the entire community, until Lauderin, Ludivine's wealthy suitor, falls immediately in love when he first sees her in the street (166). From the start, Lauderin plays a passive role in his relationship with Ludivine.

Ludivine soon realizes her power over both men: Delphin is her "proie sans défense, sa possession" [defenseless prey, her possession] that she can torture and watch suffer (Delarue-Mardrus 1928a, 168). Lauderin is for her but another victim (172). When Delphin announces his plan to leave town, Ludivine suffers horribly (201). To cause him pain, she accepts Lauderin's offer, but treats the latter with increasing scorn and cruelty: "Son goût de la guerre se satisfaisait dans cette lutte qu'elle soutenait pour écraser définitivement la nouvelle proie venue se jeter dans ses pattes" [Her taste for war was satisfied in this struggle that she maintained in order to crush definitively the new prey that had thown itself under her feet] (213). Ludivine's need to dominate finds in Lauderin a particularly willing victim.

When Ludivine sees Delphin again after some time, she is shocked by his resemblance to his father, and immediately transfers her undying youthful passion to the son (Delarue-Mardrus 1928a, 227). Ludivine feels "désarmée, vaincue" [disarmed, defeated] for the first time in her life and becomes aware of the strength of her attraction, as Delphin's resemblance to his father will only increase as he ages. She knows that she will love him forever, "désespérément, furieusement, de toute son âme rebelle, enfin subjuguée, obéissante" [desperately, furiously, with all of her rebellious soul, at last subjugated and obedient] (227–28). Romantic passion is what succeeds in taming this heretofore seemingly untameable young woman. Here Ludivine makes a surprising decision: to marry Lauderin for the good of her family while keeping Delphin as a lover (230–31). Even more shockingly, Ludivine decides to sleep with Delphin before her fiancé, so that Lauderin will only have Delphin's "restes" [leftovers] (243). The rest of the novel depicts Ludivine's attempts to see Delphin, constantly foiled by Lauderin's increasing suspicion. In a climactic scene, Delphin saves their lives when they are trapped in an inlet by a sudden, violent storm. Just before Delphin's heroic appearance, Ludivine tells Lauderin that she has always loved Delphin (289). Afterward, Lauderin leaves the town in shame, after paying the Bucaille family's debts and making them a present of a boat, with which they will be able to live.

Given the choice between a man from her social class and milieu and a wealthy, worldly one, Ludivine elects to marry within her own class. Yet Delarue-Mardrus's novel makes several interesting points. First, Ludivine's love for Delphin is problematized by her masochistic relationship to the memory of his father. Second, until Delphin saves her life, she is willing to prostitute herself to a man for whom she has no respect in order to gain financial stability for her family. Most important, Ludivine makes sexually liberated decisions yet is saved from carrying them out by the novel's end, which establishes a chaste and well-matched couple from the same social class. In this way, Delarue-Mardrus presents revolutionary ideas about sexuality and social contracts, while ultimately respecting class boundaries and moral codes.

In *Le Pain blanc*, as in *L'Ex-voto*, Delarue-Mardrus sets up two models of love in direct opposition to one other. The first is the traditional, socially accepted love based on parental choice of spouse in accordance with certain economic codes. The second is based on the mutual attraction of both parties, beyond class or social convention. Elise is flattered when her stepmother first suggests that the Count of Villevieille may be in love with her. She still feels too young for love, but knows that male attention means that she is leaving childhood forever, which she experiences with a mix of emotions (Delarue-Mardrus 1923, 177). Elise's ambivalent reaction to her suddenly discovered desirability is interesting. She experiences both "embarras immense" [immense embarrassment] and "fierté stupéfaite" [stupefied pride]. Like Ludivine, Elise experiences pleasure in viewing her admirer as a possession: "Il faisait partie de son domaine, il était à elle comme le reste de ses amusements" [He was part of her domain; he was hers like the rest of her amusements] (194). Somewhat like Cady, Elise sees seduction (for a time, at least) as a game, an "amusement." Elise soon learns the ways of the *monde*, but not without a certain level of discomfort. Her education culminates in the discovery that her stepmother has been having an affair with her fiancé. After a brief illness, Elise adjusts to the news by avoiding her stepmother as she would an enemy (209). Frustrated at her lack of confidants, she decides to handle her disappointment herself so as not to hurt her father.

Elise's discomfort with her experience in the *monde* is a reaction to the first model of love. Elise reflects on her maturity, believing that, at almost twenty, she is old enough to make her own decisions about love (Delarue-Mardrus 1923, 209). Her stepmother takes an opposite view, suggesting that Elise's reaction reveals her natural immaturity but that she will understand many things in time (211). Elise reacts to her stepmother's attempts to justify her behavior with a sensation of extreme fatigue and confusion. The world she had come to enjoy loses its savor, leaving her temporarily jaded, and she dreams of a romantic partner who will change everything. This first model of love has left her feeling lost, and yet she has hope that someone will come and "repair" and "save" everything and restore her smile (218). In other words, the first model has partially destroyed her youth. Her father's death, which immediately follows his discovery of his wife's infidelities, leaves Elise alone and worried about her place in the world. She has lost her illusions about fashionable society and retreats from it, preferring to find happiness and love honestly and without the support of the world that has betrayed her and her father. When her personal moral code is violated, she begins to develop a new understanding of love, based on respect and affection rather than appearances and social standing.

Elise's new love interest, based on the second model, is a poor but honest and truly gifted musician. His simplicity, contrasting so strongly with the pretension of her former fiancé, concretizes her disgust with high society and pushes her to reject the offer of marriage, which her former fiancé has not withdrawn. Her new experiences with life and love based on immaterial pleasures have led her to aspire to a higher, more spiritual ideal (Delarue-Mardrus 1923, 278). Given her new set of values, a life spent pursuing moral and artistic goals with a husband truly worthy of her affection appeals to her more than a life of superficial luxury. The novel ends when she refuses her former fiancé's proposal, meant to appeal to her desire for social status and wealth. The narrator tells us that Elise has made up her own mind for the first time (278). Elise has learned to choose love and moral uprightness over fashionable but shallow relationships based on social standing. She protests the immorality of the *monde* and is rewarded with a more promising chance at love and happiness.

In these novels, as in the others studied, love in various forms is always the central preoccupation of the adolescent heroine. Yet here, more than during the fin-de-siècle or Belle Epoque, these thinking heroines wish to be happy, even if happiness means refusing a rich suitor (*L'Ex-voto*, *Le Pain blanc*) or giving up their sexual innocence (*Le Blé en herbe*). Life without happiness and love may prove too difficult to bear (*Son Printemps*). These heroines are more than equal to their male counterparts, both mentally and physically. They challenge sexual mores while protecting themselves from corruption. Most important, they pave the way for an increasingly egalitarian version of the marriage union that remains the French social ideal as the end of the second decade of the twentieth century comes to a close.

Elizabeth Roudinesco underlines the year 1930 as one of a marked attitude shift in France: "It must be said that in 1930 a mutation happened in French society. When the repercussions of the Wall Street storm were felt in Europe, the folklore of the roaring twenties was already part of a faraway horizon and a perfume of disappointment reigned over the growing intellectual class" (Roudinesco 1994, 37). Indeed, Justin O'Brien declared that 1930 marked the end of novelistic interest in adolescence. In this final phase of my study, it is easy to locate some shifts in the portrayal of adolescents since the end of the nineteenth century. Female adolescent characters from 1910 to 1930 take more risks, demand more, and have more freedom and an increased sense of control over their lives. They also reveal a strong sense of self, reflected in their ways of observing and thinking about the world. Rather than passively accepting what Norbert Elias has explained as adult-imposed civilizing forces,[45] these characters observe societal tensions and pressures firsthand, developing their own behavioral codes and occasionally imparting them to others. Whether stated outright or merely suggested, there is more going on in these portrayals of adolescents than mere description of physical development or conquering of social space. Beneath the surface, their minds are opening, closing, fitting themselves around new ideas and concepts, recovering from trauma and yearning for joy, giving shape to adult personality.

Yet despite this progress in the portrayal of female adolescents, in some ways these depictions oddly resemble those of sixty years before. Though this period witnessed massive strides in the voicing of feminist concerns, the only brand of feminism that stuck was the moderate kind, that which avoided challenging traditionally superimposed sex and gender roles (Bard 1995, 457) and encouraged above all the natural feminine desire for husband and children. It has been pointed out again and again that these novels tend to reinforce the roles of wife and mother by showing young girls whose main preoccupation is finding love. True, this love nearly always entails marriage and the creation of a family. What cannot be underestimated, though, is the significance of these characters' insistence upon love on their own terms. Gone is the "belle proie soumise" [beautiful submissive prey] of the Belle Epoque or the neurotic teenager of the fin-de-siècle.[46] In their place is a young woman more like the *garçonne* than feminists of the day would care to admit, one willing to defy social convention in the name of personal values and needs, and above all, one who refuses to relinquish emotional well-being in the transition from adolescent to adult. These characters may not be the dynamic adolescents readers of more recent novels have come to expect, but their apparent stillness conceals a depth at which psychologists, writers and scholars continue to guess.

Throughout this study, novelistic portrayals of female adolescence have been linked to the sociopolitical climate of the time at which they were written. More specifically, the novels reveal the principal sources of concern to French society in general, and literary culture in particular, at a given period. Whereas the decadent portrait of 1870 to 1890 reveals anxiety about new medical understanding of the female body, that of the Belle Epoque shows emotional reaction to the new spaces opening to women, while the novel of the period dealt with in this chapter demonstrates concern about the psychological formation of identity. As in the last chapter, the young female protagonist allows novelists to explore subjective experience in the context of changing gender roles in newly provocative ways. Each period can be seen as a progressive reaction to the one before it; while the Belle Epoque novels put a more dynamic spin on female adolescence after the moral authority and fatalism of the decadent period, the last phase is the most socially realistic, and certainly the most psychologically accurate, view of adolescent subjectivity. The progression in the sexes of the writers creating these portraits of female adolescence, from largely male in the first chapter to balanced in the second, followed by largely female in the last, suggests that increasing familiarity with the category of adolescence, along with larger numbers of published women writers, allowed female novelists to stake a broader claim to the territory of female adolescence. This occupation of the territory by women facilitated the more nuanced, psychologically subtle, portraits of this final chapter.

Conclusion

This is an exploration of the rich world of novelistic representations of female adolescence, a world that often reflects adolescent reality at the time of writing, as shown by nonliterary documents. In many ways, the notion of female adolescence was in the hands of politicians, novelists, and social and literary critics, who all struggled to define it as a distinct period of life with an important role to play in French society. Many nonliterary studies of adolescence have shown it to be a threatening and threatened time, particularly for females. In her book about female adolescent experience, for instance, Constance Nathanson observes that the girl's passage from childhood to adulthood has been continually perceived as fraught with danger (Nathanson 1991, 81–82). When adolescence was still a vague concept, female idleness was considered necessary for preventive health, sexual safety, and reproductive development, yet young women suffered from the period during which they did not attend school or go to work (86–87).[1] The controversy over educating girls arose partly because the girl's need for mental stimulation was not met at home.

In the late 1950s, psychoanalyst Anna Freud corroborated the idea that adolescence was a difficult period. Freud attempted to fill what she considered to be a void in analytic study of adolescence[2] with an article in which she claims "adolescent upset" to be inevitable and especially difficult for parents (Freud 1960, 10, 22). She explains such "upset" as follows:

> I take it that it is normal for an adolescent to behave for a considerable length of time in an inconsistent and unpredictable manner; to fight his impulses and to accept them; . . . to revolt against [his parents] and to be dependent on them; . . . to thrive on imitation of and identification with others while searching unceasingly for his own identity. . . . Such fluctuations between extreme opposites would be deemed highly abnormal at any other time of life. At this time they may signify no more than that an adult structure of personality takes a long

181

time to emerge, that the ego of the individual in question does not cease to experiment and is in no hurry to close down on possibilities. (21–22)

Though Freud uses the requisite masculine pronoun, her observations about adolescence can easily be applied to female adolescents, as this study shows. Wildly fluctuating or illogical adolescent mood and behavior thus can be understood positively, as an attempt to embrace as many options as possible. In more modern terms, the adolescent can be compared to a reader of an interactive adventure book where each page offers new choices, new paths to explore, and where bad decisions can always be reversed with the flip of a page. Adolescent turbulence, though difficult for family and educators, both marks and masks the fundamental optimism of the period, the sense that anything is possible, that a hidden surprise waits around every bend in the road.

Though this analysis focuses particularly on the thirty-year periods preceding and following the turn of the century, no modern reader would claim that literature has abandoned the female adolescent character. In his book on what he calls the "generation of 1914," Robert Wohl refers to the worldwide economic crisis of 1929 as a landmark for many intellectuals, who saw in it a confirmation "that the world of their childhood was dead and that a new postwar world was being born" (Wohl 1979, 226). Indeed, in terms of the French novel of female adolescence, the end of the 1920s did signal a temporary calm in production, which provoked Justin O'Brien to write in the conclusion to his 1937 study of the novel of adolescence that French literature had entered maturity, leaving adolescence behind. In a 1936 essay entitled *Up-to-date*, novelist Lucie Delarue-Mardrus states that the kind of worry-free adolescence she and her contemporaries experienced, where young men and women could dream without anxiety and cultivate a "vie intérieure," is a thing of the past (Delarue-Mardrus 1936, 55). She associates the multiplicity of choices open to modern young people with increased stress and worry, a perspective that echoes in key respects Margaret Mead's 1928 study. Perhaps the fact that female adolescence was by 1930 a well-established social category, less open to debate than in earlier years, affected the number of novels dealing with young heroines. Another theory is that the surge in literary representation of adolescence was linked to French nationalism; concern for the future of France before the relative stability of the 1920s led to increased literary production about girls and their social role. Whatever the cause may be, novelistic interest in adolescence waned after 1930.[3]

This book traces such themes as physical transformations, evolving family dynamics, the influence of nature, access to education, and changing attitudes toward romance, sex, and marriage through a series of novels from 1870 to 1930. It shows through the progression in portrayals of adolescents during those sixty years, from static and ideological to dynamic and complex, that the novel both reflects and affects societal values and understanding of the young woman. I have demonstrated that France's literary interest in the adolescent can be traced to the birth of female adolescence as a social category in the latter half of the nineteenth century. I have also shown that the novel of female adolescence gains from being analyzed in terms of the social, political and aesthetic undercurrents at the time of its writing. From its conception, French female adolescence, at least in its literary form, has been a sign of the times, of the societal and literary preoccupations at a given historical moment. This analysis has made use of the novel as a prime literary indicator of the female adolescent's social status, but other genres, such as autobiography, the short story, theater, and poetry, also reveal interesting and pertinent information about female adolescence and could be used for further inquiry. Many of the concerns detailed here are specific to France in the sixty-year period examined; parallel studies of other world literatures from the same or from different eras would doubtless reveal some similar and other very different cultural preoccupations.

It cannot be denied that many of the novels examined in this study enjoyed mitigated success in France when they were first published, and are all but forgotten today. I have made clear that particular societal conditions gave female writers secondary status and repressed the expression of subversive ideas regarding young women. These novels deserve the closer look that some have begun to receive in recent scholarship, as they mark the birth of French interest in the documentation and shaping of young female experience through literature. That female adolescence has been a continuing cultural obsession in France and elsewhere can be partially attributed to its increasing social importance.[4] The parameters of adolescence continue to widen as children mature earlier and achieve financial autonomy later. As various countries turn their attention to early life as the breeding ground for social ill as well as good, adolescence continues to occupy the thoughts of politicians, social scientists, teachers, and writers. Adolescence itself has changed drastically in the past one hundred years: today sexual innocence can certainly no longer be considered a requisite quality of adolescence. Yet the struggles traced here in fictional adolescents over a century old still exist, in France and elsewhere. Adolescents still yearn to create for themselves a unique identity, fighting the bonds of family, school, and state in a paradoxical search for affection and/or acceptance from those very same institutions. Literary portrayals of the unique space of female adolescence continue to reveal hopes and fears about the future, gender relations, social institutions, and a country's place in the world.

Appendix: Plot Summaries

CHAPTER 1

Edmond (1822–1896) and Jules de Goncourt (1830–1870)
Renée Mauperin (1864)
Renée is a spirited, tomboyish young woman, close to her father, who finds her amusing, and criticized by her mother, who wishes she could be more attractive and feminine and less intelligent so as to find a mate. Renée refuses all proposed suitors but considers a relationship with a close family friend, who believes in educational reform for girls. After she organizes a chain of events that leads to her brother's death in a duel, Renée becomes ill and dies of remorse and heart disease.

Edmond de Goncourt (1822–1896)
Chérie (1884)
Young Chérie, whose father has died and whose mother has gone mad, lives with her paternal grandparents. They move to Paris, where Chérie halfheartedly follows lessons that do not inspire her. She contracts scarlet fever, after which she develops a passion for religion and music. After her first communion, she begins to dream of love and gets her period. When she is ready to marry, she realizes that her grandfather's lack of fortune and her mother's madness are obstacles to finding a good match. She gradually loses her lust for life, gets increasingly ill, and dies.

Rachilde (1860–1953)
La Marquise de Sade (1887)
Mary Barbe, traumatized by scenes of violence during her youth, has become cruel and sadistic as an adolescent, experiencing pleasure by causing pain and humiliation. After the death of her parents, she lives a lonely life with her libidinous uncle, then marries a baron with the condition that there will be no children. She inherits her uncle's fortune after his death and poisons her husband.

185

Minette (1889)
Hermine de Messiange, or "Minette," is sixteen and has just lost her baroness mother, making her the last member of the family line. She is cursed by werewolf blood on her father's side and becomes close to a parish priest who proves to be her biological father. She falls in love with married Laurent Bruon, but denies her feelings out of a sense of morality and goes mad. Laurent's wife gives the would-be lovers her blessing, but when Minette is about to commit adultery, she imagines she sees the curate, goes outside, and dies in the snow.

Emile Zola (1840–1902)

La Joie de vivre (1884)
Orphaned Pauline Quenu comes to live with her depressed and ill relatives, the Chanteau family, who slowly strip her of her inheritance and blame her for their misfortune. Despite her many losses, including a sacrificed love affair with Lazare Chanteau, Pauline remains optimistic and giving in the face of the illness and unhappiness that surround her.

Le Rêve (1888)
Young Angélique Marie is adopted by religious embroiderers, and becomes obsessed with the lives of the saints, dreaming of being saved by a prince. She falls for Félicien d'Hautecoeur, the last member of a noble family, whose father refuses to bless their union. When he agrees at last, they marry, but as Angélique prepares to leave the church, she kisses her husband and dies, overcome with joy because her dream has come true.

CHAPTER 2

Colette (1873–1954)

Claudine à l'école (1900)
Fifteen-year-old Claudine lives in a village with her absent-minded father. Claudine has an affair with her headmistress's assistant, Miss Aimée Lanthenay, but the headmistress, Miss Sergent, breaks them up and takes Miss Lanthenay as her own lover. Claudine seeks revenge with her friends Anaïs and Marie, then mistreats Miss Lanthenay's sister Luce. The novel follows the school year, with exams, a new school building, and an important political visit playing key roles.

Claudine à Paris (1901)

Seventeen-year-old Claudine moves to Paris with her father after an illness, where she meets her distant cousin Marcel and his charming father Renaud. She struggles with her feelings for Renaud and considers being his mistress so as not to deprive Marcel of his inheritance, but ultimately accepts Renaud's proposal of marriage.

Francis Jammes (1868–1938)

Clara d'Ellébeuse (1899)

Clara becomes obsessed with the love story of her great-uncle and his fiancée, Laure, who killed herself because she believed that her lover would not accept her pregnancy. Clara flirts with her poetry-writing boyfriend Roger Fanchereuse, becomes convinced that she is pregnant after hugging him, and falls ill. Like Laure, she poisons herself with laudanum and dies.

Almaïde d'Etremont ou l'histoire d'une jeune fille passionnée (1901)

Almaïde is an orphan who lives in virtual imprisonment with an authoritarian uncle. Her only joy is to take walks outdoors, where she experiences a sensual awakening, meets a young goatherd, falls in love, and becomes pregnant. After the deaths of her lover and her uncle, Almaïde is taken in by Mr. Astin, who violates societal expectations by agreeing to give his fortune to her child, who is born just as Astin dies at the end of the novel.

Pomme d'Anis (1904)

Laure (Pomme) d'Anis is convinced that no one will love her because of her slight limp. She falls in love with Johannes Arnousteguy, who returns her interest. Convinced that he is pretending to love her out of pity, she tells him that she promised God not to marry. Johannes ends up marrying her best friend Luce, which breaks Pomme's heart. She resolves to cut her hair and to become a nun.

Anna de Noailles (1876–1933)

Le Visage émerveillé (1904)

A young nun lives in a convent, separated from the outside world, and falls for a visitor, Julien, because she believes that he resembles Jesus. Their clandestine affair fills her life and she justifies her actions by linking romantic love with religious and familial love. When Julien asks her to leave with him, she decides that his desire is only fueled by obstacles, and chooses to stay at the convent, where she experiences superiority based on the power of her youth and her imagination.

Marcel Prévost (1862–1941)

Les Vierges fortes. Léa. (1900)

Romaine Pirnitz, an unfeminine critic of traditional social roles, runs a school for girls based on a philosphy that empasizes financial and emotional autonomy from men. Her student, Léa, is torn between the mission of the school and her love for a man named Georg. Ultimately, Léa chooses love, but too late: her health has been compromised, the school fails financially, and Léa dies.

Romain Rolland (1866–1944)

Antoinette (1908)

Antoinette is a happy, curious adolescent who loves music and teasing her younger brother, Olivier. After her father's financial ruin and suicide, the family moves to Paris where her mother works too hard and dies. Olivier wants to die too, so Antoinette decides to work as a governess to save him, denying herself pleasure so that he can be happy. She refuses a marriage proposal to stay with her brother, but when he fails an exam, she moves to Germany to stay with relatives. She falls for Jean-Christophe, a musician, but becomes ill soon thereafter and dies.

Marcelle Tinayre (1870–1948)

Avant l'amour (1897)

Orphaned Marianne is adopted by a family in Paris. Her older "brother" Maxime becomes a love interest. She is uninspired by religion or the economic nature of marriage, preferring to read forbidden novels and to dream about love. She attempts several love affairs, but is abandoned by one young man when he discovers her illegitimacy. She falls for Maxime, but refuses his marriage proposal because she sees marriage as a form of domination. He leaves in despair, but they sleep together just before his departure. She writes, saying that she will love him one day, and waits, happy with her decision to choose her path in life on her own terms.

Hellé (1899)

Hellé de Riveyrac is an orphan raised by her aunt and uncle. The latter becomes her tutor, and rejects typical education methods for girls.

After her aunt's death, Hellé moves to Paris for practical education in how to be a woman at the hands of his acquaintance Madame Marboy. Antoine Genesvrier, an older bachelor who is Marboy's nephew, inspires her to use her education to help others. She becomes engaged to Maurice Clairmont, a poet, and several ladies try to prepare her for traditional married life, but Hellé imagines a more modern, balanced union. After her split from Maurice, who reveals himself to be less than ideal for Hellé, she finally understands the egalitarian marriage model that Antoine proposed, realizes that he is much closer to her imagined hero, and accepts him.

Chapter 3

Marguerite Audoux (1863–1937)
Marie-Claire (1910)
After her mother's death and her father's departure, the title character spends nine dismal years in a convent orphanage, brightened only by beloved Sister Marie-Aimée. Marie-Claire moves to a farm, where she is employed as a shepherdess. She falls in love with Henri Deslois, her employer's wealthy second wife's brother, but his mother forbids Marie-Claire to see him again. Broken-hearted Marie-Claire sees sister Marie-Aimée once more before leaving for Paris.

Rachilde (1860–1953)
Son Printemps (1912)
Miane is fifteen and spends her time playing outside with her girlfriends and dreaming of a prince who will sweep her away. She "educates" herself, since her grandmother curtailed her formal education (after a series of chatty "lessons" with an older friend). Miane is obsessed with death and fears marriage. She compares herself with a servant, Fantille, and realizes her luck to be born into a family with money. After the deaths of her good friend and her cat, Miane becomes increasingly solitary and detached from reality. Her grandmother spies on her and destroys her beloved engraving of Cupid, which pushes her to commit suicide by drowning herself.

Camille Pert
La Petite Cady (1914)
Young Cady gets a new teacher/governess, Miss Armande, because her remarried mother has no time for her and prefers her little sister, Baby.

Cady spends time with men who smoke and drink. She meets Maurice Deber, who is shocked at her lack of education and structure. Cady rejects Armande's attempts to discipline her but tries to get her father interested in Armande, then regrets the success of her plan. Cady enjoys seducing various older men. Maurice leaves for six years, but says that, if Cady becomes a true young woman in that time, he'll marry her. After the mysterious murder of Armande and the political success of her stepfather, Cady decides to become a polite young woman.

Colette (1873–1954)

Le Blé en herbe (1923)

Longtime friends Philippe and Vinca, on vacation at the seaside, struggle with the conflict between their nascent desires and the social conventions governing their relationship. When Phil discovers carnal pleasures with an older woman, Vinca's initial feelings of betrayal give way to calm acceptance of her desire and she seduces Phil.

Lucie Delarue-Mardrus (1874–1945)

L'Ex-voto (1920)

Fourteen-year-old Ludivine lives in Honfleur, surrounded by a band of admiring children of fishermen, including her true love, Delphin. Because of the financial pressures on her family, she accepts the marriage proposal of an unappealing but wealthy man, Lauderin, but sleeps with Delphin before the wedding. After Delphin saves their lives during a violent storm, Ludivine confesses her love for him to Lauderin, who accepts his defeat and leaves, after ensuring her family's financial security.

Le Pain blanc (1923)

Elise's father leaves the family, but asks for Elise. Her bitter musician mother sends her to a boarding school. After a period of transition, Elise learns to appreciate school and becomes a young woman during the war. After learning that her unhappy mother killed herself, she makes peace with her mother and decides to study music. After learning of her disinheritance, she goes to live with her father and his new wife, who introduces her to a world of taste and class and a young suitor, Julien Villevielle. Elise prefers to spend her time with a poor musician named Hachegarde. Engaged to Julien, she realizes that he is having an affair with her stepmother. When he learns the truth, her father dies suddenly. Elise has no money, friends, or way of earning her living. She chooses to spend her time with struggling musicians and rejects Julien's renewed offer of marriage.

Graine au vent (1926)
Alexandra has a closer relationship with her sculptor father than with her mother. She loves to hunt and has no interest in Charles, a young suitor, whom she considers to be beneath her. Her mother dies in childbirth, creating a rift between Alexandra and her father. Alexandra realizes that her mother was the breadwinner and takes on the task of raising her young sister and running the household while her father drinks. Reconciliation comes when Alexandra starts to become an artist like her father.

Notes

INTRODUCTION

All translations are mine unless otherwise noted.

1. In his article on adolescence and youth in nineteenth-century America, Joseph Kett postulates that adolescence as we know it was born at the end of the century:

> The modern concept of adolescence was created by Hall and his colleagues at Clark University in the 1890s and given full expression in Hall's two-volume *Adolescence*. Hall described adolescence as a second birth, marked by a sudden rise of moral idealism, chivalry, and religious enthusiasm . . . . Weird and psuedo-scientific in retrospect, Hall's concept had a profound impact in his day. . . . One can also argue that adolescence has become a unique topic of interest in the twentieth century because of social conditions peculiar to our own time—specifically, the emergence of a yawning time gap between the onset of sexual maturity and the full incorporation of young people into the economic life of the adult world. (283)

Though Kett's article deals with nineteenth-century America, his idea that adolescence covers the period of time between biological adulthood and social autonomy is of key importance to this study. Patricia Meyer Spacks gives a very similar definition of adolescence in *The Adolescent Idea* (10).

2. Justin O'Brien's study of the French novel of adolescence concentrates on the period from 1890 to 1930. I argue that the novel of specifically female adolescence appears earlier than 1890.

3. Philippe Ariès writes that, in the early nineteenth century in France, people were unfamiliar with what modern society calls adolescence (29–30).

4. In Larousse's *Grand dictionnaire universel du XIXe siècle*, the entry for "adolescence" suggests that the earliest common use of the term was pejorative, implying youthful lack of experience.

5. In her book *Dangerous Passage*, Constance Nathanson writes, that in the United States, a country in which the emerging shape of adolescence mirrored that of France, young women of 15 to 24 appeared in the census as a separate category in 1870, at which point they represented one-third of the female population (Nathanson 1991, 85).

6. John Neubauer suggests that frequent literary use of the words "adolescent" and "adolescence" can be traced to the nineteenth century (Neubauer 1992, 5).

7. See *Eugénie Grandet, Albert Savarus, Pierrette*.

8. For more on Sand's female characters, see Schor 1986.

9. Interestingly, in many of the cases covered in this study, mother figures are either absent or problematized in some way.

10. Zola's wording, "even for peasant girls," recalls the class-based notion of adolescence discussed earlier.

11. Lloyd gives several examples of works that consider the child in literature, such as Braunschvig in 1903, H. Bordeux in 1904, and, in around 1930, J. Calvet and A. Dupuy (Lloyd 1992, 4).

12. This phenomenon is clearly not limited to France. Adolescents in the United States and elsewhere also embody the future of their respective countries, and anxiety about that future, but space does not permit an exploration of cross-cultural adolescence in this study.

CHAPTER 1. THE DECADENT VISION

1. Louis Marquèze-Pouey, in his book on *Le Mouvement décadent en France*, locates the movement from 1870 to 1889. Françoise Gaillard, of l'Université de Paris VII, considers the principal wave of decadent thought to take place from 1870 to 1890.

2. For more on this debate, see Gabrielle Houbre, 155–56, or the introduction to Yvonne Knibiehler's book *De la pucelle à la minette.*

3. In her book, Houbre traces the concept of adolescence etymologically, both for boys and for girls, and explores the significance of the historical transformations thereof (Houbre 1997, 22–24).

4. For more on the mother's role in preparing her daughter for marriage, see Houbre1997, 249–50.

5. See Houbre 1997, 156 and Knibiehler 1983, 188.

6. The reference is to Paul Bourget's *Essais de psychologie contemporaine: études littéraires* (1882), in which he outlines the notion of decadence and its manifestations in literature, starting with Baudelaire.

7. The novel by Joris-Karl Huysmans entitled *A Rebours* (1884) gives myriad examples of this particular decadent vision.

8. The term "enquête sociale" [social inquiry] comes from the Goncourt brothers, and corresponds to the goal they state at the beginning of *Renée Mauperin* (and that Edmond states in his preface to *Chérie).*

9. By this, I refer to one definition of adolescence discussed earlier, that of biological maturity combined with an inchoate social role.

10. Though it is today possible to draw distinctions between the "jeune fille" [young girl] and the "adolescente" at the time period discussed here, the social factors already discussed made these two categories overlap, if not coincide perfectly. Though Renée Mauperin is twenty years old, she corresponds in every respect to the category of adolescence that is being shaped at the time the novel appears on the literary scene. For more on Renée as "modern virgin," see Gale 2006.

11. The Goncourt brothers were known to correspond with girls and their mothers in order to gain information in the interest of perfecting their portraits of young women. It is therefore highly likely that this sentiment expressed by Renée came directly from actual girls. The brothers were no doubt smiling as they wrote "imagi-

nation d'auteur," a subtle criticism of the many mawkish nineteenth-century novels about youthful romance.

12. Emma Bovary is an excellent example of this phenomenon.

13. Ricatte 1953, 230. The expression comes from a play by Taine called *Le Fils de Giboyer* (1862), in which a young female character speaks of her "sentiment d'honneur viril" [sense of virile honor] (act III, scene 14).

14. Certain critics, such as Enzo Caramaschi, have seen in Renée's death a positive transformation, as opposed to certain other characters of the Goncourt brothers: "Suffering changes her, purifies her, matures her . . . : in a sense, she accepts death instead of being subjected to it" (Caramaschi 1971, 241). I insist on reading her death as an expression of pessimism, of bitter disillusionment in the face of societal values she cannot understand.

15. The course of Françoise Gaillard, "Penser la fin-de-siècle," at Paris VII in fall 1997 helped isolate some of the basic tenets of decadence, and notably established the period from 1870 to 1890 as the height of the decadent movement.

16. Diana Holmes acknowledges Rachilde's place as the only woman in the late nineteenth-century decadent movement (Holmes 2001, 1). In her book on *Fictional Genders*, Dorothy Kelly gives a reading of the "Decadent Reversals" in another Rachilde novel, *Monsieur Vénus*.

17. *La Petite Sœur de Balzac*, chapter 2.

18. With the discovery of the body comes the plague of body image concerns. Annelise Maugue locates the birth of the "mode de la minceur" [the fashion of slimness] at the end of the nineteenth century, a fashion that unfortunately has continued to play a principal role in the lives of adolescent girls up until the present (Maugue 1991, 540).

19. Pertinent medical studies on puberty and on marriage include those of Dr. Raciborski, *De la puberté et de l'âge critique chez la femme* (Paris: Ballière, 1844), and of Dr. Serrurier, *Du mariage considéré dans ses rapports physiques et moraux* (Paris: Ballière, 1845).

20. Brumberg cites examples of people who made links between girls' bodies and cultural values: Elizabeth Cady Stanton, who, in an 1870s speech entitled "Our Girls," advocated loose clothing, vigorous exercise, and intellectual challenges (Brumberg 1997, xxxii). In a similar vein, Dioclesian Lewis (1871) wrote a book called *Our Girls* in which he argued that girls need to develop greater confidence in their bodies to become effective teachers, students, and mothers (212). Yet Dr. Albert F. King, a professor of medicine at Columbia University in Washington, D.C., wrote in the 1870s that menstruation was something new, the result of higher education, later marriage, and deliberate family limitation: what he called "cultural interference" linked to modern life (7–8). Another medical doctor, Dr. Edward Clarke, wrote in 1873 a book entitled *Sex in Education; Or, a Fair Chance for the Girls*, in which he argued that girls should pay close attention to monthly demands in order to keep healthy. Clarke also argued against higher learning, or any excessive and improper kind of learning (8). For most Victorians, Brumberg concludes, reproductive life being the main purpose of the young woman, it must start correctly, with a minimum of instruction. Though Brumberg's study focuses on America, there are distinct parallels between girls' lives in France and in the States during the latter half of the nineteenth century, as evidenced by her references to France in the book.

21. In 1882, American Marion Harland wrote *Eve's Daughters, Or Common Sense for Maid, Wife and Mother* (1882), which decried the "pseudo-delicacy" that kept mothers from preparing their daughters for the onset of menstruation (Brumberg, 14).

22. Knibiehler 1991, 361.

23. See Ellis, Havelock. *Sexual Inversion*. Vol. 2 of the *Psychology of Sex*. Philadelphia: Davis, 1926.

24. Goncourt uses this term to denote certain inner aspects of a young woman's being.

25. Goncourt quarreled with Emile Zola over who would be the first to publish an in-depth study of the first menstrual period. In his journal entry from December 15, 1883, he writes:

> Aujourd'hui, je réponds à Zola qu'il est vrai que dans les chapitres que je lui ai lus de mon livre ne se trouvait pas le chapitre de l'apparition des règles chez Chérie, mais que je suis embêté qu'il ait choisi justement le temps où je faisais une étude de jeune fille pour en faire une, et d'autant plus embêté que comme il travaille plus vite que moi, j'aurai l'air de m'être inspiré de lui. (Goncourt 1956, 1034)

26. Earlier novelists, such as Honoré de Balzac in *Pierrette* and George Sand in *La Petite Fadette*, did treat the changing female body, though Goncourt's *Chérie* shows a far greater interest in medical documentation and scientific precision, as well as emotional realism.

27. See *Claudine à l'école*, a novel considered in greater detail in chapter 2.

28. These passionate relationships between women will be discussed further in Chapter 3.

29. Alain Corbin writes that Chérie's perfume-induced sensual dreams are part of a larger onanistic project, and that dying a virgin was, in the context of late nineteenth-century literature, the assumed fate of masturbating women (Corbin 1982, 244).

30. Corbin suggests that, for the female characters of Zola and the Goncourt brothers, smelling themselves is an aid to self-awareness and comprehension (Corbin 1982, 239).

31. For more information on the goals and methods of female education in the nineteenth century, see Vinson, *L'Education des petites filles chez la Comtesse de Ségur* and Mayeur, *L'Education des filles en France au XIXe siècle*.

32. Jennings observes the contradiction in Zola's position on female education. Though Zola appears to advocate emancipation of woman, arguing against severe and narrow-minded education because it encourages stupidity and superstition, his goal is to raise women to be better wives and mothers for the good of society, and more specifically that of men (Jennings 1969, 263, 300, 485, 486). Zola's ideal young woman is familiar with her body, is capable of exact scientific study, and spends her time in the home nurturing her family (488).

33. Michelle Perrot's article "Sortir" traces the gradual outward movement of female spaces, both physical and mental, during the nineteenth century.

34. In his chapter on *Renée Mauperin* in *La Création romanesque chez les Goncourt*, Robert Ricatte points out that Renée's bedroom, which reveals certain aspects of her secret self, is shown to the reader only as she lies dying: "The life of a middle-class adolescent gathers her secrets and her memories in her personal room; the Goncourts

understand this to be so, since they describe Renée's sanctuary so precisely. But they wait until everything is over before they let us in" (Ricatte 1953, 209).

35. Houbre 1997, 219. It is important to note again the repercussions of such a construction of adolescence in terms of class. Only girls of the middle and higher social classes would have their own rooms and the luxury of spending time lost in thought. Working-class girls would share space with siblings, if not the entire family, and would have little time for daydream between all the chores of daily life.

36. For more on the spaces of adolescence in Rachilde's novels, see Gale 2001.

37. Houbre, 1997, 174.

38. Ibid. 172.

39. Though this episode occurs after what can be considered Mary's adolescence, it nonetheless reinforces the idea of the female adolescent as nonreproductive, often by choice.

40. Françoise Gaillard has suggested that writers such as Nietzsche, Barrès, Huysmans, and Zola contributed to this ideological link between the end of the century and real and imagined infertility. Such subthemes as androgyny and mental and physical illness gave added dimension to the notion of stunted reproduction in works by these and other writers, including Rachilde.

41. Pauline is described repeatedly as weak and ill, but this is not the principal reason why marriage seems unlikely for her.

42. Zola believed in a link between physical vigor, mental health, and moral balance in young heroines (Jennings 1969, 222). The physical fragility of these two heroines might then suggest some mental or moral disorder.

43. Lucienne Frappier-Mazur has pointed out that this belief is the basis of all pathology in Balzac. In the context of this project, Goncourt merits attention for suggesting links between decadent thought and adolescent reality, creating a mix of scientific observation, social fact, and literary fabulation.

44. For more on the end of *Minette*, see Hawthorne 2001, 26–28.

45. Justin O'Brien, *The Novel of Adolescence in France* and John Neubauer, "Adolescence Comes of Age."

Chapter 2. Shifting Spaces

1. In his book on *France: Fin de Siècle*, Eugen Weber discusses the difference in meaning between Belle Epoque and fin de siècle, though he admits that people often tend to confuse the two. Weber establishes the Belle Epoque as the period from about 1904 to 1914, the ten years or so before the First World War, "robust years, sanguine and productive." (Weber 1986, 2). The fin-de-siècle period preceded them: "a time of economic and moral depression, a great deal less redolent of buoyancy or hope" (2). Because this chapter deals with both of these periods, I will distinguish between the two whenever necessary.

2. This authorial ambiguity is perhaps best exemplified by Colette. An enthusiastic reviewer of "Willy's" novel is Charles-Henry Hirsch, who wrote in an article for the *Mercure de France* in 1902 that Claudine is a rare, animalistic, sensual character, whose "mystery resides in the very sensation that she has not felt" (Hirsch 1902, 583–84). He praises both her epicurean nature and "Mr. Willy" for creating the kind

of wife "we would like our sons to have at thirty years of age" (584). Another example of confusion over Claudine's authorship is André Billy, who wrote in his *La Littérature française contemporaine* that the author of Claudine, Willy, suffers from "wordplay" that ruins his best pages, but that he is a "man of great wit, a man of letters and a true writer" (Billy 1927, 112). Less than eighty pages later, he lauds Colette for being one of the five literary "stars on the horizon" of the time (120), praising her Claudine novels, and again referring to Colette's Claudine in his section on the theme of childhood in the contemporary novel (142).

3. In his 1911 book on the current evolution of the novel, André Billy asked male and female writers to give their opinions on the new directions taken by the novel. While female novelists such as Aurel and Jeanne Landre commented on the new and necessary role of literary women, Edouard Quet pointed out the increased "curiosity" of the female readership, and Charles Pettit noted that the "great major-ity" of novel readers were women (Billy 1911, 51). In his conclusion, Billy attributes the transformations in the novel to shifts in societal attitude demanding that the novel be a "life lesson" (84), leading to a new relationship between the novel and its reader. Billy also nods to the influence of increasing numbers of female readers who found life more fascinating than coquetterie, and of female writers, who were readers themselves and therefore were well placed to cater to the demands of the increasingly female public.

4. Anne Sauvy evokes two vocal critics of female writers: Lucien Auger from Larnac's *Histoire de la littérature féminine en France* (1929) and Alphonse Karr from Gachons, Jacques, "Les femmes de lettres françaises" (1910), from whom Sauvy quotes the following: "A woman who writes has two faults: she increases the number of books and she decreases the number of women" (Sauvy 1985, 453).

5. In his 1927–28 book on French contemporary literature, André Billy asserts that there were two periods that were particularly conducive to what he calls "female literature": the "romantisme sentimental" of 1820 to 1830 and the "naturisme impres-sionnant" of the 1900s to 1920s, which was fueled by an interest in love as a key theme (Billy 1927, 120). Billy claims that the "stars" of such "female literature" are Colette, Mme de Noailles, Marcelle Tinayre, Gérard d'Houville, and Lucie Delarue-Mardrus, whose novels will be considered later in this study. Billy does not, however, anticipate further development of this "feminine" novel, which he esteems to be a dead or at best gravely worn-out genre: "We have witnessed the birth, the development and the decline of the female novel in the space of twenty years–from 1900 to 1920" (119). Later critics have drawn some of the same conclusions as those reached by Billy, some sixty years later. Elisabeth Ceaux writes in her article on the early twentieth-century woman as seen in Tinayre's novels that there was indeed a new feminine literature at the beginning of the twentieth cenutry, naming the same five writers that Billy men-tioned in his study. Ceaux then turns her attention to Marcelle Tinayre, observing that James Joyce wrote an article praising Tinayre along with such writers as William Blake and Oscar Wilde (Ceaux 1984, 209).

6. Elsewhere in his book, Bertaut attempts to explain the young girl's enigmatic appeal: "Where does the child stop? Where does the young girl begin?" (Bertaut 1909, 166).

7. This tendency to find in the female adolescent some greater principle occasion-ally spills over to female-penned characters, at least in the eyes of male critics. Jules

Bertaut considers Colette's Claudine to be the "portrait of an era" with her love of nature, her frankness, and her capacity for love. In his attempt to classify all literary "young girls," Bertaut accords Claudine her own category (Bertaut 1912, 185). Romain Rolland's Antoinette earns similar praise from Bertaut: "But here is Antoinette, and she is the most delicious of all of these women. What can be said of this exquisite young girl, the true example of the young French woman?" and:

> Nice, honest, sensitive, Antoinette possesses all of the great qualities of the French woman. Gifted with perfect balance, she knows moderation as well as grace. She is a being of reason and of courage, in whom sensitivity does not dominate, but she is also a creature of love and made for love that has learned all womanly delicacy, and that practices the principle virtue of woman, the art of consoling those who suffer. She is an admirable little courageous one who is not afraid of the word duty. She is the very example of the French woman of the middle classes, a type barely refined by contact with Paris, a solid, true, definitively admirable example . . . (*Romanciers*, 185–86)

8. Some critics, such as Jean Larnac, considered this "I" to be confirmation of the autobiographical nature of these novels: "Most of our women novelists only know how to confess or to write their more or less fictionalized memoirs. They say *I*, like Madame Colette in *Claudine*, . . . like Madame de Noailles in *le Visage émerveillé*" (Larnac 1929, 231–32). In her article on the construction of the female subject in Colette's writings, Angie Ryan analyzes the problematics of the pronoun "I" (Ryan 1995, 95).

9. This quote refers to Marcelle Tinayre, singled out by Bertaut and by André Billy as the leading female novelist of her time. Billy called Tinayre "more classic, more moderate, more virile too; she is a novelist in the most technical sense of the term. Without lacking in the natural grace of her sex, she refuses to give in to easy impressionism. She knows how to construct and compose, but is not averse to sometimes arbitrary romanticism" (Billy 1937, 123–24).

10. For critic Anne Sauvy, the "roman de moeurs" [novel of customs] was the ideal form for women writers:

> In this literary genre, women will excel for it allows them to speak of what they know well. While stigmatizing pedants, Charles Nodier had foreseen this early: "Not only are women likely to shine in a large number of literary genres, but there are certain in which men gifted with the sharpest and most delicate wit will never equal them." And he was referring notably to the analysis of female psychology and the way of making women speak, that he judged "the greatest pitfall of dramatic poets and of novelists." (Introduction à la *Biographie des femmes auteurs contemporaines françaises*, Paris, 1836). This novel of customs written by women for other women offers us in fact a remarkable sociological tableau, far more credible than that of theory novels [romans à these], always suspect of voluntary or unconscious distortions. It is not yet frozen, distorted, marked by elementary psychology . . . . The world that it presents to us reflects, on the contrary, without manicheism, the society of the time that can be found there in its entirety: daily life, the smallest details of existence, home décor, the order of meals, medical treatments, trip organization, education, religious prac-

tice, but also questions of money, at a time when there was no social security nor any inflation or dowries or inheritances, guarantees of security, bring along a whole set of moral and affective behaviors; that unite the different people of this society, parents and children, pupils and tutors, suppliers and shoppers, masters and domestics. (Sauvy 1985, 448)

11. Jean Rabaut describes this new, more subtle form of feminism:

To tell the truth, the first women writers of the Belle Epoque, in whom one eas- ily recognizes genius in the expression of instinct, barely touched on the Code civil and suffrage: as a rule, they situate themselves beyond those demands. They think that they have achieved independence, from the moment where they took the right to express melodiously how painful the conquest of amorous freedom is or was. (Rabaut 1978, 156)

Rabaut cites such writers as Anna de Noailles, Marcelle Tinayre, Gérard d'Houville, and Colette as examples of this phenomenon. Like other critics such as Juliette Rogers and Caroll Smith-Rosenberg (whose article on the New Woman deals with the same period in England and America), Rabaut identifies two waves of feminism, the second, less radical form taking over around 1900: "At the turn of the twentieth century, for about sixty years feminism of a virulent and gallant style, radical in all senses of the term, was eclipsed by another feminism, prudent and socially conservative, presented by a generation of ladies of good society who often distinguish badly the demand of philanthropy and of charity" (Rabaut 1978, 215).

12. Though *Antoinette* is one of the ten tomes constituting *Jean-Christophe*, I intend to consider it here as an autonomous work.

13. See John Neubauer, *The Fin-de-Siècle Culture of Adolescence*.

14. There are in fact few cityscapes in the novels by women. Claudine has adven- tures in village or city streets, as does Hellé.

15. Bertaut refers to Antoinette as representing the ideal "respectable young girl."

16. Lucienne Frappier-Mazur has observed that the young heroine is an orphan according to the novelistic model throughout the nineteenth century, with the notable exceptions of George Sand, whose heroines may have adoptive mother figures, and Balzac.

17. The designer Poiret is credited with abolishing the corset in 1905 (Knibiehler 1991, 356).

18. Brumberg's book deals largely with the United States; yet, because of her fre- quent references to France, I have chosen to consider her broad generalizations about the changing status of girls to be applicable to most western countries.

19. The articles by Annelise Maugue and Yvonne Knibiehler in *Histoire des femmes en Occident* give more information about the social and medical advances of the end of the nineteenth century that gave girls a new awareness of the body and of its effect on others. Eugen Weber briefly discusses the new fad in his book on fin-de-siècle France (Weber 1986, 104).

20. For more on the bathing practices of young women, see Alain Corbin and George Vigarello.

21. Again, see Alain Corbin and George Vigarello for a discussion of the nine- teenth-century conception of bathing as immoral and prurient.

22. In chapter 2 of his book, Havelock Ellis lists twelve sexologists and outlines their contributions to the field of sexual inversion.

23. In the *Grand dictionnaire universel du XIXe siècle*, the entry for "woman" includes the following statement: "Celibacy appears to be more contrary to women's health than to that of men. Observe chlorotic, langorous girls, looking like pale flowers waiting for the fertilizing rays of the day star. We see them spend sad days far from the fires of love. Amenorrhea and anomales of menstrual flow, general inertia of all of their functions, countless accidents of hysteria, disgust or strange desires alter their health" (VIII, 203). The entry for hysteria explains that symptoms most often appear in pubescent girls: "A great influence has been attributed to puberty. Without a doubt, independently of the age at which this phenomenon takes place, the age at which hysteria is most frequently observed, the changes that happen in the girl's genital organs act notably on the production of the illness" (IX, 524). Both extremes of sexual behavior are considered pernicious. In fact, the example of Geneviève in the novel suggests that sexual repression can lead to an explosion of licentious sexuality. The societal ideal in the context of the novel is to find a husband for the adolescent girl, that she may express herself sexually in a socially acceptable manner.

24. In his book on *La littérature française contemporaine* (1927), André Billy writes that Marcel Prévost "specialized in the analysis of the female soul" (Billy 1937, 74).

25. For more on French attitudes toward cleanliness in the nineteenth century, see George Vigarello and Alain Corbin. Both discuss the concern that, for girls, bathing led to prurient behavior. Corbin also discusses in more detail the theme of various smells in relation to sexual purity. For a consideration of cleanliness and body maintenance in the United States, see Joan Jacobs Brumberg, *The Body Project*.

26. According to critic Alfredo Diaz Castro, the subversiveness of Claudine's actions lies in their ambiguity/androgyny, which he considers to be a *leitmotif* of the early Claudine books (Diaz Castro 1996, 49). Diaz Castro cites Claudine's short hair and feminine clothes as signs of this ambiguity, saying that she has "a markedly masculine adolescence"(58). Yet for him, adolescence is naturally morally ambiguous: "Morally the Claudine character is complex and contradictory like that of any adolescent" (49). Interestingly, Diaz Castro places the Claudine books under the sign of decadence, which would support his reading of the novel in terms of ambiguity.

27. This wording, "un domaine où j'étais maîtresse" [a domain where I was mistress], recalls that of Rachilde in *La Femme-Dieu*: "Elle semblait habiter un monde à part où elle demeurait seule maîtresse de ses actes ou de ses secrets" [She seemed to live in a world apart where she alone governed her acts and her secrets] (Rachilde 1934, 180). Tinayre develops the metaphor by suggesting that such a realm excludes male desire.

28. Zola's *Le Rêve* is an excellent example of a novel in which dream replaces reality in a young woman's life.

29. Other equally impressed critics and readers include André Billy and James Joyce. (See notes 5 and 9).

30. Like other male critics, Bertaut assumes that the only explanation for the quality of Tinayre's writing, its compelling verisimilitude, is a necessarily autobiographical component. The word "confession" reveals his conviction that Tinayre is merely recounting her personal experience.

31. This comment echoes the theme of religious fervor as a parallel of physical passion, as discussed in chapter 1.

32. In France, this social phenomenon was referred to variously as "la femme nou-velle," "la femme moderne, " or "Eve nouvelle" [the new woman, the modern woman, or the new Eve].

33. Waelti-Walters' book briefly discusses the low birth rate in France toward the end of the nineteenth century, remarking that marriage and motherhood were enthu-siastically encouraged at this time by uneasy politicians (Waelti-Walters 1990, 8). Jean Rabaut gives some of the figures in his *Histoire des féminismes français*:

> Because of the development of abortion and especially of contraception, France was first in Europe to see its population stagnate; the surplus of births to deaths is declining: from 64,500 from 1891–1895, it falls to 46,100 from 1906–1910. From 89 children born alive for 1000 women of 15 to 49 from 1886-1895, it changes to 76 from 1906–1913. A reaction happens, fueled in part by patriotic worry, perhaps also by the desire to continue to find sufficient or even ex-cess workforce, but also and especially by an ultra-traditionalist conception of woman's role. (Rabaut 1937, 253)

In his study of the contemporary novel, André Billy quipped that the number of young characters in novels from the first two decades of the twentieth century should be some consolation for the dwindling birth rates (Billy 1937, 142). The problem of course, was not whether or not these characters existed, but whether they were good role models for other young people—that is, whether the female adolescent charac-ters chose to become "good" wives and mothers. Echoes of the New Woman in any young female character from a popular novel risked triggering population anxiety in conservative readers.

34. The New Woman phenomenon occurred at about the same time in France, the United States, and England. Though Smith-Rosenberg refers specifically to the situ-ation in America, the parallels between French and American society in this regard make her comments appropriate and valid for France as well.

35. In his book on the history of education in France, Antoine Prost confirms that this was the general attitude toward female instruction during much of the nineteenth century: "Destined for the home, girls only need to learn how to run a household, and school is for them a useless and dangerous luxury" (Prost 1968, 103).

36. Other works by Jules Bois also deal with the role of woman in society. *Eter-nelle Poupée* from 1894 discusses the doll image plaguing the woman as the product of the fin-de-siècle period, while *Le Couple futur* of 1912 weighs the impact that the new woman will have on the couple. While Bois insists that marriage will remain the principal vocation of the young woman, he presents the image of the young girl reading as the new ideal of femininity.

37. Rogers states that between 1900 and 1905 alone there were more than a dozen novels about female students and teachers published, and that all writers of those novels except for Colette are forgotten today (Rogers 1994, 322).

38. The idea that adolescence can be linked to social class is not a new one (see Introduction). If female adolescence was defined as a period of time between physi-cal maturity and marriage, which slowly became linked with access to education, as chapter 1 suggests, Pelletier's restriction of education to middle and upper classes, albeit shocking to the twenty-first-century reader, can be read as a natural expression of contemporary class distinctions.

39. In this light, the fervent participation in religious rituals on the part of deca-
dent-era adolescents, including the building of shrines to the Virgin and the organiz-
ing of religious clubs, appears to be less a sign of personal devotion and more a mark
of socialization, seasoned with mysticism and eroticism.

40. This sensuality associated with religious fervor is not a new phenomenon at the
turn of the century (see chapter 1). Emma Bovary also experienced the sensual thrill
of devotion in Flaubert's 1857 novel.

41. For Elisabeth Ceaux, Hellé is an example of a New Woman who belongs more
to the past than to the present, a paradox that the novel elaborates. "She is a modern
young girl, rebelling against traditional morality, convinced that woman is forced to
play a different role in the heart of society than that which was hers before; however
her great humanist culture leads her to belong more to the ancient world than to the
contemporary one" (Ceaux 1986, 226). In an interesting paradox, Hellé's "modern"
education places her at once far ahead of, and at odds with, her contemporaries. As
Lucienne Frappier-Mazur has pointed out, humanist education was not rare for male
adolescents in period literature. The education given to Hellé, however, is extremely
unusual for young women at the time.

42. Continual references to the first female philosopher reveal the goals of the
educational project undertaken by Hellé's uncle.

43. See George Vigarello and Alain Corbin for more on historical attitudes toward
odors and cleanliness in France.

44. Elizabeth Ceaux notes the same phenomenon of supplementary, often forbidden, reading on the part of Marcelle Tinayre's adolescents.

45. In the period covered by this study, sexual innocence is a requisite quality for
female adolescence.

46. The melodrama and dysfunction inherent in Jammes' descriptions of adolescent girls escaped critics such as Charles-Henry Hirsch, who wrote of Jammes'
portraits of "the sentimental young girl" (Clara and Almaïde): "They represent rather
precisely the two poles that limit the natural evolution of the feminine being, from the
moment of puberty to that where the rite of love frees her sensitivity" (Hirsch 1902,
582). Hirsch avoids any consideration of the decidedly unnatural aspects of these girls'
lives (suicide, imprisonment, madness, unhealthy family relationships), preferring to
consider them perfect examples of the "feminine being." Hirsch's attitude toward
young girls is further revealed by his assertion that most romantic "young girls" are
the same, and that the only way of distinguishing them is to see how they escape
partially from the discipline that holds them in line (582).

47. Though love and sex are also primary concerns in the lives of male characters
of the same period, the attitude with which they are approached and the importance
accorded to them in the context of the narrative differ from what one finds in novels
about women. Male characters are less apt to make love the primary focus of their
lives, and are more likely to regard love as a game or a challenge. Also, their other
pursuits overshadow that of love, whereas for women characters, thoughts and dreams
of love accompany, and occasionally replace, other experiences.

48. Jean Chalon comments in his 1970 article on "Colette's world" that, in the
world portrayed in Colette's novels, love is always strictly monogamous (Chalon 1970,
15–16). It is true that, during her periods of infatuation with Aimée and with Renaud, Claudine spares no thoughts for other romantic pursuits. Another interesting

commentary on Claudine comes from Alain Roger, who writes that Colette's female adolescents are not sexualized, but rather sensualized, as though the latter excludes the former in the adolescent girl (Roger 1996, 178). Roger also evokes the interesting hybrid quality of Colette's adolescents, between maturity and childhood, the masculine and the feminine (179). This hybrid quality recalls the comments of Alfredo Diaz Castro on Claudine's androgyny and ambiguity (see note 10). Interestingly, Roger links the enthusiasm for androgyny—which he finds particularly prevalent as centuries end—to adolescence: "One might wonder whether the glorification of androgyny, that seems peculiar to ends of centuries—the nineteenth as well as ours—is not a sublimation of adolescence, whose grace it usurps and idealizes, purifying it of an anecdotal disgrace" (181).

49. In France, young girls were often boarders in convents, where the same type of intense relationships tended to develop.

50. The concept of the "crush" in Vicinus's terms would find its equivalent in Colette's novel in what the characters refer to as being someone's "préférée" [favorite] or "grande amie" [great friend] (Vicinus 1989, 95).

51. Renaud married Claudine's cousin, and is the father of Claudine's "neveu à la mode de Bretagne" (Colette 1989, 201), or second cousin once removed, Marcel, with whom she establishes camaraderie before meeting Renaud. Because of their respective ages, Claudine refers to Marcel as her cousin and Renaud as her uncle, or as "mon cousin l'Oncle" (215).

52. Negative reactions to Claudine and her sexuality include that of Marvin Mudrick, who attacks Claudine's immorality as demonstrated by her erotics based on voyeurism and homosexuality: "Claudine speaks in her own pert voice, and she tells us—or so she implies—all. She prides herself on being a free spirit, an informed and unscrupulous gossip. She is licentious in anticipation and in trivial experiment, she invents and searches out dubious situations, but her eroticism . . . tends to be meanly vicarious . . . . The trouble is that, characteristically, Claudine has no imagination, only predictable impulses" (Mudrick 1963–64, 561).

53. Bertaut 1919.

54. *La Revue*, 65, no. 13 (July 13, 1903): 19–24.

55. Waelti-Walters, 176. Another example is Jean Larnac, who writes a long chapter on "l'intelligence féminine" and the ways in which it differs from male intelligence. Female minds develop more quickly, Larnac contends, but reach a point at which they can no longer develop, turning from advanced subjects, which they leave to men, to notions such as love and fashion: hence, for Larnac, the importance of love and sensitivity in the female novel. Larnac concludes his chapter on intelligence by stating that men and women naturally write differently, and that they should simply learn to appreciate and respect one another (Larnac 1929, 265).

56. Jean Larnac writes in his *Histoire de la littérature féminine en France* of the gap between educational progress and the actual educational background of the writers of the time: "There has never been such a large number of female writers in France, and one might be tempted to seek the cause in the organization of secondary education for girls and the accession of women to higher education. But many of our women writers—and not the lesser of them—had no secondary or higher education: for example, Madame Colette" (Larnac 1929, 223).

57. "Only feminist or engaged literature interests researchers. It is not well viewed to consider that domestic happiness might exist for women, in parallel with domestic unhappiness, and it is badly accepted that many women might have wanted to find in their readings the little adventures, the tribulations, the dreams, the joys or the grief that made up their daily lives, rather than fighting to get the right to vote. It is necessary to take a lucid and serene look at this near past and to understand it in its multiplicity and richness. Women's causes have nothing to lose by this" (Sauvy 1985, 448–49).

58. Elisabeth Ceaux confirms this seemingly contradictory new freedom within traditional structures, citing the case of Marcelle Tinayre. These novels are not necessarily "feminist," Ceaux asserts, but they do present a new female reality of independence, albeit based on love: "The beginning of the twentieth century is a period of transition for woman, and the works of Marcelle Tinayre written at this time both witness the attempts at female emancipation and reflect the present contradictions" (Ceaux 1984, 218). Tinayre's anti-conformist ideas, as expressed in her novels, according to Ceaux, played an important role in emancipating women of the Belle Epoque (209).

CHAPTER 3. BENEATH THE SURFACE

1. In volume 2 of her *Histoire de la psychanalyse en France*, Elisabeth Roudinesco writes: "From 1914 on, in fact, interest in psychoanalysis exists in a large sector of French thought" (Roudinesco 1994, 19). After 1922, she writes, "The Freudian season is in full swing in Paris" (87).

2. See Jessica Benjamin's *The Bonds of Love* for a discussion of the treatment of femininity in psychoanalysis.

3. Conley's study traces the contributions of several female surrealists, including Leonora Carrington.

4. Horney gives four types of personality changes in the female adolescent: an aversion to the erotic sphere, an obsession with the erotic sphere, emotional detachment, and the development of homosexual tendencies (Horney 1967, 235–36). These changes can be traced not only in literature of the time of Horney's research, but also in earlier examples of novels of female adolescence (see Edmond de Goncourt's *Chérie* and Colette's *Claudine à l'école*). In fact, some novels portray more than one of Horney's types in one adolescent character, such as Zola's *Le Rêve* and Rachilde's *Son Printemps*.

5. See Jules Bertaut, *La Jeune fille dans la littérature française*.

6. Interesting examples of such interchangeability include the scenes where Marcel realizes that the new young woman he is feverishly pursuing is none other than his former love Gilberte (*La Fugitive*, 224) and where he reads Gilberte's signature as Albertine, temporarily and wishfully thinking that Albertine has not died (299).

7. In an article on "Mythologies de l'adolescence dans le roman contemporain," Georges Monin writes of adolescence as a time of enhanced humanity and intelligence, citing *Le Grand Meaulnes* as an example (Monin 1943, 41). Monin claims that adolescence in the early twentieth-century novel is a "lost paradise" that the adult regards with nostalgia (43). Monin criticizes Cocteau for creating a false vision of

adolescence in *Les Enfants Terribles*: "Cocteau begins with the fact that adolescence is a mysterious world, and he invents a mystery of adolescence" (45). Finally, Monin writes that novelists of adolescence create mirages or myths to escape reality, painting a rosy and nostalgic picture that hardly corresponds to reality (45). One wonders whether youthful authors would in Monin's opinion be authorized to represent adolescent reality.

8. This is the same argument used by earlier male writers such as the Goncourt brothers in the first chapter. One has to wonder, then, whether male novelists simply got to the young woman character first, or whether they simply got different things wrong when they tried to correct the misinformation in the novels preceding theirs. My reading is that both are true: for various reasons, men had the first stab at the female adolescent character, but in their zeal to portray her "realistically," they inevitably made a few missteps, which the female novelists discussed here hope to set right.

9. In volume 2 of his book *The Bourgeois Experience*, Peter Gay writes of the relationship between early experiences and the development of adult sexuality according to Freud's writings on sexuality. Sexuality consists of two parts, the tender and the sensual, the latter manifesting itself later: "This sensuality has always been there, latent, masked, powerless to translate wish into action. Its underground vegetation, from which adolescence so dramatically liberates it, explains why virtually all physicians and other observers had put the birth of sexuality at puberty—until Freud compelled the world to revise its notions and accept the shocking fact of infantile sexuality" (Gay 1984, 90–91). According to Gay, "The discovery that unconscious memories play an incalculable, often dominant role in the course of love is probably Freud's most original contribution to nineteenth-century thinking on the subject" (91). Thus, childhood experiences, particularly trauma related to absent or conflictual parental ties, affect the development of adolescent sexuality.

10. In her book on Marguerite Audoux and Rachilde, Gabriella Tegyey observes that both novelists present heroines who lack family structure: they are orphans, or are abandoned or neglected by their families (Tegyey 1995, 126).

11. Holmes goes on to suggest that Vinca's behavior reveals the specific material and social conditions that govern heterosexual love in Colette's writing: "Women do not choose marriage or cohabitation out of mere inclination: it is also their principal means of economic survival" (Holmes 1991, 63). According to this argument, Vinca willingly accepts the criticism of the man she expects to be her husband. For more on gender and subjugation from a psychoanalytic perspective, see Jessica Benjamin, *The Bonds of Love*.

12. Ludivine's precocious maturity can be attributed to her difficult lifestyle. In the initial presentation of the protagonist, the reader can already guess at the scars inflicted by her difficult life: "Quatorze ans. Ulcérée, pourtant, comme une petite femme" [Fourteen years old. Festering, however, like a little woman] (Delarue-Mardrus 1928a, 30).

13. Though Brumberg writes largely of the United States, her references to France and bibliography reveal parallel phenomena in France.

14. This is not to say that, before this time, heroines did not value physical appearance (see Balzac's *Eugénie Grandet*). Brumberg traces a general shift toward self-identification through external signs. For example, young American girls of the 1920s

tended to manipulate their handwriting, projecting the new flexibility of personal image (Brumberg 1997, 105).

15. In the 1920s, Brumberg remarks, most female dieters were in late adolescence or early adulthood—high school and college students or businesswomen—they were not as young as they are today (Brumberg 1997, xxix).

16. The American beauty ideal, for example, required that legs and underarms be shaved, that the torso be svelte, and that breasts be, ideally, small and firm (Brumberg 1997, 98). The first boneless brassière to leave the midriff bare was developed in 1913 by Mary Phelps Jacobs, a New York City debutante (109).

17. In her article, Peiss explores the role of the New Woman in the cosmetics industry. Rising numbers of young, working women were targeted by the industry in advertising campaigns that appealed to their sense of independence and desire to feel attractive (Peiss 1990, 152–53). Peiss also interestingly notes the role of Paris in American advertising. Paris, considered to be the chic capital of the early century, was evoked in product names or falsely claimed to be the origin of a product. Often, a product was claimed to be a favorite of Parisian women, a tactic that inspired emulation in young Americans (158).

18. This shift from external to internal body control is the central concept of Brumberg's book. For more on control of the body from the inside, see Peiss 1990, 147.

19. Kahane notes that this literary conception of hysteria lasted only for the first two decades of the century, but that it paved the way, in some respects, for literary modernism: "By the end of the first decade of the twentieth century, my narrative suggests, hysteria had lost much of its unconscious currrency. Indeed, by the end of the second decade, hysteria was both self-consciously thematized as a trope of literary modernism as well as formalized as a poetics that could more adequately represent the dislocations of the modern subject. In this sense one can say that hysterical narrative voice not only preceded literary modernism but made it possible." (Kahane 1995, xv).

20. One example of the identification of psychic and physical phenomena can be found in Barbey d'Aurévilly's "Le plus bel amour de Don Juan" in *Les Diaboliques*. In the story, a thirteen-year-old girl experiences such emotional and physical upheaval after sitting in Don Juan's recently vacated and still warm chair that she becomes convinced that she is pregnant.

21. In 1928, Rachilde published an essay entitled *Pourquoi je ne suis pas féministe*.

22. See such sensual descriptions of physical awareness as that of Colette's Claudine, Anna de Noailles' nun, or Francis Jammes' Almaïde d'Etremont, where the adolescent admires and enjoys her body and its sensations.

23. For more on space in Rachilde's novels, see Gale 2001.

24. "Woman must belong either to Science or to the Church" (Prost 1968, 262).

25. Mayeur 1980, 194–95.

26. In her more recent study of the twentieth-century female *Bildungsroman*, Esther Labovitz notes that the genre did not exist before women's access to education (Labovitz 1986, 7). For more on the novel of education in France, see Juliette Rogers.

27. Miane reads the Comtesse de Ségur's *Les Malheurs de Sophie*, a text commonly given to young girls from the mid-nineteenth to the turn of the century (Rachilde

1920, 94). See *L'Education des petites filles chez la Comtesse de Ségur* by Marie-Christine Vinson for a discussion of Sophie's exploits as a pedagogical model.

28. Camille Pert wrote novels following Cady through much of her adult life, including *Cady mariée*, *Le Divorce de Cady*, and *Cady remariée*.

29. As stated in Chapter 2, Jean Rabaut notes in his *Histoire des féminismes français* the strong reaction produced by the dwindling birth rate and fueled in part by concern for the workforce and by a traditional idea of woman's role. Maternity was considered, after the First World War, to be French women's first duty in order to replace citizens lost in the war (Rabaut 1978, 253).

30. As Roberts points out, many governmental officials assumed that the rising numbers of single women could be linked to the loss of French soldiers during the war, and proposed various plans to provide husbands, including legalizing polygamy and importing young men from California. In fact, the loss of Frenchmen during the war was not sufficient reason for the dramatic increase in women choosing to live alone, according to Roberts.

31. Karen Offen writes that feminism was considered by its adversaries to be part of "Anglo-Saxon cultural imperialism" (Offen 1984, 662). The New Woman phenomenon was often linked to what nervous Frenchmen perceived as the feminist threat coming from abroad. In Marcel Prévost's *Vierges fortes* books, for example, "The lesson . . . was unmistakable: feminist ideas were alien to France, imports from abroad" (663).

32. Roberts confirms that the New Woman was an ancestor of the *femme moderne* (Roberts 1994, 19).

33. Ibid. 39–40.

34. Offen refers to the many publications dealing with women's issues and the New Woman that "rolled from the presses, especially after the appearance in 1896 of Jules Bois' mystico-romantic *Eve nouvelle*" (Offen 1984, 655), citing novelists like Marcel Prévost, Paul and Victor Margueritte, and Marcelle Tinayre who presented independent female characters.

35. See Waelti-Walters 1990.

36. Like that of Brumberg, D'Emilio and Freedman's book focuses on American society, yet it suggests some of the same themes to be found in French texts of the same period. The authors interestingly link new sexuality both to the existence of high schools for girls, a recent phenomenon in America as well as in France, and to a certain social class. Only those with money for clothes and entertainment could afford the kind of social life that facilitated sexual freedom (D'Emilio and Freedman 1988, 258). In early twentieth-century French fiction, sexual liberty was a more common theme among the working class—hence, the impact of Victor Margueritte's novel.

37. Roberts points out that Ellis's writings were published in translation in France from 1908 to 1935, while Freud appeared in French during the 1920s (Roberts 1994, 199).

38. *La Fronde*, the feminist newspaper created by Marguerite Durand and run entirely by women, is an example of a publication that presented such moderate feminist ideas. Many of Durand's journalists were married with children. For more on *La Fronde*, see Rabaut 1996.

39. Bard writes: " Rachilde is another bothersome priestess of sensuality for feminists, in many ways, since her audacious writing contrasts so strongly with her an-

tifeminism" (Bard 1995, 190). André Billy wrote in *Evolution actuelle du roman* that Rachilde's reputation was scandalous but that, as a writer, she was actually much less so (Billy 1911, 120). Rachilde aroused interest from all sides, as a writer associated with decadence and an unwilling representative of various versions of feminism.

40. For more on the role of class differences in the love affairs of Rachilde's characters, see Gabriella Tegyey 1995.

41. Some readers may recognize the striking similarities between Miane's dream lover and that of Angélique in Zola's *Le Rêve*. Indeed, both adolescent girls create similar romantic-religious fantasies, yet it is interesting to note that the social classes of the lovers are reversed in *Le Rêve*. Also, the marriage does take place in the latter, which suggests that a marriage between a rich man and a poor woman may be more acceptable than the reverse. Of course, Angélique dies suddenly on the steps of the church; thus, Zola avoids the representation of her married life.

42. This slippage between erotism and religious conviction was well established by the end of the nineteenth century (see Chapters 1 and 2). In Volume 2 of his book on *The Bourgeois Experience*, Peter Gay writes that, by the end of the century, it was accepted that religious fanaticism was born of unsatisfied erotic desire (Gay 1984, 284). Gay mentions several studies of the late nineteenth and early twentieth centuries that explored this link, including that of Krafft-Ebing, who wrote in the 1880s that urges exploding in adolescence as sexuality found ways of expressing themselves, including religion and poetry (286). About sexologist Havelock Ellis's view that love and religion were linked by a process of displacement, Gay writes: "In Havelock Ellis's view, the privileged moment when the pressure for sexual gratification became most imperious, and hence most unsettling, was the time of adolescence" (286–87). Gay explains that students of sexuality in the late nineteenth century such as Ellis "defined displacement as a shift of mental qualities, as instinctual tensions secured discharge through indirect, socially acceptable paths" (290). In this way, autoerotic impulse becomes religious emotion. Gay notes that Freud expressed a similar feeling that religion was a good compromise for the unconscious mind in flight from sexuality (291).

43. For more on the young female tendency to idealize love, see Benjamin 1988.

44. In a journal article published the same year as *Son Printemps*, Paul Gaultier writes of the high number of suicides among female adolescents. The slightest shock or reprimand can push an adolescent to suicide: "This is so true that women, in whom physical and moral transformations brought by puberty are particularly important, make up a greater proportion of suicides than men from 15 to 20 years of age—only in that interval. When adolescents kill themselves, it is . . . always by virtue of a sudden impulse without premeditation" (Gaultier 1912, 282).

45. Elias 1982, 330.

46. See Chapter 2 for further discussion of the end of Marcelle Tinayre's *Hellé*, where this quote can be found (Tinayre 1926, 358).

CONCLUSION

1. For more on this concept in the French context, see chapter 1.

2. "One can hear it said frequently that adolescence is a neglected period, a stepchild where analytic thinking is concerned" (Freud 1960, 1).

3. The decade following the Second World War, however, witnessed the publication of many significant novels of female adolescence, such as Françoise Mallet-Jorris's *Le Rempart des Béguines* (1951) or Françoise Sagan's *Bonjour Tristesse* (1951). Literary portraits of female adolescence trace the evolution of social values in operation at the time of writing; the reading audience of the 1950s witnessed the introduction of elements such as violent death, adultery, incest, and lesbianism into the novel of adolescence. The novel has continued to evolve, and indeed continued to present young heroines who seek to position themselves in relation to societal norms and expectations. Marguerite Duras presented a series of semi-autobiographical accounts of a young girl's coming of age in *Un Barrage contre le Pacifique* (1950), *L'Amant* (1984), and *L'Amant de la Chine du nord* (1991). Novelists such as Annie Ernaux and Christiane Rochefort have written several novels that further develop the novel of female adolescence as a genre by plunging deeper into the problematics of family relationships and introducing more candid narrators and protagonists.

4. Francophone writers in many countries have written novels of female adolescence. The authors often trace many of the themes of the French novel, though the problematics of female adolescent identity are often inextricably linked to those of post-colonial identity. Some examples of Francophone novels of female adolescence are: *Sapotille et le serin d'argile* by Michèle Lacrosil, *Le Temps des Madras* by Françoise Ega, *Desirada* by Maryse Condé, *Un Papillon dans la cité* and *L'Exil selon Julia* by Gisèle Pineau in the Caribbean; *Georgette!* by Farida Belghoul, *Journal: Nationalité Immigré(e)* by Sakinna Boukhedenna, *Beur's Story* by Ferrudja Kessas and *Zeïda de Nulle Part* by Leïla Houari from the Maghreb; and *Les Cahiers de Pauline Archange* by Marie-Claire Blais in Quebec. I thank Renée Gosson and Pascale de Souza for their help in locating these Francophone novels of female adolescence.

Works Cited

Primary Sources

Audoux, Marguerite. 1987. *Marie-Claire*. 1910. Reprint, Paris: Editions Grasset & Fasquelle.

Colette. 1974. *Le Blé en herbe*. 1923. Reprint, Paris: Editions J'ai lu.

———. 1989a. *Claudine à l'école. Romans-récits—souvenirs (1900–1919)*. 1900. Reprint, Paris: Bouquins Robert Laffont.

———. 1989b. *Claudine à Paris. Romans-récits—souvenirs (1900–1919)*. 1901. Reprint, Paris: Bouquins Robert Laffont.

Delarue-Mardrus, Lucie. 1923. *Le Pain blanc*. Paris: J. Ferenczi et fils, éditeurs.

———. 1928a. *L'Ex-voto*. 1920. Reprint, Paris: Eugène Fasquelle.

———. 1928b. *Graine au vent*. 1926. Reprint, Paris: J. Ferenczi et fils éditeurs.

Goncourt, Edmond de. 1926. *Chérie*. 1884. Reprint, Paris: Ernest Flammarion.

Goncourt, Edmond, and Jules de Goncourt. 1923. *Renée Mauperin*. 1864. Reprint, Paris: Ernest Flammarion.

Jammes, Francis. 1899. *Clara d'Ellébeuse ou l'histoire d'une ancienne jeune fille*. Paris: Mercure de France.

———. 1901. *Almaïde d'Etremont ou l'histoire d'une jeune fille passionnée*. Paris: Mercure de France.

———. 1904. *Pomme d'Anis ou l'histoire d'une jeune fille infirme*. Paris: Mercure de France.

Noailles, Anna de. 1904. *Le Visage émerveillé*. Paris: Calmann-Lévy.

Pert, Camille. 1914. *La Petite Cady*. Paris: E. Mignot.

Prévost, Marcel. 1900. *Les Vierges fortes: Léa*. Paris: A. Lemerre.

Rachilde. 1889. *Minette*. Paris: Imprimerie A. Julien.

———. 1920. *Son Printemps*. 1912. Reprint, Paris: Mercure de France.

———. 1981. *La Marquise de Sade*. 1887. Reprint, Paris: Mercure de France.

Rolland, Romain. 1908. *Antoinette*. Paris: Ollendorff.

Tinayre, Marcelle. 1897. *Avant l'amour*. Paris: Mercure de France.

———. 1926. *Hellé*. 1899. Reprint, Paris: Calmann-Lévy.

Zola, Emile. 1928. *Le Reve*. 1888. Reprint, Paris: François Bernouard.

———. 1964. *La Joie de vivre. Les Rougon-Macquart*. 1884. Reprint, Paris: Editions Fasquelle et Gallimard.

Secondary Sources

Abel, Elizabeth, et al. 1983. *The Voyage In: Fictions of Female Development.* Hanover: University Press of New England.

Alain-Fournier. 1910. "*Marie-Claire*, par Marguerite Audoux." *Nouvelle Revue Française* 4: 616–19.

Albistur, Maïté, and Daniel Armogathe. 1977. *Histoire du féminisme français de l'empire napoléonien à nos jours.* Tome 2. Paris: Editions des Femmes.

André, Jacques. 1995. *Aux origines féminines de la sexualité.* Paris: Presses universitaires de France.

Apter, Emily. 1991. *Feminizing the Fetish: Psychoanalysis and Narrative Obsession in Turn-of-the-Century France.* Ithaca: Cornell University Press.

Ardis, Ann. 1990. *New Women, New Novels: Feminism and Early Modernism.* New Brunswick: Rutgers University Press.

Ariès, Philippe. 1960. *L'enfant et la vie familiale sous l'Ancien Régime.* Paris: Plon.

Auerbach, E. 1968. Mimesis: *La representation de la réalité dans la littérature occidentale.* Paris: Gallimard.

Auerbach, Nina. 1985. *Romantic Imprisonmen.* Vol 4, *Gender and Culture*, edited by Carolyn G. Heilbrun and Nancy K. Miller. New York: Columbia University Press.

Balzac, Honoré de. 1965. *Eugénie Grandet.* Paris: Garnier Frères.

———. 1976–81. *Pierrette. La Comédie Humaine.* Paris: Gallimard.

———. 1978. *Albert Savarus.* Paris: Nizot.

Bard, Christine, ed. 1992. *Madeleine Pelletier: Logique et infortunes d'un combat pour l'égalité.* Paris: Côté-femmes éditions.

———. 1995. *Les filles de Marianne. Histoire des féminismes 1914-1940.* Paris: Fayard.

———. 1998. *Les Garçonnes: Modes et fantasmes des années folles.* Paris: Flammarion.

———, ed. 1999. *Un Siècle d'antiféminisme.* Paris: Fayard.

———. 2001. *Les Femmes dans la société française au 20e siècle.* Paris: Armand Colin.

Barrows, Susanna. 1981. *Distorting Mirrors: Visions of the Crowd in Late Nineteenth-Century France.* New Haven: Yale University Press.

Baruch, Elaine Hoffman, and Lucienne J. Serrano. 1988. *Women Analyze Women in France, England, and the United States.* New York: New York University Press.

Beasley, Wallace. 1980. *The Self as the Source of Knowledge: A Philosophical Study of the Identity Theme in the Adolescent Novel.* Knoxville: University of Tennessee.

Beauvoir, Simone de. 1949. *Le Deuxième Sexe.* Paris: Gallimard.

Beizer, Janet. 1993. *Ventriloquized Bodies: Narratives of Hysteria in 19th Century France.* Ithaca: Cornell University Press.

Bem, Jeanne. 1991. "Colette Baudoche et la 'matrie' de Barrès." In *Barrès: Une Tradition dans la modernité.* Actes du collogue de Mulhouse, Bâle et Fribourg-en-Brisgau, avril 1989. Paris: Librairie Honoré Champion, 193–202.

Benjamin, Jessica. 1988. *The Bonds of Love: Psychoanalysis, Feminism, and the Problem of Domination.* New York: Pantheon Books.

Bertaut, Jules. 1909. *La littérature féminine d'aujourd'hui*. Paris: Librairie des Annales.

———. 1910. *La Jeune fille dans la littérature française*. Paris: Michaud.

———. 1912. *Les Romanciers du nouveau siècle*. Paris: Sansot.

———. 1919. *Le Paris d'avant-guerre*. Paris: Renaissance du livre.

———. 1920. *Le Roman nouveau*. Paris: Renaissance du livre.

Billy, André. 1911. *Evolution actuelle du roman*. Paris: Eugène Rey.

———. 1937. *La Littérature française contemporaine*. 1927, Reprint, Paris: Librairie Armand Colin.

Blanchard, Phyllis. 1926. *The Adolescent Girl: A Study from the Psychoanalytic Viewpoint*. New York: Dodd, Mead and Company.

Bois, Jules. 1894. *Eternelle poupée*. Paris: Ollendorff.

———. 1895. *Eve nouvelle*. Paris: Flammarion.

———. 1912. *Le Couple futur*. Paris: Librairie des annales politiques et littéraires.

Bourget, Paul. 1993. *Essais de psychologie contemporaine: études littéraires*. 1882. Reprint, Paris: Gallimard.

Bowlby, Rachel. 1992. *Still Crazy After All These Years: Women, Writing and Psychoanalysis*. London: Routledge.

Bricard, Isabelle. 1985. *Saintes et Pouliches. L'éducation des jeunes filles au XIXe siècle*. Paris: Albin Michel.

Brumberg, Joan Jacobs. 1982. "Chlorotic Girls, 1970-1930: A Historical Perspective on Female Adolescence." *Child Development* 53: 1468–77.

———. 1997. *The Body Project: An Intimate History of American Girls*. New York: Vintage Books.

Buckley, Thomas, and Alma Gottlieb, eds. 1988. *Blood Magic: The Anthropology of Menstruation*. Berkeley: University of California Press.

Bullough, Vern, and Martha Voght. 1973. "Women, Menstruation and Nineteenth-Century Medicine." *Bulletin of the History of Medicine* 47 (January-February): 66–82.

Butler, Judith. 1987. *Subjects of Desire: Hegelian Reflections in Twentieth-Century France*. New York: Columbia University Press.

Cabanes, Jean-Louis. 1991. *Le Corps et la maladie dans les récits réalistes (1856-1893)*. Tome 1, chap 3. Paris: Kincksieck.

Cahné, Pierre. 1994. "Pourquoi treize ans?" *Littératures* 31 (Automne): 207–10.

Caramaschi, Enzo. 1971. *Réalisme et impressionnisme dans l'œuvre des frères Goncourt*. Pisa: Editrice Libreria Goliardica.

Carassus, Emilien. 1991. "Idéologie et sensibilité barréiennes dans Le Jardin de Bérénice." In *Barrès: Une Tradition dans la modernité*. Actes du collogue de Mulhouse, Bâle et Fribourg-en-Brisgau, avril 1989. Paris: Librairie Honoré Champion, 19–30.

Carles, Patricia, and Béatrice Desgranges. 1995. "Emile Zola, ou le cauchemar de l'hystérie et les rêveries de l'utérus." *Les Cahiers Naturalistes*. Dir. Alain Pagès. Coll. Emile Zola. Lectures au féminin, avatars du roman naturaliste. 69: 13–32.

Caron, Jean-Claude. 1996. "Les Jeunes à l'école: collégiens et lycéens en France et en Europe (fin XVIIIe-finXIXe siècle)." in *Histoire des jeunes en occident*, edited by Giovanni Levi and Jean-Claude Schmitt. Tome 2, *L'époque contemporaine*, Paris: Seuil. 143–207.

Ceaux, Elisabeth. 1984. "La Femme au début du XXe siècle à travers les premiers romans de Marcelle Tinayre." *Quaderni di filologia e lingue romanze.*

———. 1986. "Voyages dans le passé avec Marcelle Tinayre" *Quaderni di filologia e lingue romanze.* 221–43.

Chalon, Jean. 1970. "Le monde de Colette." *Magazine Littéraire* 42 (July): 15–16.

Charasson, Henriette. 1925. "La littérature féminine." In *Vingt-cinq années de littérature française*, edited by E. Montfort, 65–98. Paris: Librairie de France.

Charrier, Edmée. 1931. *L'Evolution intellectuelle féminine.* Paris: Editions Mechelinck.

Chauvin, Danièle, ed. 1996. *L'Imaginaire des âges de la vie.* Grenoble: Université Stendhal.

Chombart de Lauwe, M-J. 1971. *Un monde autre, l'enfance. De ses représentations à son mythe.* Paris: Payot.

Citti, Pierre. 1980. "La Notion de milieu: le roman et l'idée de décadence vers 1870." In *L'Esprit de décadence* 41–52. Colloque de Nantes, April 21-24 Paris: Librairie Minard.

Cixous, Hélène, and Catherine Clément. 1975. *The Newly-Born Woman*, trans. Betsy Wing. Minneapolis: University of Minnesota Press.

Clark, Linda C. 1984. *Schooling the Daughters of Marianne. Textbooks and the Socialization of Girls in Modern French Primary Schools.* Albany: State University of New York Press.

Compagnon, Antoine. 1993. "Zola dans la décadence." *Les Cahiers Naturalistes.* Dir. Alain Pagès. Coll. Emile Zola. Bilan et Perspectives. (97): 211–24.

Conley, Katherine. 1996. *Automatic Woman: The Representation of Woman in Surrealism.* Lincoln: University of Nebraska Press.

Corbin, Alain. 1982. *Le Miasme et la jonquille. L'odorat et l'imaginaire social: XVIIIe-XIXe siècles.* Paris: Aubier Montaigne.

Crubellier, Maurice. 1979. *L'enfance et la jeunesse dans la société française 1800-1950.* Paris: Armand Colin.

Dalsimer, Katherine. 1986. *Female Adolescence: Psychoanalytic Reflections on Works of Literature.* New Haven: Yale University Press.

Danahy, Michael. 1982. "Growing Up Female: George Sand's View in La Petite Fadette." In *George Sand Papers: Conference Proceedings 1978*, 49–58. New York: AMS Press, Inc.

Dauphin, Cécile, Arlette Farge, et. al. "Women's Culture and Women's Power: Issues in French Women's History." In *Feminism and History*, edited by Joan Wallach Scott, 568–96. Oxford: Oxford University Press, 1996.

Dauphiné, Claude. 1991. *Rachilde.* Paris: Mercure de France.

Davidson, Cathy N. 1986. "Female Education, Literacy, and the Politics of Sentimental Fiction." *Women's Studies International Forum* 9 (4): 309– 12.

Davis, Natalie Zemon, and Joan Wallach Scott. 1985. *Women's History as Women's Education.* Symposium at Smith College, April 17. Northampton: Sophia Smith Collection and College Archives.

Décaudin, Michel. 1980. "Définir la décadence," 5–12. In *L'Esprit de décadence.* Colloque de Nantes. 21–24 avril 1976. Paris: Librairie Minard.

DeJean, Joan E. 1989. *Fictions of Sappho: 1546-1937.* Chicago: University of Chicago Press.

———. 1991. *Tender Geographies: Women and the Origins of the Novel in France.* New York: Columbia University Press.

———, and Nancy K. Miller, eds. 1991. *Displacements: Women, Tradition, Literatures in French.* Baltimore: Johns Hopkins University Press.

Delarue-Mardrus, Lucie. 1927. *La Petite fille comme ça.* Paris: J. Ferenczi et fils, éditeurs.

———. 1936. *Up-to-date.* Paris: Editions Roger Allou.

D'Emilio, John, and Estelle Freedman. 1988. *Intimate Matters: A History of Sexuality in America.* Chicago: University of Chicago Press.

Diaz Castro, Alfredo. 1996. "La Saga de Claudine: una apologia de la androgynidad?" *Káñina: Revista de las artes y letras* 20 (1): 49–60.

Didier, Béatrice. 1981. *L'Ecriture femme.* Paris: PUF.

Dottin-Orsini, Mireille. 1993. *Cette femme qu'ils disent fatale: Textes et images de la misogynie fin-de-siècle.* Paris: Grasset.

Driscoll, Catherine. 2002. *Girls: Feminine Adolescence in Popular Culture and Cultural Theory.* New York: Columbia University Press.

Elias, Norbert. 1978. *The Civilizing Process.* Vol. 1, *The Development of Manners: Changes in the Code of Conduct and Feeling in Early Modern Times,* trans. Edmund Jephcott. New York: Urizen Books.

———. 1982. *The Civilizing Process.* Vol. 2, *Power and Civility,* trans. Edmund Jephcott. New York: Pantheon Books.

Ellis, Havelock. 1926. *Sexual Inversion.* Vol. 2 of the *Psychology of Sex.* 1897. Reprint, Philadelphia: Davis.

Faguet, Emile. 1910. *Le Féminisme.* Paris: Société française d'imprimerie et de libraire.

Farge, Arlette, Christiane Klapisch-Zuber, et al. 1984. *Madame ou Mademoiselle: itinéraires de la solitude féminine 18e-20e siècle.* Paris: Arthaud-Montalba.

Fargue, Léon-Paul. 1987. *Portraits de famille.* Paris: Fata Morgana.

Feldman, S. Shirley, and Glen R. Elliot, eds. 1990. *At the Threshold: The Developing Adolescent.* Cambridge, Mass. Harvard University Press.

Ferlin, Patricia. 1995. *Femmes d'encrier.* Paris: Christian de Bartillat.

Flat, P. 1909. *Nos femmes de lettres.* Paris: Perrin.

Flower, John. 1991. "Langage et politique dans *Colette Baudoche.*" In *Barrès: Une Tradition dans la modernité.* Actes du collogue de Mulhouse, Bâle et Fribourg-en-Brisgau, avril 1989. Paris: Librairie Honoré Champion, 203–11.

Foucart, Claude. 1991. "La Jeunesse 'tout nûment.'" In *Barrès: Une Tradition dans la modernité.* Actes du collogue de Mulhouse, Bâle et Fribourg-en-Brisgau, avril 1989. Paris: Librairie Honoré Champion, 103–12.

Foyard, Jean. 1991."Images de la femme chez Barrès." In *Barrès: Une Tradition dans la modernité*. Actes du collogue de Mulhouse, Bâle et Fribourg–en-Brisgau, avril 1989. Paris: Librairie Honoré Champion, 81–89.

Freud, Anna. 1960. "Adolescence." In *Recent Developments in Psychoanalytic Child Therapy*, edited by Joseph Weinreb, M.D., 1–24. New York: International Universities Press, Inc.

Friedenberg, E. Z. 1959. *The Vanishing Adolescent*. Boston: Beacon Press.

Gale, Beth W. 2001. "Female Adolescent Spaces According to Rachilde." *Romance Notes* 16 (3): 311–18.

———. 2006. "Renée Mauperin as 'Vierge Moderne': Documenting Adolescence." *Romance Quarterly* 53 (1) (winter): 43–48.

———. 2008. "Education, Literature and the Battle over Female Identity in Third Republic France." *Culture Wars and Literature in the French Third Republic*, edited by Gilbert D. Chaitin. Newcastle: Cambridge Scholars Publishing, 103–27.

———. 2009. "Ni rebelles ni soumises : les presque révoltées du roman d'adolescence en France." In *Portraits de jeunes filles: images de l'adolescence féminine dans la littérature et le cinéma francais et francophone*, edited by Daniela di Ceccço. Paris: Les Editions de l'Harmattan, 17–32.

Gallagher, Catherine, and Thomas Laqueur, eds. 1987. *The Making of the Modern Body*. Berkeley: University of California Press.

Garreau, Bernard-Marie. 1997. *Marguerite Audoux: La Famille réinventée*. Paris: Editions Indigo & Côté-femmes éditions.

Gaultier, Paul. 1912. "L'Adolescence." *La Revue de Paris* 19 (4): 256–86.

Gay, Peter. 1984. *The Bourgeois Experience: Victoria to Freud*. Oxford: Oxford University Press.

Gemie, Sharif. 1995. *Women and Schooling in France, 1815-1914. Gender, Authority and Identity in the Female Schooling Sector*. Keele: Keele University Press.

Gilbert, S., and S. Gubar. 1979. *The Mad Woman in the Attic*. New Haven: Yale University Press.

Gilman, Sander, et al. 1993. *Hysteria Beyond Freud*. Berkeley: University of California Press.

Giorgio, Michaela de. 1991. "La Bonne Catholique." In *Histoire des femmes en occident. XIXe siècle*, edited by Geneviève Fraisse and Michelle Perrot, 169–198. Paris: Plon.

Goncourt, Edmond de. 1956. *Journal: mémoires de la vie littéraire*, edited by Robert Ricatte. 1989. Reprint, Paris: Robert Laffont.

Gossy, Mary S. 1995. *Freudian Slips: Woman, Writing, the Foreign Tongue*. Ann Arbor: University of Michigan Press.

Gourmont, Rémy de. 1923. *Le Chemin de velours*. Paris: Editions G. Crès.

Greaves, Anthony F. 1980. "Zola et l'esprit décadent." In *L'Esprit de décadence*, 89–98. Collque de Nantes. April 21–24, 1976. Paris: Librairie Minard.

Gregory, Thomas West, ed. 1980. *Adolescence in Literature*. New York: Longman.

Gyp. 1894. *Le Mariage de Chiffon*. Paris: Calmann-Lévy.

Hall, Granville Stanley. 1904. *Adolescence: Its Psychology and Its Relations to Physiology, Anthropology, Sociology, Sex, Crime, Religion and Education.* New York: D. Appleton and Company.

Hawthorne, Melanie. 2001. *Rachilde and French Women's Authorship: From Decadence to Modernism.* Lincoln: University of Nebraska Press.

Hirsch, Charles-Henry. 1902. "De Mademoiselle de Maupin à Claudine." *Mercure de France* 42 (June): 577–88.

Hollingworth, Leta Stetter. 1928. *The Psychology of The Adolescent.* New York: D. Appleton.

Holmes, Diana. 1991. *Colette.* New York: St. Martin's Press.

———. 1996. *French Women's Writing 1848-1994.* London: Athlone.

———. 2001. *Rachilde: Decadence, Gender and the Woman Writer.* New York: Berg.

Hoock-Demarle, Marie-Claire. 1991. "Lire et écrire en Allemagne." In *Histoire des femmes en occident. XIXe siècle*, edited by Geneviève Fraisse and Michelle Perrot, 147–68. Paris: Plon.

Horney, Karen. 1945. *Our Inner Conflicts.* New York: Norton.

———. 1967. "Personality Changes in Female Adolescents." In *Feminine Psychology*, 234–44. New York: Norton.

Houbre, Gabrielle. 1997. *La Discipline de l'amour: l'éducation sentimentale des filles et des garçons à l'âge du romantisme.* Paris: Plon.

Houville, Gérard de. 1908. *Le Temps d'aimer.* Paris: Calmann-Lévy.

Icard, S. 1890. *La femme pendant la période menstruelle, essai de psychologie morbide et de médecine légale.* Paris: Alcan.

Ihring, Peter. 1989. *Die Jugendliche Gemeinschaft zwischen Mythos und Wirklichkeit: Motivtypologische Studien zum Französischen Adoleszenzroman von 1900 bis 1940.* Bonn: Romantischer Verlag.

James, Henry. 1958. *The Awkward Age.* New York: Doubleday.

Jennings, L. Chantal. 1969. *Les Romanciers naturalistes et la question de l'émancipation féminine.* Ph.D. diss., Wayne State University,

Joran, Théodore. 1905. *Le Mensonge du féminisme. Opinions de Léon H.* Paris: H. Jouve.

Jullien, Dominique. 1993. "Cendrillon au grand magasin (*Au Bonheur des dames* et *Le Rêve*)." *Les Cahiers Naturalistes* 67: 97–106.

Kahane, Claire. 1995. *Passions of the Voice: Hysteria, Narrative, and the Figure of the Speaking Woman, 1850-1915.* Baltimore: Johns Hopkins University Press.

Kaminskas, Jurate. 1995. "Le Rapport mère-fille dans quelques romans des Rougon-Macquart." *Les Cahiers Naturalistes* 69: 33–48.

Kauffman, G. 1900. *Questionnaire sur les sujets suivants: Revendications féministes, Education, Mariage, Prostitution, Charité, Politique.* Paris: Imprimerie Richard.

Kelly, Dorothy. 1989. *Fictional Genders: Roles and Representation in Nineteenth-Century French Narrative.* Lincoln: University of Nebraska Press.

Kennedy, Helen P. 1896. "Effects of High School Work Upon Girls During Adolescence." *Pedagogical Seminary* 3 (June): 469–82.

Kett, Joseph F. 1971. "Adolescence and Youth in Nineteenth-Century America." *Journal of Interdisciplinary History* 2 (2 Autumn): 283–98.

———. 1977. *Rites of Passage: Adolescence in America, 1790 to the Present.* New York: Basic Books.

Kiell, Norman. 1959. *The Adolescent Through Fiction: A Psychological Approach.* New York: International Universities Press, Inc.

Knibiehler, Y., et al. 1983. *De la pucelle à la minette: la jeune fille de l'âge classique à nos jours.* Paris: Temps Actuels.

———. 1991. "Corps et cœurs." In *Histoire des femmes en occident. XIXe siècle,* edited by Geneviève Fraisse and Michelle Perrot, 353–387. Paris: Plon.

Knight, Chris. 1991. *Blood Relations: Menstruation and the Origins of Culture.* New Haven: Yale University Press.

Labovitz, Esther Kleinbord. 1986. *The Myth of the Heroine: The Female Bildungsroman in the Twentieth Century.* New York: Peter Lang.

Lanson, G. 1951. *Histoire de la Littérature française.* Paris: Hachette.

Laqueur, Thomas. 1990. *Making Sex: Body and Gender from the Greeks to Freud.* Cambridge, Mass. Harvard University Press.

Larnac, Jean. 1929. *Histoire de la littérature féminine en France.* Paris: Editions Kra.

Larousse, Pierre. 1982. *Grand dictionnaire universel du XIXe siècle.* Paris: Slatkine.

Laslett, Peter. 1971. "Age at Menarche in Europe Since the Eighteenth Century." *Journal of Interdisciplinary History* 2 (2 Autumn): 221–36.

Le Cormier, Pauline. 1950. *Confidences à une jeune adolescente.* Paris: Editions familiales de France.

Lerman, Hannah. 1986. *A Mote in Freud's Eye: From Psychoanalysis to the Psychology of Women.* New York: Springer Publishing Company.

Levi, Giovanni, and Jean-Claude Schmitt, eds. 1996. *Histoire des jeunes en occident.* Tome 2, *L'époque contemporaine.* Paris: Seuil.

Lévy, M-F. 1984. *De mères en filles: L'éducation des Françaises 1850-1880.* Paris: Calmann-Lévy.

Lloyd, Rosemary. 1992. *The Land of Lost Content: Children and Childhood in Nineteenth-Century French Literature.* Oxford: Clarendon Press.

Lupton, Mary Jane. 1993. *Menstruation and Psychoanalysis.* Chicago: University of Illinois Press.

Margerie, Roland de. 1976. "Rostand, Claudel, Anna de Noailles, Valéry, Gide . . . " *Nouvelle Revue des Deux Mondes* (August): 292–99.

Marquèze-Pouey, Louis. 1986. *Le Mouvement décadent en France.* Paris: P.U.F.

Maugue, Annelise. 1991. "L'Eve nouvelle et le vieil Adam: identites sexuelles en crise." In *Histoire des femmes en Occident. Le XIX siècle,* edited by Genevieve Fraisse and Michelle Perrot, 528–43. Plon.

Maus, Octave. *Les Préludes. Impressions d'adolescence.* Brussels: 1921.

Mayeur, Françoise. 1977. *L'Enseignement secondaire des jeunes filles sous la Troisième République.* Paris: Presses de Sciences Po.

———. 1979. *L'Education des filles en France au XIXe siècle.* Paris: Hachette.

————, and Jacques Gadille, eds. 1980. *Education et images de la femme chrétienne en France au début du XXième siècle*. Lyon: Editions l'Hermès.

McCarty, Mari. 1981. "Possessing Female Space: 'The Tender Shoot'." *Women's Studies: An Interdisciplinary Journal* 8: 367–74.

Mead, Margaret. 1928. *Coming of Age in Samoa: A Psychological Study of Primitive Youth for Western Civilization*. New York: William Morrow.

Mendès, Catulle. 1891. *La Femme-enfant*. Paris: Charpentier.

Mendousse, Pierre. 1963. *L'Ame de l'adolescente*. Paris: Presses universitaires de France.

Michelet, J. 1859. *La Femme*. Paris: Hachette.

Miller, Nancy K., ed. 1986. *The Poetics of Gender*. New York: Columbia University Press.

Modell, John, and Madeline Goodman. 1990. "Historical Perspectives." In *At the Threshold: The Developing Adolescent*, edited by S. Shirley Feldman and Glen R. Elliot. Cambridge, Mass. Harvard University Press.

Monin, Georges. 1943. "Mythologies de l'adolescence dans le roman contemporain." In *Problèmes du roman*, edited by Jean Prévost, Lyon: 36–52. Confluences.

Montherlant, Henry de. 1936. *Les Jeunes filles*. Paris: Gallimard.

Moses, Claire Goldberg. 1984. *French Feminism in the Nineteenth Century*. Albany: State University of New York Press.

Mudrick, Marvin. 1963–64. "Colette, Claudine, and Willy." *Hudson Review* 16: 4 (winter). 559–72.

Nathanson, Constance. 1991. *Dangerous Passage: The Social Control of Sexuality in Women's Adolescence*. Philadelphia: Temple University Press.

Neubauer, John. 1986. "Adolescence Comes of Age." *Sensus Communis: Contemporary Trends in Comparative Literature*. Tubingen: Narr.

————. 1992. *The Fin-de-Siècle Culture of Adolescence*. New Haven: Yale University Press.

Noel, Françoise. 1995. *Vivre son âge*. Paris: Magnard.

Nordau, M. 1894. *Dégénerescence*, trans. Auguste Dietrich. Paris: Alcan.

O'Brien, Justin. 1937a. "Gide, Mauriac and Cocteau. Portraitists of the Adolescent." *French Review* 10: 377–85.

———— 1937b. *The Novel of Adolescence in France*. New York: Columbia University Press.

Odem, Mary E. 1995. *Delinquent Daughters: Protecting and Policing Adolescent Female Sexuality in the United States, 1885-1920*. Chapel Hill: University of North Carolina Press.

Offen, Karen. 1983. "The Second Sex and the Baccalauréat in Republican France 1880–1924. *French Historical Studies* 13: 2 (fall): 252–86.

————. 1984. "Depopulation, Nationalism and Feminism in Fin-de-siècle France." *American Historical Review* 89: 3 (June): 648–76.

Olivier, Christiane. 1989. *Jocasta's Children: The Imprint of the Mother*, trans. George Craig. London: Routledge.

Ozouf, Mona. 1963. *L'Ecole, l'Eglise et la République: 1871–1914*. Paris: A. Colin.

Pageaux, Daniel-Henri. 1973. "*Colette Baudoche* et le 'lotharingisme' de Maurice Barrès." *Missions et démarches de la critique*: Mélanges offerts au professeur J. A. Vier. University de Haute-Bretagne. 403–10.

Peiss, Kathy. 1990. "Making Faces: The Cosmetics Industry and the Cultural Construction of Gender, 1890-1930." *Genders* 7 (spring): 143–69.

Pelletier, Madeleine. 1978. *L'Education féministe des filles et autres textes*. 1914. Reprint, Paris: Syros.

Pereire, Anita. 1957. *Nous les jeunes filles*. Monaco: Editions du Rocher.

Périllon, Marie-Christine. 1981. *Vies de femmes: les travaux et les jours de la femme à la Belle Epoque*. Roanne: Horvath.

Perrot, Michelle. 1986. "Journaux intimes. Jeunes filles au miroir de l'âme." *Adolescence Ecrire*, 4: 1.

———. 1991a. "Production des femmes, imaginaires et reelles." In *Histoire des femmes en Occident. Le XIX siècle*, edited by Genevieve Fraisse and Michelle Perrot, 118–120. Paris: Plon, 1991.

———. 1991b. "Sortir." In *Histoire des femmes en Occident. Le XIX siècle*, edited by Genevieve Fraisse and Michelle Perrot, 467–94. Paris: Plon.

———. 1996. "La Jeunesse ouvrière: de l'atelier à l'usine." In *Histoire des jeunes en occident*. Tome 2, 85–142. Paris: Seuil.

Perrot, Philippe. 1981. *Les Dessus et les dessous de la bourgeoisie: Une histoire du vêtement au XIXe siècle*. Paris: Fayard.

Planté, Christine. 1989. *La Petite sœur de Balzac: Essai sur la femme auteur*. Paris: Seuil.

Prévost, Marcel. 1900. *Les Vierges fortes: Frédérique*. Paris: A. Lemerre.

———. 1901. *Les Demi-Vierges*. Paris: Lemerre.

Prost, Antoine. 1968. *Histoire de l'enseignement en France: 1800–1967*. Paris: Armand Colin.

Proudhon, P. J. 1875. *La Pornocratie ou les femmes dans les temps modernes*. Paris: Lacroix et Cie, éditeurs.

———. 1876. *Amour et mariage*. Paris: Lacroix et Cie, éditeurs.

Quella-Villéger, Alain. 2000. *Belles et rebelles: le roman vrai des Chasteau-Tinayre*. Bordeaux: Aubéron.

Rabaut, Jean. 1978. *Histoire des féminismes français*. Paris: Stock.

———. 1985. *Feministes à la Belle Epoque*. Paris: France-Empire.

———. 1996. *Marguerite Durand (1864–1936). 'La Fronde' féministe ou 'Le Temps' en jupons*. Paris: L'Harmattan.

Rachilde. 1904. *Le Dessous*. Paris: Mercure de France.

Raciborski, A. 1843. *La Puberté*. Paris: Baillière.

———. 1868. *Traité de la menstruation*. Paris: Baillière.

Ravoux-Rallo, Elisabeth. 1989. *Images de l'adolescence dans quelques récits du XXe siècle*. Mayenne: José Corti.

Raynaud, E. 1899. "Frères de Goncourt et la femme." *Décadent* 15: 1.

Ricatte, Robert. 1953. *La Création romanesque chez les Goncourt, 1851–1870.* Thèse. Paris: Armand Colin.

Richard, Jean-Pierre. 1954. "Deux écrivains épidermiques: Edmond et Jules de Goncourt." *Littérature et sensation.* Paris: Seuil.

Rivière, Joan. 1991. *The Inner World and Joan Rivière. Collected Papers 1920–1958.* London: Karnac Books.

Roberts, Mary Louise. 1994. *Civilization Without Sexes: Reconstructing Gender in Postwar France, 1917-1927.* Chicago: University of Chicago Press.

Roger, Alain. 1996. "Naissance de l'adolescence. De l'âge ingrat à l'état de grace." In *L'Imaginaire des âges de la vie*, edited by Danièle Chauvin, 174–83. Grenoble: Université Stendhal.

Rogers, Juliette M. 1994. "Educating the Heroine: Turn-of-the-Century Feminism and French Women's Education Novels." *Women's Studies: An Interdisciplinary Journal* 23: 4 (September): 321–34.

Romain, Yvonne de. 1909. *Semeurs d'idées.* Paris: Sansot et cie.

Roudinesco, Elisabeth. 1982. *La Bataille de cent ans. Histoire de la psychanalyse en France.* Vol. 1. Paris: Editions Ramsay.

———. 1994. *La Bataille de cent ans. Histoire de la psychanalyse en France.* Vol 2. 1925–85. Paris: Fayard.

Ryan, Angie. 1995. "The Construction of the Female Subject: Belghoul and Colette." In *Women and Representation*, edited by Diana Knight and Judith Still, 92–105. Nottingham: University of Nottingham Press.

Sagan, Françoise. 1981. *Bonjour Tristesse.* Paris: Julliard.

Sand, George. 1856. *Histoire de ma vie.* Paris: Michel-Lévy.

———. 1880-1. *La Confession d'une jeune fille.* Paris: Calmann Lévy.

———. 1979. *La Petite Fadette.* Paris: Hachette.

———. 1981. *La Mare au diable.* Paris: Garnier Frères.

Sauvy, Anne. 1985. "Une Littérature pour les femmes." *Histoire de l'édition française.* Tome 3, 445–53. Edited by Roger Chartier. Paris: Promodis.

———. 1986. "La Littérature et les femmes." In *Histoire de l'édition française.* Tome 4, 242–55. Edited by Roger Chartier. Paris: Promodis.

Schor, Naomi. 1985. *Breaking the Chain: Women, Theory, and French Realist Fiction. Gender and Culture* Vol. 2. Edited by Carolyn G. Heibrun and Nancy K. Miller. New York: Columbia University Press.

———. 1986. "Reading Double: Sand's Difference." In *The Poetics of Gender*, edited by Nancy K. Miller, 248–69. New York: Columbia University Press.

Scott, Joan Wallach, ed. 1996a. *Feminism and History.* Oxford: Oxford University Press.

———. 1996b. *Only Paradoxes to Offer: French Feminists and the Rights of Man.* Cambridge, Mass. Harvard University Press.

Shorter, Bani. 1987. *An Image Darkly Forming: Women and Initiation.* New York: Routledge and Kegan Paul.

Showalter, Elaine. 1985. *The Female Malady: Women, Madness, and English Culture, 1830-1880*. New York: Pantheon Books.

———. 1990. "New Women." In *Sexual Anarchy: Gender and Culture at the Fin-de-siècle*, 38–58. New York: Viking.

Silve, Edith. 1996. Préface à *La Marquise de Sade*. Paris: Gallimard. i-xiv.

Slipp, Samuel, M. D. 1993. *The Freudian Mystique: Freud, Women and Feminism*. New York: New York University Press.

Smith-Rosenberg, Carroll. 1972. "The Hysterical Woman." *Social Research* 39: 652–78.

———. 1989. "Discourses of Sexuality and Subjectivity: The New Woman, 1870-1936." In *Hidden from History: Reclaiming the Gay and Lesbian Past*, edited by Martin Duberman, Martha Vicinus, and George Chauncey, Jr., 264–80. New York: Penguin.

———, and Charles Rosenberg. 1973. "The Female Animal: Medical and Biological Views of Woman and Her Role in Nineteenth-Century America." *Journal of American History* 60 (September): 332–56.

Sohn, Anne-Marie. 1972. "La Garçonne face à l'opinion publique: type littéraire ou type social des années 20?" *Movement social* 80 (July-September): 3–27.

Spacks, Patricia Meyer. 1981. *The Adolescent Idea: Myths of Youth and the Adult Imagination*. New York: Basic Books.

Stewart, Joan Hinde. 1981. "The School and the Home." *Women's Studies* 8: 259–72.

Stubbs, P. 1981. *Women and Fiction, Feminism and the Novel 1880-1920*. London: Methuen.

Sussmann, Hara. 1978. *Balzac et les débuts de la vie: étude sur l'adolescence dans la comédie humaine*. Paris: A. G. Nizet.

Tegyey, Gabriella. 1995. *L'inscription du personnage dans les romans de Rachilde et de Marguerite Audoux*. Debrecen: Kossuth Lajos Tudományegyetem.

Tetu, J-F. 1978. "Remarques sur le statut juridique de la femme au XIXe siècle." *La Femme au XIXe siècle. Littérature et idéologie*. Lyon: P.U.L.

Thibaudet, Albert. 1912. "Réflexions sur le roman." *Nouvelle Revue Française* 8: 213–20.

Thiesse, Anne-Marie. 1984. *Le Roman du quotidien: Lecteurs et lectures populaires à la Belle-Epoque*. Paris: Le Chemin vert.

Thurman, Judith. 1999. *Secrets of the Flesh: A Life of Colette*. New York: Ballantine Books.

Tilly, Louise A., and Joan W. Scott. 1978. *Women, Work and Family*. New York: Holt, Rinehart and Winston.

Uzanne, Octave. 1881. *La Gazette de Cythère*. Paris: A. Quantin.

———. 1894. *La Femme à Paris, nos contemporaines*. Paris: A. Quantin.

———. 1910. *Etudes de sociologie féminine. Parisiennes de ce temps en leurs divers milieux, états et conditions*. Paris: Mercure de France.

Veblen, Thorstein. 1899. *The Theory of the Leisure Class*. New York: Macmillan.

Viallet, B. 1925. *Il Romanzo femminile francese contemporaneo*. Milano: Alpes.